CONFIDENTIAL
SOURCE NINETY-SIX

CONFIDENTIAL SOURCE NINETY-SIX

A MEMOIR

The Making of America's Preeminent
Confidential Informant

ROMAN CARIBE

and

ROBERT CEA

NEW YORK   BOSTON

Copyright © 2017 by ZOMNP Entertainment LLC.

Jacket design by Jarrod Taylor
Cover copyright © 2017 by Hachette Book Group, Inc.

Hachette Books
Hachette Book Group
1290 Avenue of the Americas
New York, NY 10104
hachettebookgroup.com
twitter.com/hachettebooks

First Edition: August 2017

Hachette Books is a division of Hachette Book Group, Inc.
The Hachette Books name and logo are trademarks of
Hachette Book Group, Inc.

The publisher is not responsible for websites (or their content) that are not owned by the publisher.

Library of Congress Control Number: 2017931873

ISBNs: 978-0-316-31537-1 (hardcover), 978-0-316-31538-8 (ebook)

Printed in the United States of America

LSC-C

10 9 8 7 6 5 4 3 2 1

To my Lord and savior Jesus, my beautiful wife, and my wonderful children. You are the reason I decided to do the right thing and become the man I am today.

CONTENTS

Prologue

I parked my whip—a straight-from-the-showroom triple black Mercedes SEL 500—at a safe distance, just in case these OG Rastafarians decided on ripping me off of the thousand pounds of weed I had stored in the car's oversized trunk: eight 125-pound, hermetically sealed bales of Mexico's finest. So I had to walk the six blocks to the initial meeting place, a big mistake. East Harlem is not the place you want to find yourself when you've got hundreds of ruthless enemies hoping to jack you.

It was one of those late August nights New York City is famous for, so hot and muggy you felt as though you were plodding through a torpid bowl of pea soup. The quicker I was off the street and back in the whip, a/c jacked to the max—or inside the hotel's rooftop pool—the better.

The blazing sun slid behind a wall of decaying tenements offering little relief. The streets were teeming with people, every block, every corner; every doorway satiated with steerers, lookouts, slingers, shooters, and the occasional hooker; every one of them looked suspect to me—the paranoia growing inside me threatened to subsume every other part of me.

On my walk to the meet I was hawked everything from nickels, dimes, halves, and whole grams of *"primo perrico,"* or cocaine. I was offered blow jobs for twenty, straight-up fucks for forty, and the special of the evening, a half-and-half, for fifty. I'm sure if I asked any one of those street hustlers where I could buy a rocket launcher, within ten minutes I'd be in some alley deciding between a Russian- and a North Korean–made RPG. But I had no time to chat with any of these young enterprising businessmen and women; I had my own business to attend to.

Our meet for the trade-off was at my customer's restaurant, Caribbean Sea Cuisine on Second Avenue. The closer I got to the restaurant the more sweat I found myself swabbing off my face and neck. I worried I was being followed but did not look back. The very last thing anyone in my position wants to do is appear nervous, because these are the type of cats who can smell fear a mile away. And fear on a first buy with $400,000 and a half ton of marijuana at risk would be the deciding factor between whether these Rastas were going to torture me until I brought them to my $90,000 whip, where they'd certainly take the weed they assumed was in the trunk and put a bullet in my head, or whether we would have a friendly transaction that would lead to bigger and better endeavors—for me at least.

I knew exactly who and what Anthony Makey was long before I got off the jet at JFK. His reputation as a ruthless Jamaican hit man, as well as a major weed distributor and rip-off artist, was legendary all over the country. I'd been introduced to him by a very reputable gang of coke dealers out of LA whom he'd done business with in the past. My reputation was that of a sound, standup player with deep connections to the Bel-trán Cartel based out of Sinaloa, Mexico. I, for all intents and purposes, was a responsible businessman who could deliver as much weight as needed, tons in fact, on a mere day's notice.

I'd studied Makey and his crew of ruthless rip-off artists and killers the way I would any other dealer or buyer before making a transaction: I'd rehearsed this sale over and over in my mind. I'd talked to Makey at least a dozen times, and had seen him once in Santa Barbara, California, on what we'd called a "meet and greet," though my real intent was the chance to look into his eyes and size him up, see if he could be the next guy I'd cut a deal with. I'd evaluated him as a businessman first and killer second. My first impression of the man was that he didn't kill for sport. My second was that he always seemed to wear a strap, as did his cabal of Jamaican ex-pat security goons. I may have never carried a gun, but my ace in the hole—and one Makey was aware of—was that I represented some very dangerous people with a very long reach. If anything happened to me, or the primo weed I was selling, these Jamaicans, including every one of their family members, would be tracked, caught, tortured—and only afforded the luxury of a bullet through the eye.

As I approached Caribbean Sea Cuisine I noticed the restaurant was a storefront establishment—shabby in accordance with the rest of the neighborhood. It stood between two prewar four-story tenements. The lights were on, and from the street I could see no customers other than three light-skinned black men, two with dreadlocks the length of jump ropes, and the third a bespectacled man with short cropped hair whom I immediately recognized as Anthony Makey.

They appeared to be in quiet conversation, sitting at a four-top table next to the counter.

This was not how our meet was to go down. I was to meet Makey *alone* in his restaurant. Once he flashed me the money, I was to get my car, come back, and make the switch. It was never a good sign for a customer to be changing the rules of engagement before the meet began, but if I walked away now I was sure he would've gotten a call and I'd have been grabbed before I made it to the corner. No, now I had to switch up and go off book just like him.

The street-side establishment looked like any other fast-food roti den. Above the counter, covered by grease-stained Plexiglas, were faded pictures of jerk chicken, oxtail, beef roti, and other Jamaican delicacies I did not recognize nor had any desire or proclivity to eat.

As I got within a couple meters of the shabby restaurant I pulled out my phone and pretended to make a call. I set my cell phone to record everything that was about to happen.

I spoke into the phone and gave the exact address and quick description of the men inside the restaurant.

Makey, like every other drug dealer on the planet, had become very paranoid behind the inception of all the new technology that law enforcement now had at its disposal. My colleagues guaranteed me that the modified phone I was using would not read as a bug—in fact, they wanded the transmitter in front of me and it registered nothing—from the outside, it appeared to be just another cell phone.

I entered the restaurant, and though I'm sure Makey knew exactly where I was once I stepped onto Second Avenue, if not the moment I parked my car, he feigned complete surprise.

Makey had a big personality to match his big evil. He stood up, hugged me tightly as if we were old friends, and in his thick

Jamaican brogue said, "Ya, Mon, here come da big mon all da wey from da sunny coast 'a Californ'a. Roman, meet me business par'nahs Zeek and Colin."

Both men had dead eyes—glassy and bloodshot, though behind the apparent partying they'd been doing and their anemic look, I could tell they were very aware and furtively sizing me way the fuck up. They stared hard, but in deference to their boss, nodded hello.

I had to read out as much information as I could about my environment, whom I was with, any guns in view, if and when I saw the money, where it was, what it was held in, color of bag—without making it sound like I was bugged. A one-on-one meeting would've been hard enough to keep under control.

I shook hands with Zeek and Colin. "Damn, how long it take you guys to grow those dreads?" It was the best partial description I could give under the circumstances.

Makey told me to sit down and asked if I wanted something to eat, which I definitely declined.

Makey suddenly dropped the friendly decorum rap and seemed to grow pensive. After an agonizingly long silence he said, "Ya mon, ya be wantin' to get right'a business. I can respect that. Cool." He stood up and moved to a glass-encased refrigerator stocked with soda, water, and the obligatory Jamaican staple in every roti den—Red Stripe beer. He looked into it for a moment then turned back to me and said, "Well, let's go den."

I was confused; he was standing in front of a refrigerator situated against a wall. Where was he expecting me to go?

Suddenly Makey skillfully pulled on the large icebox and

I realized it was on recessed wheels; it slid easily from the wall revealing a hole large enough to walk through.

Moving out of the restaurant and into the adjacent building was a big problem. If this phone wasn't transmitting and these Rastas did in fact have larceny and murder on their minds, I had no one to keep an eye on me.

Before I moved to the hidden passageway the one named Colin held his hands out indicating he was going to frisk me, which I fully expected. I took my hand out of my pocket holding onto the phone, leaving it in plain sight. As he tossed me I noticed he had what appeared to be a Beretta 9mm tucked under his t-shirt, my level of paranoia now spiking almost out of control. I had to get this information out immediately. My throat went dry.

I stopped and said, "Whoa, let's take a step back for a second. A hole in the wall behind a soda machine, are you guys kidding? Before I walk into that building I want to know exactly where the fuck you're taking me." Just as I relayed that bit of information I heard the iron gates being pulled down in front of the restaurant. It was a loud clanging noise ending with a BANG! and easily cloaking my transmission—I was now, without question, completely on my own.

"By the way," I said, turning to Colin, "there's no need for fucking weapons, bro. You saw I came clean?"

The metaphor of entering a dark black hole was not lost on me. I could only hope my boys on the other end of the cell phone caught my description of it.

At that point Colin indicated my phone. I handed it to him to inspect. To my absolute surprise and horror, he removed the battery and handed it back to me. That was it. My lifeline, the only hope I had of communicating beyond these walls, was gone. I felt that cold familiar chill run up my spine.

The contingency plan was that if I didn't leave the storefront to retrieve the car with the weed in fifteen minutes, one of my boys would walk in to check out the menu. That plan was now completely off the table, as the restaurant was shuttered and locked.

I was completely at Makey's mercy. He and his friends had played me perfectly—they were professionals. I could only hope to be their match.

I followed Makey and Zeek up a darkened stairway with garbage everywhere; there were syringes, crack vials, broken glass, and suddenly I was hit with that putrid unforgettable odor, the smell of death. And there it was, a dead cat being ravaged by a horde of rats as big as the cat.

BOOM! A rat exploded less than six feet in front of me. I nearly jumped out of my shoes as the rats scattered. I spun on Colin, who was tucking the smoking Beretta back into his pants. "What the fuck!" I screamed. "Let a brother know when you're going to bust off a shot."

Makey and Zeek laughed. "Hey, cat got your tongue?" Makey said.

I had to take control of the situation. I stopped following them. "No, no, no! This isn't cool, bro. Where the fuck are we going? It was supposed to be just you and me in the restaurant, Makey, and now I'm following you and two of your boys through an abandoned building. No, brother, that's not how I do business."

Makey looked down the landing at me. He was suddenly calm again, back to the businessman. He told me the cash was too big a load to show me in the restaurant—we were going to an upstairs apartment, and he wanted to show me some of the Jamaican weed they were hopeful I'd peddle back to LA.

"All right," I said. "Let's just do this. Show me the cash and I'll bring back the fucking material!"

I'm not sure if it was the bullet ringing my head, the exploding rat, the other rats, the half-eaten dead cat, the eerie building, or the absolute insanity these three hitters displayed, but I began shaking. Before I got into a lit room with these three I had to calm down—my life depended on it.

We reached the top floor where two apartment doors were side by side; we entered the one on the left. The apartment was characterized by the same filth as the halls and stairwell. It was a railroad-style apartment, abandoned, walls torn out, closet doors missing. I noticed a fireman's pole in the front closet that led straight down to the first floor, making note of this potential escape route. There was a narrow hallway or foyer, kitchen to the right, living room beyond that, and a side-by-side bathroom and bedroom in the back. On the floor of the living room was a bloody king-sized mattress.

Makey pulled an old-fashioned chain affixed to an ancient, greasy balustrade and the ugly white fluorescent bulb blinked to life. I noticed it was jerry-rigged through a line that ran across the floor and through a wall presumably jacked into the restaurant's electric box.

Makey looked at me for more than a few seconds. Then he turned, and from behind a wall extracted a large canvas bag, unzipped it, and pulled it open for me to see: stacks of cash. He elegantly moved his hands through it so I could see the bills, all hundreds wrapped in ten-thousand-dollar ID bands.

It was all there.

"I don't have to count it, do I?" I laughed, slightly relieved.

Suddenly Makey did something that shocked me: He pulled out a large kitchen knife and held it up, very close to my face. He wasn't going to shoot me, he was going to slit my throat. How could I have been fooled into taking this meeting, thinking I could beat a legend like Makey?

I was about to drop-kick him and hit that fireman's pole as fast as I could when suddenly he bent down and produced a huge block of marijuana. It was wrapped in plastic and looked like a square block of gingerbread. He handed me the brick and the knife.

"Ga'head, cut it, smell it," he said. "Da best Jamaican ganja on da planet."

I cut into it and it felt as though I was cutting into a block of clay, though its odor—undeniable. I split it, sniffed it, and looked up at him—that's when the lights suddenly snapped off and all hell broke loose.

I quickly shuffled back to the wall, dropped low on my haunches with the knife out in front of me. The first person I could detect close enough was going to get slashed and stabbed in the face. My heart was now pounding. This couldn't be happening, but it was. I was waiting for the flash of a gun so I could determine who was closest. If I was going to die, I was taking at least one of these motherfuckers with me.

I was trying to see, gripping the sweaty knife.

Then suddenly the lights came back on.

Colin and Makey were standing in the same position as they were before the lights went out. Zeek was gone and so was the bag of money. When they saw me in that prone position, terror in my eyes, shaking hand gripping the knife, they both started laughing.

I felt the blood pounding through my ears. I wanted to get up and hack both men to pieces, but I calmed. This wasn't a rip, just an elaborate plan to keep *them* from getting ripped. Now, I was back in control.

I looked into Anthony Makey's eyes and I started laughing, too, hysterical laughter, insane laughter.

And why not? I wasn't laughing for the same reason these guys were—that business was good. I was laughing because I would leave this building to pretend to retrieve all that good Mexican weed they were expecting, and when I got back to the restaurant, I'd hesitate by the door, bend down, and pretend to pick up a coin—the signal for my colleagues to move in—and as soon as I was safely outside, about fifty federal agents and cops would swarm the place. Just about the time these guys were getting fingerprinted, I'll be on a jet back to California with a money belt filled with about $40,000 in hundred-dollar bills, the same bills they'd just fronted me in that bag.

I
The Escape

Thin Ice

I drove to the safe house in Temecula, California, about forty miles northeast of my home. It was a sprawling, hard-edged suburb of San Diego, lying at the center of a two-county region known as the "Inland Empire"—the perfect location to set up a drug-smuggling ring. It was beyond any customs checkpoints, clear sailing to all points north throughout the country.

I worked for a man named Tony Geneste, who often went by "Tony Loco Tony" for reasons that quickly became obvious when you met him. My job was to manage all the logistics of our operation—to devise the circuitous, off-the-beaten-path routes we used for transporting the hundreds of millions of dollars' worth of illegal narcotics we were distributing for the Beltrán Cartel in Mexico, all in an effort to circumvent seizures north of the Inland Empire. And I excelled at it, at knowing the police stations, sheriff's offices, state trooper barracks, checkpoints, hot spots, and speed traps. Through weeks, sometimes months, of reconnaissance and due diligence I even acquired the names and shifts of the cops that worked in most of the precincts and sheriff's offices my men drove through—the backwater towns and exurbs and suburbs of minor and major cities. Yes, *my* routes took longer to spirit the material to its final destination—but when they were followed to the letter, they worked.

Finding someone who could follow directions wasn't as easy as it sounds. The biggest problem Tony and I faced was finding and indoctrinating clean drivers who were fearless and smart, men and women who could think on their feet and not fall apart during a random police check of their car, truck, or person. And our inability to recruit enough good drivers was the reason I was forty miles from home.

As I pulled down the quiet, nondescript cul-de-sac, I noticed Tony walking back and forth in front of the safe house, phone jammed tightly against his ear in what seemed like animated conversation. Odd because Tony *never* spoke on the phone—he preferred two-way walkie-talkies or medical pagers. After all, his were usually *yes-or-no* conversations.

The leader of our American cartel, subsidized by the powerful and feared Beltrán Cartel, Tony Geneste looked like a cartel leader straight out of central casting. If you were to see him on the street, or in a nightclub, you'd know this man's whole life just by looking at him, and he didn't give a shit that anyone knew because Tony was careful, and very dangerous. He had that aura that read: *back away or die.*

By the way Tony was pacing, I knew the phone call wasn't going how he hoped. He was throwing around his fireplug physique in frustration. He had naturally broad shoulders, massive biceps, a hairless barrel chest covered with jailhouse tattoos, and thighs thick as tree trunks. His enormous cinderblock hands—callused and seemingly overworked—were capable of squeezing a man's head until it popped. He wore a Pancho Villa–like mustache covering both lips and when untrimmed it drooped ridiculously to the bottom of his chin; his receding hairline was always greased back and pulled into a tight ponytail.

Tony was built for the profession he was in, and he had the mind-set—I'd seen him tear men limb from limb with his bare hands. If there was a way to hurt another human being without the help of a weapon, he could do it—Tony *was* the weapon, every inch of him.

Beyond Tony's insatiable quest to be the *baddest mothafucka* on the planet—which in my estimation he was, and believe me it was nothing to be proud of—the man was an oddball of sorts. He had zero taste in clothing. I'd like to say he was a throwback of some kind, but the era to which his taste aspired, to this day, it's still indecipherable to me. He favored colorful alligator boots, carefully pressed starched black jeans, and colorful silk shirts opened to his breastbone. He wore jewelry that was garish even for a drug lord, thick gold chains affixed with an assortment of diamond crucifixes, a not-so-mini diamond-encrusted AK47, and a gold Christ head the size of an infant's fist, its thorny crown adorned with seven karats of diamonds and rubies.

Yet despite his bizarre appearance, Tony was never a man who liked to waste time, so I couldn't help but wonder what he could still need to say to the person on the other end of the phone. Even when he was in prison for seventeen years, he didn't waste a minute. I'm sure he had plenty of leisure time to do what abnormally strong psychopathic killers do—prey upon the rest of the inmates with shakedowns and contract murders, swing deals with corrupt guards. But Tony didn't do those things. Instead, while incarcerated, he became a licensed paralegal. And had he not been a predicate felon and convicted killer he could've easily passed the bar exam in any state of the country.

I parked the car and walked cautiously to him, and when he snapped the phone closed it sounded like the report of a .25-caliber pistol, business end pointed at my head. Tony didn't look at me, he just screamed, *"Puta pandejo!"*

I knew Tony's moods all too well; it was best to let him vent and not say a word. Waiting for him to catch his breath, I watched as he walked in small tight circles muttering some Cuban Santeria-like hex. I did catch the name of its recipient, *Raul.* That's when I knew that the day had gone sideways.

Raul, one of our drivers and the bane of all our existence, was the older brother of Tony's closest friend and business partner, Hector, and that was the only reason Raul still stood amongst the living, because Raul was a stone-cold crackhead who at times was not above liberating some of Tony's product for his continuous objective—working the crack pipe four, sometimes five days straight. This, it turned out, was why I was summoned to the suicide king's safe house that early Sunday morning.

Hector and Tony went back so far that not even Raul's absurd antics could get between them. Hector had introduced Tony to the heads of the cartel, Abel and Eliseo Beltrán, our benefactors in the drug business who just happened to be savage killers, too. Tony, the more aggressive between himself and Hector, made a good impression on the brothers and he supplanted Hector as their "go-to-guy," thus becoming the leader of the American distribution arm of the Beltrán Cartel. I knew this was a thorn in Hector's side and wondered how long it would take for their tense alliance to dissolve. Tony and Hector seemed able to cooperate so long as they were getting paid.

But Hector and his brother Raul were two very different breeds of men. Though Hector didn't own Tony's fearsome look, he was as ruthless and dangerous, whereas Raul was a nonconfrontational free spirit, and, as I mentioned, a crackhead.

It was Hector's job to deal with the Beltrán's acolytes, making sure the drugs passed through San Diego's San Ysidro border safely, then were ferried to Los Angeles where the parcels would be secured—without incident—at our safe houses. Once the drugs were secured, it was my job to supervise our workers breaking down the product into manageable packages, sneak them into our refrigerated trucks, and then have them transported across the country to our many clients in the East, mainly New York and Detroit. Upon delivery, I'd fly east, pick up the cash from our clients, make sure the count was right, load the massive amount of cash on pallets, and send it all back to Hector in San Diego via the refrigerated trucks the drugs had been delivered in. Hector would break off what we owed to the Beltráns and deliver them the balance, sending the profits back to our safe houses all over California. A simple operation that netted us tens of millions of dollars a year.

But it never ended up so simple. Originally this was Tony's job, but he began staying in New York for longer stretches at a time, so he delegated this über-important part of the operation to Hector—which was the biggest operations mistake he'd ever make. At one point, I thought it'd cost us our lives.

When Tony was in San Diego, he'd take over the job of handing off the cash to the cartel couriers, and the consequences of his giving Hector so much latitude hit us in the face on one such trip down there. At this point Tony was dating a beautiful, thirty-something woman, Rosaria, who, unfortunately for us, was also from Sinaloa, the headquarters of the Beltrán brothers' cartel and a place where everybody knows everybody, especially if you're in *the life*. She was the manager of a beautiful boutique hotel—The Sweet Water—situated directly on the beach in San Diego. The Sweet Water wasn't listed with any travel agents— you needed to have a connection to someone in management to get a room. Needless to say, its array of guests were wealthy Mexicans and South Americans trying to maintain a very low profile while staying in the United States. All, certainly, were friends of the Beltráns, and, I'd learn, mostly all in the drug business in one capacity or another. I'd come to learn that The Sweet Water Hotel was financed and built by the Beltráns, but whether they were using it to launder money or as a discreet location—situated very close to the border—to relax undisturbed when they were in town, I would never know.

We thought The Sweet Water was the perfect place for downtime while Tony and I waited for our next shipment of drugs to arrive from Mexico. One early evening, just before heading out for dinner, we were relaxing on the large patio deck watching the sunset over the Pacific. Drinks in hand, we were discussing the potential of new clientele in Miami, Florida, and at the moment life was very good. So good, in fact, we wondered if we really needed more clients. The answer, we decided, was no. We had loyal, very buttoned-up clients who were making us wealthy beyond our wildest dreams. We were wealthy and the business ran with the expedience of any Fortune 500 company, and we were seemingly untouchable.

There was a soft knock on the door. Tony and I looked at each other, perplexed, as a knock on our door at this particular hotel was odd. Odd because there was an understanding between the guests of the hotel and security-conscious management to never send any members of the staff or guests of the patrons to these rooms unless requested, so Tony and I were immediately on guard. We were unarmed, which made the situation worse. I was looking around the room for anything I could use as a weapon just in case this was an attempted kidnap-and-ransom setup—we were in the drug business, after all, and where there are drugs, there is money, and a lot of it.

I quietly made my way to the door, looked through the peephole, and I was shocked when I realized who the two well-dressed men standing outside were—the Beltrán brothers, Eliseo and Abel, the heads of a worldwide drug empire that netted billions of dollars a year thanks to distributors like Tony and myself.

Now it made sense. They were the only two men—without search warrants and a posse full of federal agents—that would be able to circumvent the rules and regulations of *their* hotel, with a little help from Rosaria of Sinaloa.

I whispered, a little confused and worried, "It's the brothers."

Tony stiffened up immediately, smoothing out his shirt and pants; he was excited by the visit. In his mind it must've made all the sense in the world: We were making them boat-loads of money, always on time with our payments, and our solid client base was steadily increasing their orders. They must've been in town, Rosaria gave them our room number, and they wanted to pop by say hello.

I, on the other hand, wasn't feeling Tony's warm and fuzzy euphoria. No, a surprise visit from these two, in our world, would be like the mayor of New York City racing over to Macy's department store to hand over the key to the city to a mall security guard for catching a shoplifter—it just didn't make sense. Yes, we were making the brothers millions upon millions of dollars a year, but we were one of many. We were clients, and they were gods in the drug business. The Beltrán brothers were a combo of Pablo Escobar, Pol Pot, and Attila the Hun all rolled into one.

Eliseo and Abel entered the room and made small talk. Tony poured drinks for these two ruthless killers responsible for thousands of murders in Mexico and the United States. They were also two of the wealthiest men in the world, though *Forbes* magazine wouldn't catch on and add them to their list for a number of years. Two psychotic killers of the same bloodline, billions of dollars in their bloody coffers, with judges, politicians, as well as federal and local Mexican cops on their payroll. They weren't exactly the ideal bosses you wanted to receive a surprise visit from. The brothers had found the soccer game that Tony had on, and when Eliseo raised his arm to point at something on the screen, I noticed that he was strapped with an intricately designed .45-caliber pistol.

When Tony brought them their drinks, they turned their attention on us. "Let's get down to business at hand, *sí*?" Eliseo said. "Apparently there's a serious problem with our accounting."

Eliseo grinned at Tony, moving his bejeweled hand back and forth, indicating Tony and Eliseo.

I saw Tony's demeanor change in a flash; he went from cool and somewhat relaxed to twitchy and hot. This wasn't the president of the company coming down to Earth, bearing goodwill and salutations to his star salesman, it was just the opposite.

Tony was not going to roll over and plead for his life to *anyone*. It just wasn't in his nature. He'd rather die fighting than kiss *anyone's* ass.

Tony rose up. "What the fuck are you talking about? Accounting? I pay back every dollar I owe," he said without fear of retribution.

Abel simply shook his head *"no."* "You owe us $2,466,000." Eliseo sat forward now, pulling out his large pistol and laying it down on the glass table in front of him. All eyes turned to the gun. Tony just sneered at Eliseo, almost daring him to reach for the weapon. I felt my heart pounding in my throat. Tony was a badass but he didn't have wings; if Eliseo decided he was tired of the interrogation he could snap up that .45 in a hot second, killing us both.

Tony turned to look at me in complete shock, wondering if I knew what in the hell they were talking about, which of course I did not. He shook his head, *"no."* "There's a mistake with your accounting. Like I said, we pay back what we owe, what would be the purpose? We're in business for almost twenty years; we can make that in a couple of weeks. Why would we cheat you on such an insignificant amount of money? There's got to be a mistake, fuck, man, no way!" He wasn't talking to them directly: I could see he was trying to work through this: *How could we owe these* "pandejos" *money?* My eyes drifted back to the gun on the table.

Abel continued, "Every week it's another story, you had to pay someone off, you had a confiscated load, some *puta* didn't pay you on time, you had a—"

Tony stood up, cutting him off, face now flushed red with anger. Again I looked around for something I could use as a weapon, finding nothing. Tony said, "I don't know where you got that number from but there's a mistake…"

Now it was Eliseo who cut Tony off, slamming his hand on the table, jolting all of us back a bit. He said, voice climbing with every word, "Yes! Every fucking week Hector gives our people another story, we'll catch up next week, and then it's another week; week after fucking week after week. It ends now. We want the money *tonight.* Eight months of this back-and-forth bullshit." He clapped his hands together a number of times to drive home his point. "Time's up!"

Tony and I were speechless, coming to grips with the fact that Hector, who we'd entrusted with so much, had been skimming from right under our noses. Tony shook his head. "I don't know anything about this, but we're going to find out right now what the fuck is going on."

Tony had to calm himself down for this phone call; the last thing he wanted to do was alert Hector to the fact that *the* Beltrán brothers were sitting directly in front of him, guns at the ready, claiming we were short a lot of money, because if Hector *was* skimming and he knew the brothers were confronting Tony, he'd be in the wind—for good. Tony poured a large tumbler of excellent Scotch, drained it, then waited a few more moments before dialing Hector's number.

Hector picked up the call on the first ring. Tony was calm but added just a little urgency to his voice. Tony told him there was an emergency with a delivery and he had to meet us at The Sweet Water immediately. He didn't wait for Hector to respond, he clicked the line dead, and we waited.

While we were waiting, the brothers turned back to the Mexican soccer game. They were having fun, feet kicked up on the coffee tables, cheering on the players as if they were in their own living rooms relaxing, as opposed to their true mission, which was to potentially whack three of their distributors for stealing money. The calmer and more boisterous they were watching the game, the further my anxiety spiked. To them, killing us was just one of the many trivial chores they had to do to keep the business running smoothly. They didn't seem to care who ripped them off; they were here to get their money back and send a message to the rest of their dealers: *This is what happens when you fuck with the Beltrán organization.* Three hacked-up bodies found in the trunk of my car on some desolate street would certainly make the evening news, sending a very clear and chilling message to the hundreds of other distributors they were selling to.

Tony was walking back and forth like a caged tiger.

There was a quick series of raps on the door. Tony ran to it, ripping it open. Tony backed into the room as Hector followed him in, not realizing who was sitting just feet from him. I moved behind Hector and closed the door, standing in front of it just in case Hector decided to take off running.

He was confused, asking Tony what the emergency was, when he noticed the two men seated in front of the TV. They were staring at him, zero emotion. And then one of the brothers clicked off the remote. Hector started shaking, his bottom lip was quivering so fast it appeared as though he were either about to start crying or take off in flight.

Tony broke the unbearable silence, keeping his cool until he unearthed the truth. "I'm hearing something for the first time, something very disturbing, and Hector, if you lie to me so help me God…" He didn't finish the threat, didn't need to. Hector knew Tony—knew the things that he'd done—better than anyone.

Hector had but one choice: tell the truth and pray that Tony would be the one to kill him, because the Beltráns would make an example out of him, torturing him for weeks before ending his life in a ten-gallon drum of hydrochloric acid. He was now shaking uncontrollably, as if his core body temperature had dropped, nearing hypothermia. Then he broke down crying, stammering, explaining how he needed the money to pay for the child support he owed all over the country but that he was going to pay it all back. It went on and on. I was no longer watching him; I was watching Tony, who dropped his head forward and slumped his shoulders, as if all the air was suddenly sucked out of him.

Hector's excuse was partially true—he did have twelve or more kids with an assortment of women—but I also knew Hector had other enterprises outside of the drug business as well. He owned homes and properties all over the country, and he liked to spend big-time.

Hector's scam wasn't even a good one. He had to know the lies would eventually catch up to him, or he simply deluded himself into thinking this could go on forever. As long as we were paying the Beltráns back *most* of their money, every month, they'd let it slide. But as I said, the Beltráns knew every dollar owed to them. Hector's ridiculous scam was delivering the money back to the couriers in partial payments, telling them week after week one lie after another: *One of our clients got arrested and would pay us back within the month; we'd lost a load on the road behind a random stop; one of our clients didn't pick up the load and we were sitting on it.*

Hector swore that he was eventually going to pay the money back, but that did not seem to sway the brothers one way or the other. I could tell they were enjoying watching the fat man tremble with fear, but I could also tell that Tony read that, too, and it must've gotten under his skin that they were making sport of toying with his devious friend. The brothers didn't say a word; they turned to Tony, waiting to see what he was going to do.

Tony moved an inch from Hector's face, staring at him for at least half a minute. Hector understood every word of that silent communication, and I read the complete embarrassment and dejection in Hector's eyes behind the betrayal he had perpetrated against *his* closest friend. I knew this was going one of two ways: Tony would ask for a pistol and end Hector's life right there, or he was going to tell the brothers to take him with them, allowing them to make an example out of him.

What Tony did shocked me to this very day.

He casually moved to the brothers, sitting down next to them. He calmly told them that he was going to pay them back every week until the debt was paid, and he also told them he would handle this betrayal internally.

The next five seconds were the longest five seconds of my, and certainly Hector's, life. The brothers stared at Tony, again, same indifferent attitude.

So many scenarios crossed my mind. *Were they going to pull out their guns and kill all of us? Is this where it ends, in some swanky drug den on the beach in San Diego? Would my wife, Inez, be able to identify me at the morgue? What will happen to my family?* And then, like nothing had occurred, both brothers stood up, shook Tony's hand, agreed that they'd be paid back an additional $25 for every pound of weed we bought, and, without looking back, they left the room.

Tony waited a few minutes, saying nothing. Hector remained standing stoically in the same spot, knowing this wasn't over, not by a long shot, waiting for his fate to be determined. He knew Tony had every right to kill him where he stood, and I have to give Hector credit because he didn't try to talk or worm his way out of the unenviable situation he'd placed himself in—he'd either live or die, and that all depended on the level of Tony's *big evil* at that very moment.

Tony kept his distance from Hector because—I knew—if he were within striking distance of the fat man, he might not be able to stop himself from going through with it. And Tony was so combustible that once he started he would not be able to stop himself until he tore Hector fully apart. Tony could never kill Hector; he was the godfather to one of his sons and they'd been friends for too long. It was a strange symbiotic relationship, like twin brothers who could do or say anything to the other, but at the end of the day they'd die for one another. Had this been anyone else, Tony would not hesitate and that man would be dead the moment his duplicity was revealed. Then Tony went off—screaming at the top of his lungs how close he brought us to the brink of death. Telling him that if it were anyone else they'd be dead already. He laid into him for ten minutes, bringing up everything he'd done for Hector, leaving not one stone of their emotional and storied past unturned. I saw the tears dropping down Hector's thick cheeks and into the folds of his jowls.

Tony calmed down, but Hector's fate was sealed—he could never be trusted again. Tony told him that after this nut was paid off they were through. In the meantime Hector would do whatever Tony asked of him without pay. He was completely cut out of the business, not to be anywhere in the vicinity of product or money ever again. Tony also told him that if he found out Hector was working on the side selling, he'd forget he was his son's godfather and, without hesitation, find him and his loser brother Raul—also hanging on by a frayed thread—and eviscerate them both.

I knew better than to completely trust this bravado—as I mentioned, he'd never kill Hector. Raul, however, was an entirely different story, Tony was just waiting for that last snowflake to hit the snowcapped bough, which would snap it from its trunk. Hector, on the other hand, would be sidelined and he probably wouldn't touch any of Tony's money again, but eventually Tony would soften toward his closest friend and slowly Hector would be able to earn again.

Tony stopped abruptly. Then he asked Hector why he didn't come to him for money if he needed it, and Hector had no answer. Depleted of his usual energy, Tony told Hector to leave and never return to The Sweet Water again. He also told him to sell his properties because Tony wasn't picking up the nearly $2.5 million alone.

Hector agreed and left.

Raul

The reason for my trip to Temecula this early Sunday morning was Hector's older brother, Raul, the thirty-eight-year-old, rail-thin, stone-cold junkie with a twenty-year jones for crack cocaine. He had shoulder-length, inky black hair, perpetually greasy and matted, falling across his skeletal face like tattered wet shoelaces. His face was long and angular, and one could see hints of the chiseled, handsome face it once was before the interceding years of abusing the glass stem of a crack pipe. Crack had turned him into the poster boy for the *"Just Say No"* campaign of the Reagan era.

Raul was neither ruthless nor smart, and for the most part did what he was told; that is, unless he was off getting high, which occurred frequently. But Hector had a soft spot for his only brother, and, regardless of his newly revealed duplicity, Tony had a soft spot for his oldest friend, Hector. So when Raul dipped a little too deep into the company's material for his personal use, or a few thousand dollars came up short on a sale, again for his personal use, Raul got a pass. Anyone else would've been tortured for weeks until they begged and pleaded for death.

Today was one of those days; Raul had screwed up in obscene proportions.

Our resident crackhead was supposed to stay clean for the week, and on the prior Thursday was to have rendezvoused with one of our best drivers and couriers, Pedro, relaying the message that the two of them, along with Tony's common-law wife and their two children, a five-year-old and an infant, were going on a road trip in an RV at two o'clock on Sunday, *today*. They were to deliver thirty kilos of uncut cocaine to our processors and clients in Detroit.

Raul had woken, after a four-day binge, just an hour before I received my page. Raul had also failed to alert Pedro about today's run.

Our loads were on a very tight schedule; we had buyers set up to take possession of all thirty kilos in exactly five days. However, our 100 percent pure cocaine had to be stepped on, or "spanked," by 30 percent, meaning we'd dilute the pure cocaine down to 70 percent pure, still excellent street powder, giving us an additional 30 percent on top of our profit margin. That breakdown of the cocaine would take place at one of our many safe houses; this particular one was in Detroit. Combine three-and-a-half days of nonstop travel and two days to process and repackage into varying amounts of weight for our many clients, it equated to exactly five days. If we did not show with our product at 5 P.M. the next Friday night, completely buttoned up with our product intact, we'd end up losing all of the deals. Johnny-come-lately drug dealers usually brought out the paranoia in other drug dealers. Tony wasn't about to lose the deal and risk alientating solid customers.

But there was an even bigger elephant in the room. Two, in fact.

Buses were a relatively easy way to move coke across the country; however, no transport is completely bulletproof. Our last consignment of cocaine, forty kilos, from the Beltrán brothers, was seized at a Trailways bus station in a border town between California and Nevada.

Two of my female mules, chosen and trained by me because they were smart and could physically tone themselves down to avoid attention, but if needed—in a snap—sex themselves up, were each carrying twenty kilos of pure cocaine in their luggage stored above their seats. As they approached the rest stop, a targeted hot spot by the DEA and customs agents that I'd previously prepped them on, they noticed two unmarked cars following the bus. Without raising suspicion they changed their seats. The bus rolled into the station, a busy gas and food mart for tourists and gamblers, all with varying degrees of degeneration, and stopped to let the passengers out for a break. The girls separated and quickly intermingled with the crowd—as trained.

Two of the customs agents checked all of the tickets and names on the driver's manifest while the second team of agents carefully scrutinized the occupants of the bus and walked the perimeter with a drug-sniffing canine. Within minutes the dog hit on the cocaine inside the bus; the girls saw this and disappeared.

Seizures are a norm in this business and you're given a pass by the cartel if there is paperwork, such as an arrest report to back up the confiscated or lost load of drugs. With that report in hand you did not have to pay for the load because it was considered a work-related hazard, or *the price of doing business.* The problem was that since the girls were not arrested, we had no paperwork to prove that it was seized—we had to pay for the load.

We were given this second thirty-kilo load we were looking to bring to Detroit on consignment as well, worth $510,000, so this load *had* to be sold to pay for both loads. And though our relationship was *semi* solid with the Beltráns, regardless of Hector's stupidity and greed, they were definitely the *two strikes and you're out* type of operators. If we didn't get them back their $1,190,000 within two weeks, well, we were as good as dead. That's just the way it works.

The second elephant in the room—larger and far more dangerous—was, of course, the money Hector skimmed from the Beltráns. Tony had been paying down the debt, but we still owed at least half. So the grand total we owed including the cost of the seized cocaine was $2,466,000.00.

We were now at strike two, or to put it in military terms, DEFCON ONE, meaning everyone working under the umbrella of Tony Loco Tony had AKs pointed at their heads, me included. Without Pedro to drive, we had another big problem. On such short notice we would never be able to get a suitable driver who knew the routes and secondary routes as backups just in case of police activity. Raul could never be allowed to travel alone—he was just too erratic and the temptation of all that cocaine in such close proximity to a crackhead would've been like closing down an amusement park, leaving all the rides on, and sending a hyperactive nine-year-old kid whacked on Adderall in.

After explaining the situation to me, Tony just tilted his head and said, "Get packed, tool up."

I was beyond confused. I hadn't handled product in over eight years, and that was a promise I made to my wife, Inez, and a deal I'd made with Tony, which he had conveniently forgotten. I wasn't about to become a drug mule all over again.

My job was strictly oversight, facilitation, and, like any good businessman, expansion and seeking other diverse opportunities within our reliable client base. I earned that title and the respect it warranted, not based on the years I'd put in, but by the sheer money I'd made for Tony and the cartel—hundreds of millions of dollars.

I shook my head no over and over but was unable to speak.

Tony's mausoleum-black eyes were focused on mine. The pulsing energy that permeated through and around him, like a battalion of killer bees waiting to swarm, suddenly joined us together. Gone was the decorous father-son relationship, the heir-to-the-throne bullshit. This was about dollars and cents and Tony's true loyalty wasn't to me, his "surrogate street son," but to his prized offshore bank accounts he had hidden all over the world—and to his masters, the Beltráns.

My knees weakened at the thought of this and it took a moment to regain my composure when I finally said, "No way, Tony, I'm not driving 3,000 miles with a crackhead, an illegal who doesn't speak English, and two crying kids with one still in diapers, not gonna happen." It really was a recipe for disaster. And had we not owed the Beltráns for the last load I'd have called the trip off altogether. I'd developed a solid relationship with the clients in Detroit. I'd promise them a better deal on the next load, something—anything—to keep Tony from making me coordinate and participate in this suicide haul— because that's exactly what it was: fucking suicide. But Tony was like a bull in a caged pen, coiled rage and power just waiting for that gate to be opened.

Tony moved within two inches of my face and he smiled; gold blingy eyetooth so suggestive in the sun, though his eyes radiated unhinged mayhem. He said, in a very soft voice, "Not gonna happen? Roman, poppy, you get paid well, yes?" His eyes squinted and he moved in closer, for greater effect, I'm sure. "The kids, your wife, all good, *sí* or no?"

There was something in his voice when he made that simple reference to my family, a veiled threat. It felt like I'd been shanked between my ribs. My children, each of them, flashed before my eyes, and at that instant, if I had a weapon on me I might've pulled out and blown a gaping hole through Tony's face. It was at this exact moment that I knew it was time to start looking for an exit strategy. I knew all of Tony's foibles, but threats, veiled or not, weren't one of them. Something had gone off the rails inside of him. It was time to get out while I—and my family—still could.

I calmed and listened, and in that moment I knew for the first time that if I ended up trapped working for this man for another decade, I might kill him.

He continued, "You have everything you could ask for, no? When have I ever asked you for a favor in return for what I've given you and your family, huh?"

The mention of my family struck home again; I felt a blinding sting behind my eyes, a furious red flash furthering my contempt. What Tony failed to mention was that favors weren't part of the bargain between us. I'd moved his business from a mom-and-pop operation to a virtual empire—he went from the corner bodega to Walmart since bringing me on. I was loyal, trusted, honest, and I did not do drugs. I was the one who had traversed the country finding better routes, but also searched out new locations to plant our flag; in other words, more clients, more than Tony had ever imagined he'd have. At first I tripled our net profit, and then tripled that, and soon, rather than earning a very good living as a drug courier and dealer, Tony became an American kingpin worth tens of millions of dollars, all of which apparently meant nothing to him. In the beginning this was as much a start-up business venture to me as it was to him. Only difference was I wasn't a lifer, or so I told myself, and yet ten years later here I was—back to *muling.* I was living a lie I couldn't untangle myself from. And as bad as today was, something good came from it, that push I needed. Tony hadn't realized it but he opened the door for me to step outside myself and finally assess where our relationship had taken me, the life I was living.

His voice went from sotto to withering heat in a flash. "Never, that's how many fucking favors I asked from you, *cero!* And now when the motherfucking chips are down this is how you come at me? It's bad enough I have to put up with this *puta maricone* Raul, whose face I should tear off with these fucking hands."

Tony lifted his giant hands up to my face, shaking with rage, and I knew if he could get away with the total dismemberment of Raul without Hector knowing, he'd do just that. I was now certain that my existence to Tony was but a simple afterthought. He'd do to me in a hot second exactly what he couldn't do to Raul if I didn't get with the program.

Tony made it very clear who and what he was, in fact he *wanted* the world to see because he was smart, careful, and calculating. And though he looked, acted—*was*—every bit the killer and American drug kingpin—Tony was *never* getting caught with product; no, that he'd leave entirely up to someone else: Raul, Pedro, any number of our other couriers, *and now me.*

I could see there was no way around this; I was going one way or another. I stepped away from him resigned to a destiny that awaited me. Now, more than ever, I wanted out. I wanted a life of normalcy, wanted my children to know what their dad did for a living, but most of all I wanted to see the light in Inez's eyes once again, that light that told me how much she loved and respected me; one I hadn't seen in so many years—I wanted it back, and I was going to get it. Ironically, Tony had become the impetus that would set my out-of-control life on track.

I looked into his eyes, still blazing with intensity, and after an ugly awkward silence I nodded, affirming his demand.

Tony relented instantaneously, smiled, and held out his arms, *"Esa es mi ahijado, mi chico, mi pareja!"*—That's my godson, my boy, my partner: I wanted him to choke on the words.

I backed away from Tony because I couldn't bear to embrace this conniving animal. Instead, I looked directly into his eyes, unwavering and unafraid, and I said, "Okay, Tony, I'll go, but I don't want to know where the product is, and if Raul doesn't follow my orders from the start I'm throwing the dope out of the RV and I don't give a shit if it's in the middle of the desert. If I see he's getting high, I'm tossing his ass, we clear?" I spoke with as much emphasis as I could under the circumstances, because it's very hard to dance with the suicide king—the devil.

Tony was still smiling, and why shouldn't he? Sure, the business that had done so well for him had hit a few road-blocks, and they were beginning to come so frequently that you wondered if something might be amiss, but if this run went as planned he'd be out of the hole we were in. And in Tony's mind, no cop or fed could stop me. I was untouchable.

Ship of Fools

I headed home to pack for the road trip. On the way my only thoughts were of Inez; the way she walked away from me that morning when I told her I had to meet Tony. She knew what I was up to—she'd been an innocent bystander these past ten years. A victim, really, and she was at the end of her rope. I had the strangest of feelings that if she could keep walking she would, and a chill shot down my back, the first flake of a blizzard I'd never survive.

I had to convince her that my days in this life were finally over. Sure, we'd been here before and she'd heard it all time and time again. But this time was different. It was now about a compilation of wrongs I'd endured at the hands of Tony. Turning the clock back ten years sending me out as a mule once again and this sudden threat against my family, these things could not go unchallenged. In my mind, I was already out of the business. The hardest part of it all was that I could not tell Inez about how Tony had subtly threatened all of us. It would divide us even further apart.

The truth was that, though I'd realized it long ago, I had continued living a life I was never meant to be a part of, as if there were someone else at the wheel, someone who had taken control of my mind and body, acting as my ghost proxy all these years. I knew I was on the wrong side of the law, and it disgusted me to the point where I could no longer look at myself in the mirror. And every day it wore on me, grinding me down slowly, right down to a nub of the man I once was. I had to show her it was going to be all right. I somehow had to spool up all of that history between us this one last time. My only hope was that she'd listen and could understand.

I entered the house and thankfully the kids weren't home; we were alone. Inez was in the kitchen putting groceries in the cupboards and cabinets. I moved behind her and held onto her waist. She stopped moving, suddenly frigid. I whispered in her ear, "This is it, honey. I promise, today is the last run. I'm out of this miserable business for good."

Before I could explain further she unwound herself from my arms, quickly moving away, unpacking the bags as if she were on a mission. I stood there frozen, a glacier, not knowing what to say, though I had to prove to her that the sun was setting on this horrible ten-year nightmare I'd put her through.

I tried to close the distance between us and explain why this time was so definite. She felt me approaching and suddenly slammed a jar on the counter so hard it cracked a tile. Startled, I quickly retreated, raising my hands in supplication. She said, "Stop. I don't want to go over this again. You're going on a run? Really? Are you fucking kidding me?"

She turned away, busying herself with the rest of the groceries, as if working out a way to tell me this relationship was over. But she didn't have to; Inez never used foul language—ever.

And there was no denying the dispassionate resolution in her voice and her body language, like she'd already turned this page in her life and now I was getting in the way of her *new* life, a life she'd been planning for a very long time.

I was terrified of losing her, yet I couldn't blame her for finally giving up. What made me even more afraid was that she didn't even—cursing and all—sound as troubled as I'd thought she would. It was as if she'd already played through the conversation in her head a million times.

I sat down on a bar chair at our kitchen counter. I spoke without looking at Inez and I was surprised at how easily the words came. I told her of the disgust I felt just getting out of bed in the morning, how I couldn't look in a mirror for fear of spitting at my image or breaking it into pieces. How I couldn't look into her eyes without feeling so much disappointment with myself. I explained that there was a chasm that had built up between Tony and myself over the past few years and that we were both aware of this abyss, that maybe it was time for a change. I ended by telling her that after this last piece of business today it was the end of my life as drug smuggler. I stood up without looking at her. My back was to her as I stopped in the doorframe. I squeezed my eyes tightly, hoping that she'd come to me and tell me that she believed me and everything would be all right, but most important, that she still loved me.

Those words never came. She'd lost her faith in me. And frankly, as angry as I was, I couldn't find a single way to blame her.

That afternoon I went back to the safe house, because I had no choice—if I didn't go Tony might very well have killed me. Tony's common-law wife, Maria, one of about four he had children with, walked out of the house carrying her infant son on her hip and half dragging the other sleepy child by the hand. I could hardly believe he was sending each of them on a cross-country ride in a rolling cocaine dispensary.

Maria looked ragged, way beyond her years of *maybe* twenty-three. She had been beaten down by her shitty circumstances, one of the unfortunates who grew up in the slums of Culiacán, Mexico. She saw her way out with the Cubano-Americano, Tony, the man with the nice jewelry and talk of a better life. And now this poor woman, the mother of this animal's two children, had become his drug mule, his slave; she gets caught, it's jail time for her. The two babies would be off into the broken system of child services, but no matter what, Tony always rode off into the sunset.

Tony exited the house, sucking on a chicken bone while holding a nicely patterned beveled rocks glass half full of whiskey and ice. He laughed sarcastically, explaining that Raul was fueling up the RV and that if he gave me any trouble to put a bullet in his head and drop him on the side of the road. He pulled out a solid gold Walther PPK with diamond-encrusted grips, and said, "This is my baby, bring her back in one piece. Raul, you know, like I said, fuck him. I don't give a shit if you dump that dopehead off the Grand Canyon. Just bring me back my baby." He laughed, stoked with macabre. "And my mothafuckin' money."

I wondered about Maria and his two boys. He acted as if they didn't exist.

I held my hands up and backed away from the pistol. "I'm good, Tony. I got this. No need for a weapons charge, too."

Tony jammed the glistening pistol into the small of his back. "You still trippin' about getting busted, ese?" He avoided my eyes, coolly pulling a wad of cash out of his pocket, handing me two thousand dollars in crisp hundreds, fifties, and twenties. Tony then looked at Maria. "You see what happens when you teach a spic how to read?"

I laughed. I didn't want to give him the satisfaction of knowing how much his toxic words stung.

"I swear, Tony, I don't know where I'd be without you," I said. Though the truth was all I could do was imagine the better places I might be.

Tony squinted up at me. "Maybe on the unemployment line, but then again, probably not, because that would mean that you would've had a job."

He knew the right buttons to push—when I had met him I was on the unemployment line, hustling all over the city to find a job that just wasn't there.

He downshifted, back to business. "You got your clone phone, yes?"

I nodded—and that's precisely when my half-witted partner-in-crime, Raul, banked the corner. The RV he was driving skidded briefly, tipped onto two wheels, and came pulsingly to a stop. He jumped out, completely jacked up. I prayed he wasn't high again. Not with that pretty little gold biscuit in the small of Tony's sweaty back.

Raul had two speeds, hyperactive when he was straight and nuclear explosive when he was high, and this was to be my driving partner for the next six days.

Tony walked over to him, grabbed him roughly by the chin,

and looked intensely into his eyes, like a doctor searching for any sign of life, studying them for a long moment. Then, in a flash, he slapped Raul so hard across the face that he seemed to lift off both feet, shuffling back clumsily into a row of thorny hedges.

Raul was so shocked he didn't know whether to address the stinging in his face, the bloody lip he now had, or the fact that he was splayed across two bushes. He chose to do all three ineffectively, falling deeper into the sharp, ragged branches. After a few attempts to free himself, he finally emerged with deep red scratches on his arms, neck, and face, looking as if he'd been windmilled by a rabid cat.

"Where'd that come from, *primo*?" he asked. "I gassed up like you said, the material is packed away like you told me, and I got food for the trip. Why you gotta do me like that?"

Tony didn't waste a second, grabbing Raul roughly by the throat, squeezing the air from his trachea. I'm sure with the slightest tug he would've snapped the life right out of him. Raul's face was turning blue as he tried desperately to pull Tony's vise of a hand from his throat. I noticed Maria pull her children closer, hands covering their scared little eyes, herself looking away as if trained to do so by how many times she'd been put in this position. I couldn't help but feel sorry for Raul. He was a product of his environment, born into this shitty life without knowing any different. Drugs were his escape from a life he had no clue how to extricate himself from, and now Tony was bullying him, this poor junkie, the easiest of targets. I wanted to free Raul from the grip of this animal and wrap my hands around Tony's neck to see how he dealt with the humiliation, the pain, the fear of the unknown, but what would that accomplish? A bloody gunfight in front of a scared twenty-something-year-old girl and her two babies who didn't deserve to be a part of any of this? I needed to find another way out, a way in which I could guarantee my family's safety from Tony's retaliation.

Tony whispered in Raul's ear, I'm sure relaying what we'd discussed before Raul two-wheeled the truck to a stop. Raul's eyes focused and he nodded his head.

We piled into the RV. Tony didn't wait for us to drive off, not even a cursory wave. He turned, tossed the chicken bone over his shoulder, and walked back into the house.

A problem presented itself all too quickly. The RV was registered in Raul's name. If I got pulled over driving *his* RV it would've raised unwanted suspicion, unnecessary flags. So even though I was beyond nervous about the idea, it made a crazy kind of sense to let him drive.

First, I had to calm him down. Once inside the RV I gave Raul a detailed outline of our route. Using my route of moving northeast on small roads across the country we were less likely to get accosted by any random police stops or checkpoints—it was a route I'd created for Tony's drivers, and I'd dry-run it myself two dozen times without ever being stopped.

Raul, still embarrassed and humiliated, nodded absently, holding onto his throat while dabbing the blood off his face and arms with a handkerchief Maria had slipped him. "I'll stick to the map, Rome."

Raul laughed while pulling a bag out from under his seat. He reached inside the bag and produced a ridiculous-looking

Russian naval captain's hat. He seemed to have snapped out of his depression. As pathetic as Raul was, he had a good heart and wouldn't hurt a soul, and he had this incredible ability to adapt quickly.

Pulling the naval hat on his head, obviously too big as his ears flopped underneath the hat's brim, he saluted and tried his best at a Russian accent which ended up sounding much like the Spanish Ebonics he normally spoke: "This is your cap-ee-tan. We hope you enjoy your ride today. We got snacks and water for the adults and cookies and milk for the childrens onboard. Sit back and enjoy the trip."

I felt a surge of compassion for this doomed man; as I mentioned he was born into a world of misery, poverty, and pain, the elixirs the ghettos of the world perpetuate upon the young. I realized that all of the impatience and contempt I had for the man was in fact directed at myself, for I was the one continuing the ugly cycle, moving into Detroit the drugs that tore people apart, that left people as utterly hopeless as Raul must have felt.

I told myself that I needed to stay focused on the task at hand. The plan was simple: up to Vegas onto Interstate 15, across Nevada onto Interstate 70, up through Denver, and then jump onto Interstate 80 east that would take us along the northern corridor across the country. At Toledo we'd get onto Interstate 75 north, taking us right to the client's door in beautiful downtown Detroit.

I smiled at Maria, who smiled back, but it was more of a resigned, defeated smile; she was as doomed as Raul in life and she knew it, and there wasn't a damn thing she, or I, could do about it. I asked Raul one last time if he understood the route. He said, "Yes, chief, it's all good. Not my first pony ride."

I lay down on the loft bed, checked the time; it was closing in on 5 o'clock. I tried to close my eyes, hoping the rhythmic humming of the engine would lull me to sleep, but all I could think about was Inez and the kids.

Down the Rabbit Hole

O ut of the blackness I was yoked by a sharp pain over
my eye.

That's when I realized I was hit in the face with the clone
phone. Fully awake, and very pissed off, I looked out the
side window and saw that it was daylight. For the briefest of
moments the tension I'd been feeling was gone—we'd made it
a day, only two and a half to go. Then I looked over at Maria,
who appeared to be panicking, almost hyperventilating. She
waved her hands, unable to speak. She was terrified, and for
the life of me I couldn't understand why. I looked at my watch,
10:15 in the morning. I'd slept for nearly fifteen hours.

Unable to hold back her anxiety any longer, Maria shouted,
"We're getting pulled over!" Her baby erupted in tears.

That's when I noticed a stocky deputy slowly amble by the
tinted side window like he'd been here before, done this a million times. He looked to be in his mid-sixties, and his under-
sized uniform had definitely seen better days. I froze. My heart
was pounding so hard I felt it vibrate in my throat. I needed to
regain control, slow down my breathing. I carefully separated

the venetian blinds of the back window, but for the life of me I didn't recognize where we were.

The deputy's cruiser turret lights spun, as if to reaffirm this was no dream.

The officer tapped on the driver's side window; before I let go of the thin blind I noticed the cruiser's front plate—Utah.

Somehow, unfathomably—unless you happen to know Raul or somebody like him—we were hundreds of miles off track in a state we were never supposed to touch.

I heard the window slowly crank open. "Good morning, sir. I'm Deputy Phil Barney of the Sevier County Sheriff's Office. Do you know why I pulled you over?"

My mind was racing, listening for any intonation in his speech pattern that could tell me something. The deputy's voice was low and worn, as if torn up by years of unfiltered cigarettes.

Raul answered, though jittery, almost stuttering, not a good indicator for a cop who's probably seen more than his share of Rauls throughout his career on the road. "No, sir, I don't know why you pulled me over. I was driving the limit, sir, I'm sure of that. I wouldn't drive poorly, my wife and two kids are with me," he said.

"Well, son, your front plate is missing, and you were swerving a bit back there," he said calmly, matter-of-fact.

That's when I knew Deputy Phil Barney had done this a million times before: this was a profiled car stop and he wanted to get a look inside this RV. The only shred of hope I had was that Utah's finest had upgraded their deputy sheriffs with the newest technology and they were all mic'ed and wired for sound. If that were the case, all Raul had to was say "no" when asked by this cop if he could come into the RV to inspect it. Phil Barney had no reasonable suspicion to enter this RV, and if he entered it anyway, this case would be tossed before it even made it to the grand jury.

To my surprise Raul answered him back quickly. He sounded together, actually in control, a nonconfrontational man who knew his rights. "Yes, sir, I am aware of that, but in Michigan we aren't required to have front plates on our vehicles."

The deputy parried, "Well, son, that might be true in *Michigan*, but right now you're in Sevier County, Utah, and here we require back *and* front plates on vehicles driving on *our* roads. But beyond that you were swerving quite a bit back there."

He stared Raul down. Raul looked the part and though Deputy Phil Barney might've been pushing seventy years old, Sevier County was his, and no long-haired, rail-thin potential doper was getting through *his* real estate without a cursory search.

"Sir, like I said, I'm driving with my wife and two babies, I'm sure I wasn't swerving, but if you say so then I guess I must've swerved." Raul went for his wallet in his pocket.

"Son, my weapon is unholstered. Do you understand that? So please don't make any quick moves unless I tell you to. Let's take everything textbook slow now. Okay? Now you mentioned your wife and two children. Is there anyone else in the RV with you?" Barney asked with a hint of suspicion.

Raul didn't hesitate, though his voice now trembled with fear. "No, sir, it's just me, my wife Maria, and our two kids."

That's when my heart really started pumping, wildly banging against my chest cavity. Why would Raul blatantly lie when he had to know the next step was a check of the RV? And once Deputy Barney saw me the search would certainly go far beyond a quick cursory check. No, this was going to be a full-blown search, more cops, K-9, the works. The officer's next question was if he could take a look in the RV.

Raul said, "I'm not really comfortable with that. You're going to scare my kids."

The deputy said, "Well, regardless, unlock the door so I can check and make sure everything is okay with those kids."

I didn't know where the coke was, but how much trouble would they have finding it in a seven-by-twelve RV? I rolled over on the loft bed, looking away from the front. I wanted him to get a clear visual of me, my hands stretched out in the open, free of any weapons, as well as appearing to have slept through the entire encounter.

The door opened and I heard his feet ascending the steps into the cabin. He noticed me immediately. I made a show of stirring awake just as he pointed at Raul, though oddly unperturbed, saying, "I thought you said there was no one else in here except you, your wife, and kids."

"Sir, why are you pointing a gun at me?" I asked, feigning horror. "Raul, Maria what the hell is going on?"

"Son, I need you to keep your hands where I can see them." The deputy pulled his portable radio, calling for immediate backup, adding the exact highway marker we were at.

The old cop looked at me and asked, "All right, son, what's your name?"

"Roman Caribe, sir," I said with genuine concern, and that wasn't a hard emotion to pull off.

Deputy Barney then told me to slide off the platform, keeping my hands high in the air; I complied. I could hear the cavalry coming, sirens blaring in all directions. Before I knew it there were four police cars in a loose semicircle surrounding the RV. I could hear their doors swing open, and I imagined their guns were out at the ready.

I wondered how good the lawyers were in Sevier County. No doubt they weren't the Ivy League types, but I didn't need them to be great—just good enough to negotiate a way for me to help the feds, a way out of my life under Tony.

Deputy Barney ordered Raul and me to step outside the RV with our hands where he could see them and we complied. He allowed Maria to stay inside the RV with her children.

To my surprise Deputy Barney did not cuff us. He gave us a cursory frisk to see if we were carrying any weapons; there were none, of course. He moved us to his cruiser, opened the door, and we filed in. "Y'all stay here while I make sure the woman is all right and there's nothing hinky going on. Oh, and by the way, you see these boys in uniforms around us? They was raised up in these woods and they could shoot the tits clear off a bull at a thousand feet."

The request was crystal clear.

Deputy Barney waked back to the RV and tilted his head at two cops to join him inside.

I looked at Raul, who was sweating, petrified. He was about to talk, and I shook my head no. I made a circling sweep with my hand of the interior of the car then pointed to my ear. I moved in and whispered, "This car is recording everything we say. *Don't* say a word that can implicate you. And by the way, what in the hell are we doing in Utah?"

"Yo, *primo*, there was some crazy traffic on 70, lotsa police activity and shit, so I came down a little further south to, you know, bypass it. Believe me, I wouldn't have if I didn't think it was too dangerous rolling through 70 to get to 80 with all them cops."

I looked at him with murder in my eyes. He got it, and his head flopped against the side window of the cruiser like he'd just booted up a hot shot of black tar heroin.

I explained the dire circumstances to him, telling him to be, above all else, respectful and to ask for a lawyer the moment they start asking questions. Though I was crossing my fingers that I'd get the chance to speak with someone at the DEA and get out from under Tony for good, I couldn't let Raul know. I needed to act like everything was as it had always been.

Raul nodded his head, but there wasn't much life left behind his eyes. I jammed him hard with my shoulder and said, "Look at me and tell me you understand what I just said to you!"

The damage Raul could do to all of us was insurmountable. I needed to keep him on point just long enough till we were lawyered up.

Deputy Barney bounded out of the RV like a kid on Christmas morning. There was more bounce to his step, a smile even. It all seemed to be moving in slow motion, surreal, like a film, as if I'd been here before. The truth was I had been; I'd visualized this all happening the moment I agreed to go on this clusterfuck of a transport. The deputy moved to the back of the cruiser, popped open the trunk, and pulled out a large crowbar. When Raul saw this he dropped his head, resigned, shaking it back and forth. "That's it. They found it. We fucked, Rome; we fucked." His voice trailed off and back he went to the safe oblivion of nothingness.

It took under two minutes for Deputy Phil Barney to emerge, now holding two sets of cuffs. The two other deputies also emerged with big toothy grins, and one of them gave a deputy standing sentry nearby a big thumbs-up.

We were carted off in separate vehicles to the Sevier County Sheriff's Office. It was an all-in-one complex—sheriff's station, dispatch, corrections department, and courthouse. Deputy Barney separated Raul and me the moment we were cuffed. If these cops understood the bigger picture, who I was and what I was a part of, and they proved it to me, then I'd offer them nuggets of information that just might get me out of this life forever.

The good news was the sheriff's department could administer bail without having to see a judge, which they did upon my arrival—bail was set at $500,000. There are apparent guidelines that need to be adhered to. The weight of the controlled substance we were caught with was obviously an A-1 felony charge, meaning it is equal to a murder charge, but without *heinous intent*, key words enabling us to get such a reasonable bail. To most criminals living in this part of the country, $500,000 might have seemed the same as $500,000,000, but I was solvent, and using my home as collateral I'd only need to come up with 10 percent in cash, and I'd be out in a day. If I was to find a way out of this life, I was going to have to risk it all.

The desk sergeant, a tall, fit, good-looking man with a pleasant face, escorted me to the fingerprint board to start processing my arrest. "Roman? What kind of name is that?" he asked.

"My parents are from Puerto Rico so your guess is as good as mine." We both laughed.

He asked, "You think you'll make bail?"

"I believe so, but I'd like to speak to counsel if that's possible?"

"Phone's over there. Once you're printed you can make your calls." He pointed to a large empty pen filled with about forty beds and a bank of phones along the wall. He reached into his pocket, fishing out a load of change. Smiling, he continued, "I'm sure they fleeced you at the desk so here's some change."

I thanked him and the moment he finished printing me I stared at the phone bank and prepared for the worst call I would ever make. Before I moved to the phones, I asked him what they did with Maria. He told me she wasn't being charged and that she was in a motel waiting for the next bus to take her and her two kids to San Diego. I could only hope that she would get off the bus and call a family member in Mexico to pick her up and get her as far away from Tony as humanly possible. Just the thought of her and those two innocent kids reminded me of all the lives I'd destroyed. This arrest brought up from the depth of my soul all of the shit that I'd tamped down for so many years. All that denial and false justification hit me square in the face like a slug from a .45. One thing was certain: if I ever got out from under this, somehow I was going to make it all worthwhile. I prayed that these cops had relationships with feds in the area.

I asked the desk sergeant if he knew of any good lawyers in

the area—what I needed a lawyer to help me pull off was like nothing I'd ever done before. Without hesitation he moved to his desk, wrote down the name of a local who was licensed in three adjoining states, then, handing it to me, he said, "He's the best. Have someone call him now."

Inez picked up the phone on the second ring. I told her I'd been arrested. By her reaction you would have thought I'd told her I'd murdered someone. Her anguish crushed me, and I confess I began sobbing quietly into the phone. I worried the best thing I could do for her would be to disappear. That's when I gathered my nerves and told her that I had a plan. It was going to be okay. In fact, crazy as it sounded, this arrest was the best thing that could've happened to us.

After the sizable amount of paperwork was completed, Deputy Phil Barney brought me into a small eight-by-ten-square-foot interrogation room with one desk, two chairs, two-way smoked-glass window, a very visible camera mounted above a standard wall clock, and that was it, utilitarian in manner and fashion. There were no tricks, no good cop–bad cop-type bullshit. The deputy reread me my Miranda rights and then he told me that the drugs we were caught with were coming back unreadable and he wanted to know if the substance was something other than cocaine, possibly methamphetamine. I knew the drugs weren't coming back as cocaine because the rudimentary drug testing kits they used searched for additives amongst other chemicals when identifying drugs and this cocaine was 100 percent pure.

I was stuck because I wanted to talk; I wanted to rip myself open and let it all pour out, everything I'd done up to that point. But if I broke so quickly to him, a local deputy, I feared

I'd lose my leverage with the feds, and that I could not allow to happen.

Fearful of ruining my one chance at escaping Tony's deadly shadow, I kept my mouth shut and lawyered up as respectfully as I could. I needed someone to help broker the deal I had in mind.

The Way Out

I could only hope Raul had lawyered up, too. I wondered why the corrections officers and deputies were keeping me isolated from him as well as the rest of the prisoners in an otherwise empty forty-bed quad. It concerned the hell out of me. That and the fact that I'd been told that there was a federal bail hold on me, so I wouldn't be allowed to leave any time soon.

From what I had ascertained they considered *me* a high-profile prisoner, like a celebrity rolling through who had gotten caught in one of Sevier's no-tell motels firing a twelve-gauge into the TV screen while in the throes of a four-day crack binge. I'd learn later why they kept me from the rest of the local population, and it had nothing to do with my charm or celebrity. Everything that happened up to that point was a carefully choreographed operation. From the separation of Raul, to the genteel, kid-gloves way I had been treated, it was all in preparation for the sales pitch that was coming. And what a pitch it was.

A thousand miles away from my family, sleep was an impossible commodity. All I could do was fixate on the thought of twenty-plus years without them, and it started to wear me down. I was sitting on my bunk contemplating my life, how

I'd gotten to this point. Through the Plexiglas window I could watch the inner workings of the whole facility, and when I did so I witnessed something that made my blood run cold. Raul, my partner in crime, was being escorted out of the building surrounded by *cops*! Cops whom I hadn't seen up to that point, and worse still, they weren't local cops or Utah State Troopers—their suits, blinding white oxford shirts, neutral blue-and-red-striped ties, soft-sole shoes, their fucking pocket squares, everything about them read wrong—read *federal agents*. He'd beaten me to the punch.

It was bad enough having Tony, and his deceiving partner Hector, determine my fate and my every move, the money I earned, the air I breathed, but to have my freedom rescinded behind what this junkie said was too big a pill to swallow.

I gently knocked on the Plexiglas. One of the young booking officers I became friendly with unlocked the slide on the window. "Who are those men," I asked, "and where are they taking Raul?"

He smiled and reaffirmed what I already knew and dreaded. The moment Raul was questioned he fell apart, giving up the entire transport and operation. And what a tale it must've been, because the feds were called in. But the worst part was that these feds somehow convinced Raul to take them to Detroit to sell the drugs to a group that he'd called his clients—not to the clients we planned to sell to, mind you, but to Italian gangster clients he'd once been in touch with as part of a deal I'd cut. Word traveled fast in this out-of-the way jailhouse facility; this young cop knew things about our organization that I didn't think Raul even knew. Clearly I was wrong, and Raul was taking them on a very dangerous wild goose chase,

I assumed to show his bona fides. These feds, whoever they were, would soon learn that Raul did not have the juice nor the knowledge to sell anything to anyone. Raul talking first was my biggest fear. How would they trust anything I said or offered them once they'd discovered how untrustworthy my partner was?

I was face-to-face with this deputy who couldn't be much older than twenty. I knew he was searching for my response and I gave it my all to remain calm in an effort not to betray the fear and anger surging through me.

I'd dealt with Italians in Detroit several times in the past, and they weren't the sort of men you would want to try and entrap or double-deal. But our contacts for this particular load were three separate groups of drug gangs: Dominicans, Jamaicans, and American blacks. Since he was going elsewhere, I knew Raul was punting, but he was going to end up dead and, quite possibly, get the feds he was with *as dead*. He was trying to sell the coke to a third party he barely knew, hoping to curry favor with the feds. He was smart enough to know he couldn't go to my connections because they'd NEVER buy anything from him. They expected Pedro or me on this trip.

That night in the quad I tried to sleep, wondering what lay ahead for my family. I was thinking of my son, just months old—would he grow up barely knowing me? My daughter suffering with cerebral palsy—how could Inez care for her, and all the children, and pay the bills? How would they recover from the embarrassment and dejection I laid at their feet? I knew what I had done for the past ten years was illegal— everything—and I deserved whatever they would throw at me, but they didn't deserve this. I got so caught up in *the life* that I'd lost perspective of the "what if" moment—*what if* I get locked up? What happens to my family?

I tried to calm myself. I thought about Raul with all those feds. Perhaps he was not the one they wanted but the bait to get me to flip. I needed one shot to prove myself to them.

The first thing my lawyer told me was that they had cases against me, and of course I was blown away. Yes, we knew we were being watched. Hell, we were bringing in tons of weed, cocaine, methamphetamine, and heroin every week. But beyond that we'd seen the conspicuous tails on us all the time, which is why we were so buttoned up on security and street tradecraft when moving or delivering our material. They could follow us all they wanted, but we were never going to lead them to any tangible evidence to develop any real cases on us—or so I thought. But no security can stop your associates, once they have been arrested, from becoming informants and going after the biggest organizations they know. Usually, that was us.

We were the Beltráns' main supplier to the United States— and we could be sure our customers let their customers know about it. Selling dope is not only about executing sales— marketing and branding are equally important for sustaining an operation. Cocaine, weed, heroin, and meth directly from the source—the Beltráns—was considered the Ferrari of dope. The issue—what I had for so long led myself to believe would never be a problem—was that any cop or fed working in any narcotics detail knew the local purveyors of Beltrán's gack, or drugs, were out there and they wanted to stem or stop its flow.

I suddenly realized what a fool I'd been. Did I really think we were smarter than customs, the DEA, ATF, FBI, or any of the hundreds of local narcotics teams out there, all working 24/7 in a concerted effort to thwart the Beltráns and their U.S. connection?

My options were limited and none of them were good. I knew I was caught, but for some reason, after the initial shock, I felt relief wash over me because I knew at that moment I'd be free from Tony.

I finally turned to my lawyer, Tim, and very clearly announced, "I want out of here now."

Tim cut me off. "Of course you do, but first I need..."

"No, you're not understanding what I'm saying. I want out, today, this instant, and I'll do whatever it takes to get back to my wife and children, anything! Meaning I'm willing to talk."

Tim was caught off guard. He was a lawyer, after all, and it was his job to do one of two things: have the charges dropped on a technicality or get me the best possible deal. In a calm, practiced voice, he replied, "Listen, I understand your dilemma and frustration, I really do, but just hear me out. Deputy Phil Barney is an honest cop, and Lord knows he's a good man." He lowered his voice. "But he doesn't adhere to the rules of the law very well. I've been down this exact road with him more times than I can remember. He has excellent skills as a cop, and he knows when someone is..." He hesitated. "When someone is 'dirty' for lack of a better word. But nine out of ten times he reacts poorly, prejudicing the case, and nine out of ten I've easily beaten him in court. This fits the same pattern."

He furthered this by explaining that the town judge was a very law-sensitive man, and though it was a Friday, by Monday he'd get in front of the judge who, once presented with these facts, would have no choice but to throw the case out, meaning I would be home by Tuesday.

I listened, but my mind was made up. I didn't care if this was a tainted arrest and I was going free. I was done trying to beat the system. This was my chance to get out of the life, and hopefully redeem some of my past mistakes—I just needed to talk with someone who could guarantee that it was done safely. If I truly wanted out, it was going to have to start here and now. I was ready to start divulging a series of dangerous secrets, and I knew there were people out there who were going to listen, so I told Tim *everything*. He was pinned back in his chair listening. I told him about how I had been broke, nowhere to turn, making that fateful wrong decision to mule for the day, which of course turned into a ten-year odyssey of pyrrhic fantasies fulfilled, coupled with broken promises and dreams. The lie I was living, the pretense of being a good father while ruining other families' lives; it felt good to let it all out. Every word amplified, crystal clear, and by this simple first act of contrition, finally speaking to another person without cherry-picking events or reciting a scripted response, it felt liberating. I ended by telling him I wanted to speak with Deputy Barney and the agents who had this case, or cases on me.

The lawyer looked as shell-shocked as I must've looked when he dropped the bomb on me that the feds had "cases" on me. To his credit he didn't try to debate me. He simply stood, knocked on the door, and was led out.

Deputy Barney and the lawyer reentered the room about ten minutes later. I said, "I'd like to talk to the agent or agents that have cases pending against me."

True to form, Deputy Barney didn't show any type of

emotion. He simply said, "I'll get in touch with the gentlemen that were here yesterday." He turned to walk out.

Before exiting I asked, "Does Raul have a bail hold on him as well?"

"No, he does not," both Barney and Tim said simultaneously.

I shook my head in disbelief. He could've made bail; there was nothing holding him here. All he had to do was wait it out and, as Tim said, the case, in all likelihood, would've been tossed and it would've been as if nothing happened.

Reborn

T he very next morning I was visited by a customs agent I recognized as one of the men who escorted Raul to Detroit. Agent Chris Cristiana was a big man, about forty-five, blond, and he wore very casual clothes as if he'd been called out to do this interview while in the middle of weed whacking his lawn. He smiled, walked to me briskly, announced his name, and told me he was from the Salt Lake City field office. I'm not a small man, but when Chris shook my hand it was swallowed up in his killer grip. The agent pulled out a pen and a rectangular notepad that fit into the side pocket of his windbreaker. He then pulled out and unfolded reading glasses, and without looking up he said, "You're either going to tell me a story that is true, one that I can verify and corroborate, or you're not. If you tell me the truth and can help us in some investigations we're working on you'll be rewarded. If not"—he looked up at me—"you're going to remain in this place. You roll the dice. If you're convicted, you're looking at twenty-five plus."

I didn't wait for him to ask any questions, which I could tell he found unusual. I just told the same story I'd told

Tim Macinerny. I watched him carefully as he was taking notes just as fast as I spoke. The deeper I got into Mexico and the Beltráns, the more intense he became. Occasionally he stopped me, asking me to repeat a name, but for the most part he was fast and sharp. My statement took just over two hours. There wasn't much conversation other than when he stepped away to get a coffee or water, and in those brief interludes I saw a very different person emerge. I was giving him gold and he knew it. He relaxed, letting his guard down, treating me like he would any of his colleagues. After all, we were in the same business, even if we'd once played on different sides.

When I finished, he asked an unusual question, a question I was not expecting from a federal agent on a drug case: Did I know of any federal agents, border patrol, immigration, customs, DEA, or any cops anywhere in the United States that are *dirty*?

"You mean corrupt agents or cops?" I asked.

"Exactly. Have you ever, or do you know of anyone who has ever paid off a federal agent or cop anywhere, at any time?"

I didn't even have to think about that question. It was our job to stay away from cops and agents. If one cop or agent was on the pad, or was getting paid to turn a blind eye, it would just be a matter of time before he or she got sloppy and was caught. To save their own ass they might give up anyone—even their own family members—to stay out of prison. Cops don't do well in prison. So we steered clear of law enforcement in any capacity, and the truth was that in all the time I'd been smuggling in the United States, I'd never heard firsthand of bribes being practiced with American agents.

Chris stood up, shook my hand, and thanked me for the cooperation. We'd be in touch.

"Listen, Chris. I want out of this filthy business. If you give me a chance, just one chance, I promise you I'll help you in ways you never imagined."

His smile was wide and sincere. "I'm sure we'll see each other tomorrow." He walked out the door with much more information than he walked in with. I finally felt free, and I knew what I wanted to do with the rest of my life. I was going to take everything negative I'd ever been involved with and use what I learned about criminals to stop them from hurting people.

I called Inez collect. I knew the stress I was putting her under and I wasn't sure how she'd take the news that I was going to turn state's evidence, essentially becoming a rat, which, once labeled, could give you an expiration date. I held my breath for a moment and then I told her exactly what I'd done. This was my chance to get out, and it meant not just getting away from the violence and despair that follows drug lords around, but doing so with the sworn protection of the federal government. I could simply walk away from this, but it was my intention to get out of the business altogether, and my testimony would solidify that for certain. I honestly didn't know what her reaction would be, but she surprised me.

"So you're through with this business? You're out of the life?" There was a slight pause. "Roman, I'm so happy and proud of you." Her voice cracked.

"Once I do this," I said, "there's no turning back, you understand that, right?"

She said she'd been waiting for this for years.

*   *   *

Same time next morning Chris was back, smiling broadly and shaking my hand. I took this as an indication that his meeting with his superiors had gone well. Under his arm was a stack of folders the size of a phone book. He dropped the enormous file on the desk with a thud. He got right to work, pulling out photos as if he knew the exact placement of each one. He started out slowly with the least shocking, but somehow I knew the visuals were going to get far worse. First came some one-on-one photos or garden-variety mug shots, then some grainy surveillance shots. He asked if I wouldn't mind identifying *some* faces. I agreed.

There had to be a hundred photos, and as he moved through each of them the macabre got worse and worse. Some of the photos were indiscriminate of gender, one eye opened revealing a milky unfocused stare, the other eye shut, obviously taken on a morgue slab, or taken in the field, like the desert, some back alley, or hanging off a bridge in Tijuana. Others, a rather gruesome sight, were of a decapitated head, some macheted to pieces: eyes, ears, lips, and nose removed, reminiscent of a carved-out pumpkin. The close-up photos of human depravity and the desecration one human being can impose upon another was too much to handle. They put faces on the dirty and dangerous business I was in. I forced myself to look at every photo. I wanted to burn all of that blood and desecration into my brain, my psyche. Of course I knew people were getting killed all the time: rats, thieves, swindlers, gamers, and *informants*—exactly what I was about to become. Most of the photos were players I could easily identify, at least the ones that weren't totally hacked to pieces or burned alive.

Many were men and women I'd sat down to dinner with, others I'd done business with, some I hadn't seen in years, but for every photo of an intact body revealed, I had names and aliases; some I even had phone numbers and addresses on. I was getting a glimpse of the alternate future I'd so narrowly avoided.

All of it reminded me how deeply involved I was, but also who my coworkers and *friends* were, because some of those *still living* surveillance photos facilitated some of those *very dead* photos. I gave Chris all I knew about these people, and with every name and organization I gave up I felt a little more encouraged because I was finally giving myself distance. For so many years I'd watched Tony operate with impunity, stepping over body after body, intimidating anyone who got in his way until death was the only option, all the while I was playing "businessman." Now I saw, in vivid color, the business I was actually in. I was just as much a cog in a murder machine.

I knew then it'd be my mission to do what I could to jam the machine, and my first step to doing it would be through Tony.

Switching Flags

After I finished handing Chris this treasure trove of information, the pitch for me to switch flags began. He explained a couple of things to me: First off, the information I supplied him the day before went over really well with his superiors, and today's information helped debunk false intel. And then he said something I had already known—I'd ducked a bullet by getting arrested. Chris and a task force of agents had been on us for nearly two years, and he promised it was just a matter of time before he had us all painted into a corner, with nowhere to go but prison. He didn't tiptoe around the subject of flipping or switching sides; in a very straightforward manner he asked if I'd like to work with them, and if so, I could work off my case, which entailed me essentially doing what I had been dreaming about—cutting the head off the snake that was Tony Geneste. He also stated that once we decimated Tony's operation, he was going after the Beltráns, along with other cartel kingpins both here in the United States and in Mexico—and he needed my help.

"Roman, before I make any official offer I need to hear you say that you are willing to work for us." Chris pulled out a microrecorder, snapping it on. He laid it on the desk in front of me. He continued, "If what we're offering you is something you're not willing to do, then you can simply decline and I'll walk out of here like we've never met before. Before I leave, I'll talk with the judge and your arresting officer as well as the prosecutor's office; hopefully that'll give them cause to go easy if you're sentenced. So, here we go, you ready?" I agreed and Chris spoke into the recorder, stating his name and government status, my name, the date, where we were, and what I was charged with. He then said, "Roman Caribe, are you willing to work with the United States Attorney's Office Western District and all its law enforcement apparatus in an effort to combat ongoing crimes that you are knowledgeable of and others we might assign to you as a confidential informant or confidential source of information?"

I didn't even think about what I'd be doing or how dangerous a job it might've been. I just wanted out, a new life, and possibly a new identity for my wife and kids. I knew about the federal witness protection program, WITSEC, and if need be that would keep my family from becoming collateral damage. I lowered my head so there could be no mistaking my answer or my voice, "This is Roman Caribe. I understand the question clearly, and I'm willing to work as a confidential informant or a source of information for the government or whatever capacity they deem me worthy of."

Chris smiled and gave a little fist pump as he snapped off the recorder, placing it in his briefcase. He said, "Okay, let me explain to you how this works. I'll need a few days to work out all the details, but basically you and your attorney walk into court where you'll need to plead guilty to the charges of criminal possession of a controlled substance with intent to sell, first degree, conspiracy to commit a felony, crossing state lines in possession of a controlled substance with the intent to sell, first degree, and racketeering."

All of the crimes he rattled off were the equivalent to murdering a cop—there isn't a higher charge you could be hit with. The racketeering charge is where they could go after Inez, her money, and living arrangements. They could take our home from her, the cars, furniture, and jewelry, anything of value because all of it was purchased with illegal money garnered off of a criminally organized enterprise. If I screwed this up, I was putting her back in the ghetto in downtown Los Angeles, where in the year before I'd met her she'd learned to survive.

Chris looked at me for a long moment. He was waiting for me to agree; he had to because I had to be in this 100 percent.

"I need you to tell me you understand what I've said so far," he said.

"I understand exactly what you've said."

"Good. Once you plead out, your case is going to be sealed. Now you must understand that this isn't a get-out-of-jail-free card. You have to work off your case."

He told me that I'd have to bring in some "big" numbers, at least four or five times the amount of cocaine I was arrested with, which amounted to between 120 and 150 keys of cocaine. He also said, they don't work in piecemeal, a key here, and a key there; they wanted weight and needed me to pull that weight within two years. "Do you have the guns or horses to pull that kind of weight?" he asked.

It was a ridiculous question, but I wasn't about to call him out on any of it. From that jail cell I could've made a sixty-key buy or sale, and after following me and Tony's operation for two years he knew that.

Chris then explained that the charges won't go away until they were satisfied that I'd paid my debt back to the U.S. government, and if I got into any trouble, like getting caught double dealing, or getting back into the game, I was going to get the maximum sentence.

"What is it?" Chris could tell something was wrong.

I was worried about Raul—about what he could do when he found out I'd cooperated. I'll be a dead man, I told Chris, and my family will not be safe. Not from Raul, not from Tony.

"Calm down, Roman. We have it covered. Raul's on the other side of this complex in general population. The word is that you're still acting the tough guy and that there is a bail hold but your lawyer is working on it."

"How could he possibly know that?" I asked.

Chris smiled. "We had one of our undercover agents go in on a drug charge. His cover is he got busted and was remanded in here with you for two days." I was learning how brilliantly cagey the DEA could be. Chris said the undercover told Raul that "you said your lawyer thinks you both have a tainted case and you'll both be out soon. He also gave Raul a message from you: 'Stay strong and don't say anything, we're going to beat the case.' So now he's walking around in there like he's Tony fucking Montana. The assistant U.S. attorney knows this case is weak behind the faulty arrest, so they're going to have the charges dropped on Raul. And in reality it's just a matter of time before we get him solid in another case, with your help of course."

I asked, "What about Tony and the rest of the crew? What do I tell them?"

All the paperwork would read that the case was tossed on an illegal search of the RV. Plus, Chris suggested, I'd have Raul corroborating the story. "If Tony has another deal set up right away," Chris said, "call me or the field agent in San Diego, and memorize everything. You'd be surprised how many guys leave places like this with agents' cards on them. Pocket litter is the first thing they're going to check for no matter how legit your story is. Then they're going to check your phone, which you might as well dump now. Say it got broken during the arrest. If they find one business card or number on your phone that reads back to a field office...well, do I really need to scenario that one out for you?"

They had all the bases covered, but they didn't know Tony like I did. Once you were arrested you were suspect, period.

I told Chris that I had been waiting for an opportunity like this for many years and that I was not going to let them down.

Chris laughed and said, "We know that. We've been on you for two years. We've tried to get UCs in, bugs, surveillance, the whole round-robin, and we couldn't get near any of you." He stood and shook my hand. He looked me in the eyes for a long moment. "I do believe that you fell ass backwards into this business, and I believe that you want to help us and turn your life around, but you're the only one that can do it. Now's your chance." He moved to the door and left.

It took about a week to get everything solidified; my life had completely transformed in the few weeks I'd been there. I was a different person—or I was trying to be one—and it felt good. I was given all of my personal items back and Deputy Phil Barney walked me across the building to the courthouse. There was a court clerk; a tired-looking, older uniformed officer; my attorney, Tim Macinerny; and the judge, a short man in his late sixties who looked like he'd just stepped off a John Deere tractor. The clerk read the charges, and the judge quickly asked, "How do you plead?"

Tim said, "My client pleads guilty, your honor."

The judge took a minute to review the paperwork, looked up, and said, "Case temporarily dismissed." With that he slammed the gavel, stood, and exited into his chambers.

Tim shook my hand and wished me luck.

Deputy Phil Barney nodded his head; he was a man of very few words. "Make the best of this, son," he told me. "You don't get chances like this but once in a lifetime."

I nodded my head in agreement.

Freedom

Raul and I were released simultaneously at 11 A.M. He hadn't seen me yet, though I was watching him carefully as he retrieved his personal items from the property clerk's office. Raul, as usual, was acting the fool. Dancing around like a marionette with a busted string. To me he looked high. I assumed he scored a bag of meth or cocaine in gen pop, as no prison is without its own drug network. He was mocking the cops and aides, who had by all accounts treated him fairly. That's when I moved to him. He hugged me and began screaming, "Ahhh, Primo, we did it. No walls can hold us down. We's Batman and Robin, these fools didn't know who's they was dealin' with!"

I grabbed him, pulling him close to me. I hissed into his ear: "Listen to me, you little junkie prick. If you say one more word in here or on that bus ride home I'm going to snatch the life out of you. You think your troubles are over, you're fucking mistaken because *you* lost this load. And when Tony finds out *how* you lost this load, your brother Hector is going to have a really tough time convincing Tony not to do what he promised you he was going to do before we left. So shut your mother-fucking mouth and let's get out of here before they start asking questions about how you got high. We clear?"

He calmed down and did as told, received his personal belongings, dropped his head, and walked out quiet as a mouse.

We were driven to the bus depot with two tickets to Los Angeles. The RV was still remanded by the sheriff's office and it would take two more days to get processed out in order for us to drive it back, and I wasn't waiting for it. Inside that RV was the last place I wanted to be. It was the beginning of the physical separation from the life. I did get back all the money Tony gave me before we left, so we weren't totally beholden to the $20 the Sevier County clerk's office gave us for the trip back. I was actually looking forward to this long bus ride back. It would give me time to reflect, but to also prepare my story for Tony's firestorm of questions that was sure to come. He would not be happy about the seized drugs, but this one was on him, and we both knew it. I closed my eyes to try and sleep but I was too anxious about what I was about to do.

Tony was supremely careful, and behind this arrest who knows what he might think. I'd been with him long enough to know once one of our couriers was arrested they were side-lined for months, all the while being followed by highly paid private investigators. If they had snitched they would suddenly disappear, never to be seen or heard from again.

Any type of deviance or disloyalty toward Tony upset him more than a sour business deal ever could. He was, after all, in the business of obedience and rules, and without them he was just another soon-to-be property of the state. But he was also a sadistic bastard. If you broke those rules, he made an example out of you, and those horrifying examples kept everyone in line. And that was the unbreakable link of Tony's operation; he was insulated because under the harshest of interrogations, *no one talked.*

Once Tony's workers were cleared of any duplicity, he did eventually bring them back into the fold. I suspected this was going to be his plan of action with me. Getting Tony dirty, actually holding drugs, or on tape setting up a deal was going to be a monster, if not impossible, operation. I'm certain that as soon as he found out we were arrested he'd already switched safe houses, locations unknown to me, that held his product and, I'm sure, money he squirrelled away. But I knew more about Tony than he knew I did.

The bus ride back was uneventful. Once Raul leveled off from whatever drugs he huffed or smoked, he fell asleep for most of the trip. When he was awake for a few moments, he'd just look at me then drop his head, nodding off to sleep. He knew—or thought—I was livid, and my eyes relayed that to him just in case he'd forgotten, and he also knew I was willing, and very capable, of doing exactly what I said I would do to him if he didn't keep his mouth shut.

We arrived in downtown Los Angeles at 1 A.M. Raul went his way and I went mine. So much had gone unmentioned— namely that I had no idea what Raul said to Hector, and Hector in turn said to Tony, quite possibly to save his brother from a rather gruesome end—but I couldn't ask about that without drawing suspicion. I was completely in the dark. But what did I think Raul would do? I assumed he was going to hole up in some crack den for a few days before he resurfaced to face the wrath of Tony. First he'd call Hector to assess how bad the damage was and if he needed to go on the lam for a while until this all cooled down. But as it turns out, I was very wrong. The little junkie would play me, and play me good.

I took a cab from the bus terminal heading to Pasadena, where my in-laws lived. Inez's mother, Minerrands, had no idea what I really did for a living and knew nothing of my arrest. She believed the story we told her: I was an executive at a large building company. I was going to her house that day because I needed cash—in case something happened and Inez and the kids and I needed to disappear quickly. I had installed a safe in Minerrands' home years before, where I kept $30,000 in cash for emergency money, as well as a Mercedes 500 SEL, which she happily agreed to keep as long as she could use it for special occasions.

In the meantime, I would plan with the DEA agents how I could approach Tony and dispel any suspicions, a confrontation I was not looking forward to.

It was good to drive in the luxurious ride. After I picked up the cash, I got in the car, opened all the windows, and once I got onto Interstate 101 heading south toward San Diego I opened up all eight cylinders, feeling the power of the engine carry me away, as if to a different existence. The arid desert air filled my lungs. I felt alive, free for the first time since I'd left Puerto Rico at eighteen years old, which seemed like a lifetime ago. Yes, incredibly dangerous terrain lay ahead for me—the Beltráns, Hector, Tony—and I knew I had to mitigate the risks that could get me into trouble. But at that moment, nearing

100 M.P.H. on the interstate, I was smiling. I couldn't get home fast enough to tell Inez that this whole charade we were living was finally over. We were free.

It was around 4 A.M. when I pulled the Mercedes into my driveway. I noticed the lights were on in the yard. Inez was in the exact same place we had started this odyssey, just a handful of Sundays prior, sitting in a chaise lounge gazing into the pool. Yet, our whole lives had changed, come full circle in that short period of time. When I left, I was an American kingpin drug dealer, both of us unsure what the future held; upon my return I had morphed into someone completely different, a man I was sure I would become proud of, and my God, how I hoped she'd feel the same way. For better or worse I was fully committed, and there was no turning back.

I approached her; her eyes were wet, rimmed in red, though she smiled when she saw me, patting the chaise next to hers. I was afraid that while I was away she had come to the realization that this episode was just another in a series of elevating mishaps in the dirty world of drugs with more to come, same old Roman, same old tired bullshit, and that she was truly beyond her threshold of pain and anguish. I'd resigned myself to the fact that it was a possibility she was leaving me for good. And I couldn't have blamed her if she did just that.

I sat down next to her, cautious of her emotional state considering what she had to have been contemplating since receiving the call of my arrest. She sat up, grabbed both of my hands, looked me directly in the eyes, and quietly said, "Roman, you made me a promise on the phone, that you were out. I want you to know that I love you and I always will love you. But if you betray this last promise you made to me"—she paused, squeezing my hands ever so gently while continuing to look me dead in the eyes—"you'll never see me or the children again."

It was a cold, calculated statement, and I believed her.

I had a second chance, a reprieve from a fate worse than any time in prison. In that moment all I wanted to do was envelope her, feel her warmth, listen to her heartbeat.

The Angel of Death

I did exactly what I was told in Sevier County. I destroyed my phone and made sure there was nothing on my person that tied me to any federal agents. I stared at the landline phone in my study for hours. Playing devil's advocate, thinking about the way Tony, my coconspirator, my mentor, and a heartless, stone-cold killer, would think. The questions he'd ask, the traps he'd set, the clever repetitiveness of it all, just waiting to catch me in the smallest of lies that would, without question, lead me to his torture chamber where I'd be turned into a skin suit. Tony's chronicles of evil were legendary, but never had they left me so breathless.

I had to convince him the paperwork I received from the agents was legit. *It was a weak case and my lawyer got Raul and me off without a Mapp hearing.* If I could convince this brilliant, conniving savage, I would beat him at his own game—treachery. It was going to be an epic three-dimensional game of chess, playing six different personalities at once—one more devious and perverse than the other. I stared at that phone until it was an inanimate white blur, all of the back-and-forth lightning repartee between us playing out in my head till there wasn't one question I did not have the answer to. I leveled off my breathing, stood, and dialed the phone.

Tony was cool. He let it ring three times before picking it up. *Lull your target into a false sense of security, kill him with kindness, then rip his fucking heart out with your bare hands.* Tony's lessons were teeming inside of me. Considering the loss we'd just sustained and his doubtless suspicions regarding my loyalty, his demeanor was cheery, upbeat, almost happy to hear from me—*no doubt a deception.*

Tony whistled into the phone and said, "Wowy wow, wow, look at you, the prodigal son finally decides to call? Raul, yeah sure, that fucking crackhead *cabron*, yes, I'd expect that shit from him, but you, baby boy, c'mon?" He laughed, "So you had a premonition about the run, and you were right. I think maybe I should've listened to my right hand this time, no?"

If this was anyone other than the devil himself, I would've bought into the fatuous bullshit, hook, line, and sinker—he was that good on the phone. He'd ask for a meet at one of the safe houses, and I knew he'd expect that would be the last place I'd go after just escaping the drug charges. I had to stay on the offensive, rattle his cage a little—*I'm pissed off; we shouldn't have done the run; Raul should have never been allowed to drive, stuck in that shitty little town jail for a month*—I had to knock him back a bit, off balance, then make it seem like I couldn't meet at a location of his choosing without allowing him to think I was worried, a telltale sign I was hiding something. You see, I was most at risk in this organization because I was basically the brain behind all of the transports. I had the names and locations of all of our clients because over the last eight years I'd cultivated all of them—both in the United States and in Mexico. If the cops turned me, Tony's business would go tits up in a week. I knew how much he needed me. He'd have no one to sell to because without me in the picture every client would easily put together what had happened: I was either busted, in which case Tony was being watched, or I ratted or was eliminated, which also meant Tony was likely being watched. Even worse for Tony, no one (aside from me) would be stupid enough to move anything for him given Raul's and my arrest. And without cash on hand to pay back the Beltráns, Tony was as good as dead.

But I had one more wild card in my pocket that just might completely burn Tony Loco Tony to the ground. I knew where Tony kept all of his money. Safe houses, bank accounts, off-shore accounts, I had it all, and to kill Tony, I mean really *kill* Tony—to take out the thing he loved most—all one had to do was bankrupt him. That's exactly what I intended to do.

Tony's biggest mistake to date was taking himself off the street selling the product because he viewed that as dirty work, work that was beneath him, but he did not remove himself from the consignment business—buying from the Beltráns. You see, Tony had an ego the size of Inland Empire, he liked to be on *Front Street* with the Mexicans. It made him feel like one of them, as if he was actually a blood member of the Beltrán Cartel, which in reality he was not, not even close. However, Tony was a ruthless, hard-hitting Cuban thug who could, without question, do time, and he possessed a huge pair of steel balls. The Beltráns, along with their acolytes, recognized these excellent street traits, their usefulness in the United States—money, power, and above all else, loyalty to them. However, the *lowly* sales department, which by the way generated all the money for this miserable business, Tony had bequeathed to me.

The entire machination of getting the product to the buyers, as well as getting the money back to Tony and the brothers, was my department, my sole responsibility. Tony had to be 100 percent sure I flipped before actually skinning me alive. And that was the purpose of this Cuban sitdown.

Tony was always super cognizant of wiretaps, but now he had to be thinking every federal agency, including the NSA, was on the line listening, so in semi-coded language that a five-year-old could figure out, he asked for a meet at the safe house he shared with Maria.

Tony said, "So...long trip. Let's talk about it, come by Maria's bakery, we'll have a nice Cuban coffee and talk about your...*vacation*."

I shot back quickly, "First of all, I got in at four in the morning and was a little tired as I'm sure you can imagine. I was a little pissed off, too, because on the sudden—and please don't take this the wrong way, no disrespect meant—*delightful* vacation you *insisted* I take, well, let's just say the crowd there was a little rowdy and in an ensuing brawl my phone got smashed to shit. And by the way the accommodations at the alleged five-star hotel were more like some crack den no-tell-motel in fucking Port-au-Prince."

There was an extended silence on the line; I knew he was assessing every word I uttered. Then, "You're tired, Chico, I get it," he said with the slightest trepidation in his voice. I was glad I had knocked him off balance a bit. Too cool and happy, he'd know I flipped. This call would set the tone for our meeting, and without question how and when he'd kill me. This was all part of Tony's ritual, and he enjoyed it. Having the power to determine a man's fate with a simple phone call.

Even though massive amounts of adrenaline raced through my veins and I was shaking like a newborn calf, I did one of the things I've continued to learn how to do best as a CI: acted my ass off, appearing tired, ragged, with just the right amount of a pissy attitude.

"Tony, I haven't slept much these past few weeks and I'm not exactly in the mood to drive all the way to the bakery. You kidding me? I'm serious, man. I'm fucking exhausted. Let's meet halfway for a triple play." "Halfway" and "triple play" meant a Denny's restaurant about fifteen minutes from my house, a very busy and public restaurant in the middle of a busy outdoor mall. Even Tony Loco Tony wasn't crazy enough to club me over the head, drop a hood over my bashed-in skull, and kidnap me right out in the open in broad daylight. Was he?

If he insisted I come to the bakery, I would then know that if I went, I might be driving to my death. And then I'd have to move to plan B, alert the DEA field team in San Diego for protection, get Inez and the kids safely to her mother's house, and then somehow try and rendezvous with agents, whom I'd never met before, unaware of their true motivations or if they in fact could be trusted with the lives of my family, all the while trying desperately not to be located or tailed by Tony.

After an agonizingly long pause he said, "No, poppy, you right, you right. I'm askin' a lot from you. I know you had a rough trip. That sounds like a plan—let's say, uhh, one hour?"

"Perfect. And thank you, I'm really beat to shit, my brother."

I'm sure he was thinking the same thing. You can't remove the spots from a leopard.

Before I ended the call, he quickly said, "Oh and by the

way, that paperwork from the trip, you do have that with you, yes?"

He was referring to the arrest reports and the accompanying letters between my lawyer, the DA's office, the judge, and the sheriff's department; the report that would save his ass from having to pay the Beltráns for the confiscated gack, but also the paper that he'd study with a fine-tooth comb for any inconsistences.

I was already dressed, and after strapping on my ankle holster that held my Glock 17, a god-awful illegal semiautomatic pistol loaded with seventeen .45-caliber hollow-point rounds, possessing the stopping power of a runaway locomotive, I made my way briskly to the car. I needed to get to the Denny's immediately. I had to beat him there just in case I was wrong and he did plan on clipping me right there in the parking lot, then having some kid rifle through the dead guy's pockets— *mine*—to jack the paperwork from the seizure, and he'd be off the hook with the Beltráns, two birds with one bullet, knife, garrote, or club. I'd preempt that strike by getting there early, seated at our usual table with the perfect vantage point of the entire parking lot. I could see everyone who came and went. Anything I saw that was remotely suspicious, I was hightailing it the hell out the back where my car was parked feet from the kitchen's fire exit.

I was taking a big chance carrying that Glock—the feds had warned me that if I got into any kind of trouble while on the outside I was going back in, deal of the century completely rescinded, and that meant twenty years in some federal hole in the ground—but I had no choice. I needed to be able to protect myself from Tony.

*   *   *

I was positioned at our usual booth, declined coffee for herbal tea, which the waitress brought over with a smile at the exact moment I saw Tony's shiny purple, garishly refurbished 1978 Cadillac Sedan de Ville roll slowly into the parking lot. No cars entered before his, no cars followed. Could he have really come alone?

The waitress asked, "Anything else I can get you, sir?"

I was fixated on the parking lot and that purple *love boat* that just rolled in, sweat dripping from every pore of my body. It was go time. It all came down to this meeting: would I live to fight another day, or would Tony Loco Tony be true to form and lose his mind, blowing a gaping hole in my head, gray matter landing in the cheese Danish the gentleman behind me had just ordered? I felt my hands begin to tremble. I quickly grabbed hold to steady them. Noticing a knife on the table I quickly unwrapped it from its napkin, separating the spoon and fork, placing it under my left thigh while keeping my hands below the tabletop. I looked up for the briefest of moments and that's when I realized the now-terrified waitress had been watching this whole bizarre episode. I stared into her eyes, unsure of what to say. I heard the hoarse words tumble out of my cottony dry mouth, "I'm, I'm fine, the tea is all I need, thank you." Before she walked away, I conspicuously placed the knife back on the table, pretending to thoroughly wipe it down with the napkin.

She walked away quickly, though I did feel a little more comfortable knowing that she'd be carefully watching me, the crazy man with Tourette's by the window—if Tony decided to go jailhouse, she'd notice and call 911 immediately. Not that it would matter because neither the cops nor even a comic book superhero would beat a bullet to my head. That is, if I didn't beat Tony to the punch.

Tony did not disappoint anyone inside that restaurant; heads nearly snapped in his direction as he strolled in like a king meeting his court jesters. He was dressed like Robert Plant, twenty-five years in the past. He wore a floppy white cowboy hat with a colorful peacock band and matching feathers protruding from its side. In the center of the ridiculous hat he pinned two three-inch solid gold crossed .45-caliber pistols; beige leather pants flared at his ankles, which I knew was for easy access to his pistol. His gold belt buckle was the size of a turkey platter and loaded with diamonds, rubies, and sapphires replicating the Cuban national flag. Capping off his ensemble were a silk purple shirt with lavender stripes unbuttoned to the top of his rotund belly, mocha-brown velvet boots—which in all probability contained a "stinger," what we called a .25-caliber five-shot pistol—and a boot knife. I remember the first time I watched him tool up, surprised at all the armaments he carried. "You never know, *hermano*, what happens when there's just you against four *pandejos*? Always be prepared for that close wet work, daddy."

Seeing Tony enter this quiet, family-friendly restaurant, the waitress approached the hostess and whispered something to her.

Tony stood at the table, arms wide open, grinning ear to ear. He wasn't going to sit, not until he got that cursory hug to check for wires.

I stood, he hugged me, and in a not-so-veiled maneuver, those big callused hands moved expertly up and down my back and sides, he then patted my chest then began rubbing my belly up and down like a caring dad. "Poppy, you look skinnier. Food must've been for shit out there, eh?"

He'd covered my front, back, and sides in a matter of seconds. I was clean—this he was sure of. He dropped into the booth heavily, disregarding the family in the adjacent one. I saw them actually rise and fall in their seats, though they didn't dare confront him with so much as a snooty look. In fact, everyone in the restaurant, after first glance at the colorfully coordinated drug lord billboard, made it his or her business to look away from him. Though I knew it wasn't just his circus clown outfit that deterred looks; it was his demonstrative arrogance, his utter display of condescension toward the hardworking folks in the restaurant.

His demeanor goaded me. Something was bubbling up inside, overriding my preternatural survival instincts. I knew he'd kill me right there if he deemed me disrespectful or disloyal—he'd killed for much less, men *and women* he'd known a lot longer than he had known me. In fact, seventeen years of his life had been spent behind bars because he was caught with his favorite gun, which was traced back to a string of those very murders. So I had to tread lightly to cover or placate the hatred I now felt toward him, though with enough moxie he'd fall for the frustration over the whole situation that I betrayed.

How had I allowed myself to be taken in so easily by this animal, this savage beast of a man? Yes, I'd needed the money the day I'd agreed to my first smuggling run, and then, as the money grew, I'd liked what it could do for me. But somewhere along the way I forgot to leave this life behind. Tony didn't deserve to be in the company of these decent people, out for an afternoon with friends, colleagues, loved ones. Tony, without question, belonged behind bars. The irony of this situation was not lost on me. I began working for Tony all in an effort to make enough money with the hopes that one day I'd become just like these very people Tony had such contempt for. And now it was crystal clear that I had to put Tony down like the rabid dog he was. Because if I didn't, my family might end up murdered any day in his destructive wake. He was cagey and clever, and his only loyalty was to his money and himself.

The waitress, now obliterated with fear, offered us two scary, oddball men a menu, one of us a stammering mess, the other a cross-dressing torpedo who looked like he'd just walked off the stage of a '70s glam rock show.

I casually asked Tony, "You want something to eat?"

He was staring intensely into my eyes, same tight grin; after a long moment he shook his head no.

I tried to let this poor waitress off the hook. I caught her eye and shook my head, no. What I meant was, *we're okay, no menus, and as long as you stay as far away from this table as you can, you'll be okay, too.*

I sipped my tea, staring right back at Tony. Ever since we had come face-to-face, my fear had been slowly dissipating and excitement filled me all over again the way it had in Sevier County, the surge of electricity I'd felt when I was revealing all the secrets to Chris, the customs agent.

I'm going to burn down your house, I thought.

I could only hope I'd be there when Tony realized it was me all along, and he'd missed his chance on taking me out, the only man who could do so much damage, the young Sherpa who guided him up the icy crags of a sky-splitting mountaintop, and, just before reaching its summit, drop-kicked him the fuck off.

Tony held out his hands, very close to my face. I eased back in the booth, now totally in control of the situation. I said, "What, your manicure? Shiny, like always, very pretty, Tony. Has sort of a French tip thing going—très cosmopolitan."

Tony shook his head no and wiggled his fingers as if he were calling over a toddler.

"Tony, I'm not in the mood for games. What is it you want?"

"The paperwork, your wallet, and your phone," he said quickly.

I was taken off guard when he asked about the phone; I had told him it was destroyed during the arrest. Why would he ask for it? I was sure Raul hadn't seen me with it on the bus ride home, so under the harshest of tortures he couldn't have given me up, unless he lied, which was not a huge stretch of the imagination.

I stalled, pulling the folder off the seat. I slid it over to him. He didn't look at it, obviously waiting for the wallet and phone.

I tilted my head at Tony, feigning an are-you-fucking-kidding-me look. Then after a few very tense moments I simply shook my head, pulling out my wallet and sliding that over to him as well. I said, "Tony! I don't have a phone, remember? I told you it's gone. Broken during the arrest."

His eyes opened wide. "You think I ain't been arrested before, Daddy? They have to give you your phone back, your property, regardless if it's broke or not, there's still the SIM card. Once you free you get it back, so why you so nervous to give me your phone, or what's left of it?" He tilted his head at me, feigning a joke, though it was no joke. "You trying to hide something?" His smile was creepy, twisted, his blingy gold tooth glistening as always under the bright fluorescents above. I wanted to take a blowtorch to it.

I'd left the phone in one of the hidden compartments I had built into the floor of the Mercedes, an aftermarket, spring-loaded electric compartment, built and hidden into the undercarriage of the car with an opening hatch, nearly seamless, underneath the driver's seat rug.

"Yeah, they tried to give it back to me, busted! And do you honestly think I'm that stupid, that I'd keep it whether it was broken or not, or that I'd keep that fucking SIM card of all things? How do I know they didn't put a trap on it while I was in lockup, or a tracking device, or worse, some new kind of listening device?" I tried to suppress the smile blooming from inside of me.

I continued, needing to hammer this in so it stuck, "You see, that's why, until this major fuckup, which by the way I said was a disaster waiting to happen from the very beginning, I have never done one day inside because I think not one step but *three* steps ahead of everyone else. So fuck that phone. And fuck you for the accusation. What do you think, I'm working with the Dudley-Do-Right cops of Sevier County, Utah? Are you fucking kidding me?"

Tony tilted his head at me, that Hun-like smile gone, his thin sadistic lips twitching, hidden under that droopy mustache now involuntarily moving back and forth. I knew I had him. He was sold. I just prayed to God that the paperwork was as good as my lie.

Tony said, almost in a whisper, "Yeah, three steps ahead of everyone else, that's what I'm afraid of."

I shot back, "Oh, suddenly because I'm careful I'm the bad guy? My caution has made you a lot of money over the years. It's also kept all of us out of prison, if you haven't forgotten." I paused for greater effect, pretending to still—not fully—understand his accusations. "And I really don't understand what it is you're trying to get at?"

Tony pulled out a small, stylish chrome case containing delicate reading glasses; he carefully unfolded them and slid them onto his nose.

The worn leather bench seat crackled with his every move. He began to examine the documents, checking to see if there was anything off. I knew this was do or die. He would not repudiate anything he read, or give me any indication he found discrepancies between the law as he knew it and what those documents revealed, not yet anyway.

Eerily calm, Tony looked up over his lavender glasses into my eyes. He asked, "What I don't get is that you got caught with thirty keys of pure powder and they just *let* you and that fool waltz out of there without bail. That's very interesting to me."

"Well, let me help dispel any doubt you have or *accusations* you might be cooking up in that head of yours. First off, it wasn't *'they just let us waltz out.'* It took time. As you may have forgotten I was there for *weeks* on a federal hold. The cop that jumped us, Phil Barney, is apparently some loose cannon out there in the sticks, thinks he's some super trooper and a true believer, just doesn't go by the book very often, and there have been lawsuits brought up against the town by people who have been arrested by this particular superhero deputy. Regardless of what he found, it's fruit of the poisonous tree. He had no reason to enter the RV, no threat to life, any imminent danger or circumstances, nothing. He just took it upon himself to search the RV, and then, without a warrant, busts up that *incredible hiding spot* you put together with, I'll assume, Raul, because a five-year-old could've found it."

WHAM! Tony, having reached his limit, slammed his fist on the table sending silverware, my cup of tea, and sugar packets onto the floor. By this point diners had quietly asked for their checks, leaving half-eaten food, slinking their way out of the soon-to-be crime scene restaurant.

Tony pointed his finger in my face, hissing at me like a cornered rat. "Blame me? Who told you to take a nap for a mothafuckin' day? You were on that transport to watch over that *maricone*! You forget who the landlord is and the tenant is all a sudden? ME, I'm the mothafuckin' landlord, ME!" He pointed his thick shaking finger so close to my face I could smell the nicotine on it. "Don't blame me because you fuckin' checked out. That was your job staying on top a him. You were right that we should've sent him alone, because apparently for fifteen fucking hours he *was* alone!"

The waitress didn't even attempt to move to the table. I had to slow this down, calm the beast, or else we'd need to move this meeting to another venue, and I was afraid of what Tony might do to me if he got a moment alone. I casually scooped up the mess off the floor.

After a few moments I cautiously continued, "Tony, the judge knew it was a bad arrest, and my lawyer screamed bloody fucking murder that if I wasn't released on my own recognizance or the charges weren't dropped in light of the sheriff's disregard for the law, I was prepared to file suit against the county for false imprisonment." I indicated the paper, still shaking in his hands. "Read on, it's all there. He's getting the whole thing thrown out without even bringing it to a Mapp hearing. The case is getting tossed."

Tony thought about it, all seemingly calm, and he finally nodded his head. He removed the thin lavender frames from his face, slowly folding them up and placing them back into their pretty little chrome case. "Lucky? Huh. That's a good one. You know what Raul told Hector and then Hector told me?"

Here it comes, the do or die, or start blasting and run-like-hell scenario.

He didn't wait for me to answer. "He told him that you were cooperating and that's why you got out without any bail and they're dropping these charges. Now why would he say that?"

The little ratfink had to know I was going to inform Tony that *he in fact* tried to work out a deal with the feds, and furthering his duplicity by decidedly going to Detroit to sell the gack and in the process potentially blowing up our Canadian connects with the Italians. I realized then the grave mistake I'd made. I should have told Tony this as soon as he walked in. Now, for the first time, I felt cornered.

My only choice was to appeal to Tony's malevolent hatred. The hatred he had tamped down for years. I had to give him the reason to kill this predestined doomed junkie, Raul. If I was successful, I thought Raul was going to die a very unpleasant death, and even though he had tried to make me meet that same fate in order to cover his own scrawny ass, I felt terrible sending him to such a terrible end. I needed to remind myself that I no longer had a choice. It was either him or me.

I dropped my head, slowly shaking it. I started to laugh. "That little junkie rat," I said. "Do you actually think it was me that tried to set that deal up? You know both of us for how long? Think about that for a second. And if you had to pick which one of us would pull such a ridiculous boneheaded maneuver? But beyond the obvious, why would I do it when I knew the case was weak? It makes no sense. If I were the one who went out there to sell the material, *I would've sold it!* No. Raul rolled the dice because he's an idiot junkie. That's why they separated the two of us from the jump, as soon as we got there, divide and conquer. Who would you try to turn, him or me?"

Tony's face was slowly turning from a crimson red to a white complexion. The vehemence Tony had, squashing Raul like a bug, was just too overwhelming for him to think clearly. He began shaking all over again. I'm sure he was thinking of a million different ways to torture Raul, and possibly Hector, for getting caught up in the lie.

I didn't stop. I had to fully manipulate the kill cog in Tony's head, that once clicked into place could never be reversed. "Tony. Look at my paper: when asked if I wanted to talk without the presence of counsel, what's the statement read?"

He didn't answer me, just kept staring into his shaking hands.

"It reads, after subject was read Miranda rights he refused to make any statements without the presence of an attorney. Now I'll bet you my SEL outside that not only haven't you read Raul's paperwork, but you haven't even heard from or seen him. And as sure as we're both sitting here, Hector did not bring you Raul's paper. What's that tell you? And you know what, they're both going to come up with some dumbass excuse that Raul lost his paperwork, or tossed it, because he'll claim the case was weak and thrown out. But let me go one better. It was that little asshole who talked."

Tony's head shot up; eyes wild like that of a basset hound close on the trail of a fox, snout flaring in the musky air, ready to pounce, clench, and shake its prey till its neck snapped. "What are you saying?" His voice was as close to desperate as I'd ever heard from him.

"Like I said, they had us separated from the arrest on the scene all the way to the time we were released. They kept me segregated in the hole, and that prick was in gen pop. They figured him as the type of clown who would be doing a lot of talking with—I'm now sure—prison snitches or worse, undercovers inside the prison. From my cell I could see the outer offices. And who is walking out, uncuffed and surrounded by a group of guys that I can only describe to you as suits with attitudes, and not the type of suits you can purchase next to the garden hoses at Sears. No, these were feds."

Tony's eyes were darting back and forth like laser beams at some drug-fueled rave, no longer in disbelief of me, but of himself, for not eliminating this problem long ago. He said, "And you decide to let me in on this *little tidbit* of information only now? Not last night, or as soon as I walked in here, maybe a heads-up on the phone this morning?"

I shook my head no. "I don't trust the phones any longer, and last night? What would've the difference been? It was four in the morning when I got in. And the moment you walked in here you had your finger pointed at me like I was some newbie mule come up short on a load without paper."

"Did he ever return to the jail? Did he tell you he ratted?"

"He didn't have to. The COs in the facility told me. After I saw him skipping out with that troop of Eagle Scouts I asked, and they told me he gave up everything about the run. The crazy thing was, he was trying to sell it to our *Italian* connects in Detroit."

"Italians! Are you fucking kidding me?" Tony dropped his head in his hands, his giant fists balled up like two large coconuts, turning white as he squeezed the blood out of them, veins pulsing in his powerful wrists and forearms.

"Listen, Tony," I said gently. "The good news is that it was a total clusterfuck, a bust of a trip. They flew him out there and he wasn't able to make any connects, that's what I got from the inside guys. So as far as I can tell he didn't damage our relationships yet. What he gave up as far as the organization, Mexico, that I have no idea."

"So, he finally got his chance to fuck us and he did. I swear I'm gonna drop hundred fifty thousand on the street right now for anyone who can bring him to me alive."

"You can't, Tony. He's in the system and they're watching him now. Me, too. We need to put a little distance between all of us for a while. They don't know anything about you unless the asshole gave you up, but that means he'd be giving Hector up, and honestly, Tony, I don't see him rolling up his own brother."

Again, he screamed, "Guy's a fucking crack fiend, he'd give up his mother for a $10 rock!"

By now the restaurant was almost completely empty. Tony tended to clear restaurants and clubs, but only after he'd had a few bourbons and half an ounce of his own product. I noticed the manager and a few waitresses huddled in a corner talking quietly, occasionally sneaking a peek at our table to see what we were up to. If the police came, that'd be a major problem, since I was strapped and I was sure Tony was carrying as well.

We sat there quietly. I was certain Tony was only thinking how he was going to exact revenge on Raul, but also how he was going to get the Beltráns their money back for the previous load we lost, the one this load would have paid for, and of course *the other debt*, the one Hector hung like a noose around his neck.

I was worried Denny's workforce, seeing all of their tips quickly evaporating behind the crazy man screaming and cussing, might have called 911 to try to salvage the rest of their day. With that would come the inevitable toss from the cops, and they might find the gun strapped to my ankle, ending my chance at the start of the new life. "Listen, let's get out of here, Tony. I think we scared half the people out of here and one of them might have called the cops. Let's take a walk and talk about what to do next."

Tony was fuming. He stood up and looked at the crowd of employees, now gathered in a tight little huddle near the kitchen. Suddenly all of them quickly looked away and began to studiously focus on the food to a degree that for a Denny's felt almost suspicious.

Tony, doing his best Tony Montana impression, began slowly walking out. He pulled a two-inch-thick wad of bills out of his pocket, balling up a twenty-dollar bill, tossing it over his shoulder, then another twenty, and another, till he exited the restaurant, one I'd never be coming back to. In a loud voice he said, "What, we can't have a fucking conversation, that not allowed in here? Family friendly? *MI PUTO CULO, HA! CHUPAME*

EL BICHO! You fucking people heading right to the incinerators just don't know it yet, *PEDAZO DE MINERRANDS!* You all can go fuck yourselves, dying your little lives here making motherfuckin' pennies, BUNCH'A *PUTA PENDEJOS!*"

I followed with my head down.

We walked about three blocks, away from any cops that might've been called to the restaurant. I could see Tony was conflicted. Gone was that wild jump in his step, that air of invincibility.

Was Tony actually worried?

He had plenty of reason to be. He was now a man without protection. Once his crew found out he was being watched, they'd all jump ship like the rats they were. Once they found out the Beltráns were dispatching an army of fanatical killing machines to wipe out Tony and all who worked for him, they'd leave the state, some even the country.

The moment I saw the concern in Tony's face was the moment I knew I was built for this new life.

Tony agreed that we would separate for a while. He said he'd have to cash out some of his assets to pay back the Beltráns and then explain to them it was getting too hot and he needed to lay low for a while.

I pretended to have second thoughts—*if this ship is going down I'm going down with the captain* sort of nonsense. But then he said something that startled me.

"Listen, poppolitto. We can't trust these…*cops*," he spit the word out as if it were a hot load of venom, "especially these townie *putas* makin' that white man's welfare all for the sake a carrying that fuckin' *badge and gun*." He spat on the ground. "I don't trust they won't get to the judge and come up with some other booty charges sending you up for thirty years. So what about this? The United States has no extradition agreement with the Mexican government. We fucked up big-time with the Beltráns, but they always liked you. What say I give you $125,000 to get set up over there, then I'll send you another $250,000 once you're settled, and the debt I pay back to the Beltráns you don't have to worry about—I'll give you a pass on that."

He was giving *me* a pass on money *he* owed? I wanted to laugh.

He continued, "This way you become our conduit there as opposed to here, shipping the material across the border, the Beltráns will go for that, *sabe?* Less loads they'll lose on the border crossings..."

I held out my hands. "Wait a minute, Tony. What about my family? I don't want to raise my kids in Mexico. Plus, we're not Mexican citizens, we'd have to live there behind bribes and the relationships the Beltráns have with the government. That could change as fast as the wind changes direction, you know that."

"I'll watch over Inez and the kids." This he said with the tone of an old paternal grandpa, the patriarch of the family he cared for so very deeply.

My blood began to boil. Right up to the very end this prick was scheming. Inez had always suspected he had a thing for her—and now he wasn't even trying to hide it. I had to make him think my decision to stay was reasoned carefully, the pros and cons thoroughly weighed.

I turned away from him, appearing to contemplate his plan. I was startled by how naïve Tony actually thought I was, and it added fuel to the fire raging inside of me.

After a long pause of false reasoning I slowly shook my

head, "*no.*" "Inez will never go for it. She'll want to come with me and bring the kids and I'm not putting her through a life of hell. I'm going to ride this out. The lawyer I have is an ex-prosecutor and he assures me the case is over. They're not coming after any of us on some trumped-up *new* charges— that's you being paranoid. They have nothing on us. We'll be fine, okay? Right now you get in touch with the Beltráns and give them the paperwork. Tell them that we're shutting down for no more than a few weeks. I'm going to find out through my lawyer if the feds have anything at all they can leverage against us. I need to find out if Raul gave them anything. But, Tony—do *not* go after Raul. If you do, they'll start questioning me for the hit behind his treachery in Utah, and after this arrest, do we really need a murder rap following us as well? Just cool out, talk to Hector, see if he got anything out of Raul. I'll be in touch in a couple a days."

Tony acquiesced. What choice did he have?

He began walking away then stopped, turning to me excitedly. "Roman. Holy shit! I have an idea how we can get back some of the money we owe the Beltráns without actually going out of pocket for it, and it'll buy us some time. Fuck me, *maricone*, why didn't I think of this earlier?"

I knew whatever the idea was bouncing around his head like so many loose screws, nuts, and bolts, it was not going to be some easy pickup and transport, or he'd have one of our couriers do it. But I was glad to see he was ready to unknowingly set up his own sting operation. I was back within his trust, and I had him in the palm of my hand—for now.

I would've laughed at the insane request then cried if an amazing idea hadn't presented itself behind what I could only describe as the stupidest request the man had ever suggested, and Tony Loco Tony was full of them. He told me that three days ago a car was confiscated at the San Ysidro border crossing where a number of kilos were found inside its airbags; however, they missed another twenty kilos of uncut cocaine hidden inside the back two tires of a beat-up Nissan Sentra, and he wanted me to set up a team, jump the fence at the militaristically fortified facility, and recover the cocaine.

The San Ysidro Port of Entry connected San Diego to Tijuana, Mexico, and is, by far, the busiest, most guarded and watched border crossing in *the world.*

Tony laughed; back was his manic bounce, the quick hand movements, the rough excitable grab and shaking of my shoulders. There I was, Roman, his surrogate son all over again, the only one he trusted enough that would even consider going on this suicide mission.

I told Tony that I'd need to survey the area and come up with a plan. "I think I know how to do this, but it's no smash-and-grab. I'll need to pick my own men. You get word to the Beltráns that we're going to try and recover it."

He moved in to hug me and said, "We going to be all right, Roman. We back, and there ain't no one out there gonna stop us now!" Tony started to dance around slowly, pretend-swinging his dance partner in a '70s hustle movie.

I laughed, backed away, and said, "I'll get started on this. I'll be in touch."

We parted ways. I looked back and the fool was still dancing in the street. There was no demarcation line in the man's psyche differentiating sanity from insanity. Tony lived with a false sense of security based on his own delusional mind that made it impossible for him to fear anything. But, as I would learn happens to most street-smart and devious people in the two decades of undercover work I was embarking upon, all the people harboring that sense of security while living a dangerous, drugs-driven life—all the ones I sniffed out, anyway—would eventually fall prey to their complacency.

And just like that I received a call from Tony later that night. I didn't want to pick up the call, but I had to pretend that we were still on solid ground, and I was truly planning the most reckless heist in the history of theft. Pretending to be woken up from the call, I whispered groggily into the phone, "Hello?"

He mumbled something. I could tell he was high on his blow. "Roman, poppy, I woke you? Oh man, I'm sorry, daddy, I didn't wake up the little *mejos*, did I?" Tony showed great love and affection to me when he was jacked up on cocaine and bourbon.

He didn't let me answer, all motored up. "I just want you to know you're the only one I trust, and you the one gonna run this operation once we get through all this bullshit. I'm gonna take a step backwards and relax a bit, get out of the day to day, you know I'm getting too old for this!" He laughed and slurred and laughed some more. He cleared his throat and said, "Listen, that thing we was planning over there at Ysidro. Well, I talked to the brothers about it and they didn't think it was such a good idea, so we gonna put that on hold a while."

And just like that the line went dead.

Burning Down the House

For the next two days I remained at home waiting for my phone to ring. Though I knew Tony had bought everything I told him, he was still—always—a wild card. And there was also Hector to contend with. With the information I gave him about Raul, I knew Tony wanted him dead. But certainly Hector wasn't about to allow me to send Raul to his untimely death. Needless to say, while waiting for that call from the feds I slept in my downstairs family room well-fortified with three guns and plenty of ammunition.

And then my phone rang—one of the burners Tony knew nothing about.

The coded message I was to receive, which Chris gave to me before I left Sevier County, was easy to remember. A man would say he was calling from a bank in San Diego, which was the signal I was talking to a customs agent from the San Diego field office. Then he would give me a number of an alleged account I had at the bank with the message that there seemed to be a problem with the account. The account number would start with two zeros, the next set of numbers was the address; then he would tell me his name, which was the street where we were to meet, and finally he would ask if there was a better time to call, give me a time, and that was the time we would meet.

I took all the information down, and at eleven that morning I was on my way to San Diego.

I left two hours earlier than I normally would so I'd be able to decipher if I were being followed by one of Tony's PIs, one of Hector's hitters, or, worse, a carload of them. Once I determined I was clean I headed to San Diego's National City neighborhood—or, as it was known, "Nasty City"—to meet an agent, oddly enough, at another Denny's. Chock-full of predicate felons, wanted men and women, hookers walking the track, illegals running numbers, and dealers hawking every high imaginable, the place felt like it was fortified with more illegal weapons than the entire LAPD had in its arsenal—it was a gangbanger's paradise. I'd done many deals in this neighborhood, and I was *always* strapped.

I parked my car on the roof of an enclosed parking lot about four blocks away from the proposed meet. I wanted to get a 360-degree view of the area—alleys, main streets, the quickest and also the most secluded ways to and from my spot. The last thing I needed was to run into anyone I knew, even peripherally. I was starting to think like an undercover operative, trying to enjoy the cat-and-mouse of it all. It was exciting to have a chance to channel my instincts for good.

The moment I walked into the mildly busy restaurant I saw him, way in the back, facing the entrance across the dining area away from the bathrooms, close enough to the hot, busy kitchen to keep customers away, and most important away from any windows; the exact place I would've chosen had I called this meeting.

I truly hoped he'd understand the risk and magnitude of danger an undertaking like this was going to be. What I could give the feds could potentially tear apart a billion-dollar-a-year entity and destroy the lives and careers of many monsters. I was as close to the point of the spear in the world of narcotics smuggling as this guy or any of his buddies would ever get, and if he didn't realize that, I'd have to show him.

He was watching me as I slowly made my way to the table, as nonchalant as my pounding heart allowed. He gave me the slightest of head nods.

I sat down facing him. At first glance he looked like he was on his lunch break in between cutting down redwoods up north. He wore a red plaid shirt, worn dungarees, and, just in case there were any doubters that he was anything other than a blue-collar dude meeting up with an old buddy for lunch, a yellow hard hat sat atop the table. He had shoulder-length dirty blond hair, a full beard of blonde curls, and he was as big as a redwood at about six-feet-four and close to three hundred pounds.

He smiled, did not shake my hand because that would indicate a first meet to anyone watching. Instead, he gave me a perfunctory slap on the shoulder as normal friends might do and said, "Rome, man, how've you been? Long time, brother." On the table in front of him was a newspaper and he quickly indicated the top of the paper with a gentle tap of his finger. There scribbled in legible ink it read, Tim Dowling.

I smiled and went along with the game, "Tim-Tim, my brother from another mother. How are you? I've been well."

"Inez, the kids—all good?" he asked.

"Same old, same old. Kids are getting big, man. Inez started her new job at the clinic…" The conversation went on, more of the same theatrics to create the appearance of two old friends hooking up just in case Tony had a private investigator glued to me. After a few minutes, Tim asked, in a low voice, if I thought we were okay to chat.

I nodded. "We're good. I got clearance from Inez and the boss to take the afternoon off."

Then I noticed Tim relax, just enough to focus on the conversation we were about to have. Though his eyes kept surveying the restaurant for any signs of a threat, his shoulders sagged. He began assessing me, smiling, almost amused, and I'd find out why soon enough. He checked out the Daytona I was wearing, smiled, and gestured to it. "Business must be as good as ever." I shrugged.

"I feel like I know you so well," he said. "I do, in a way; we've been on you and your organization for over two years. I'm sure Chris briefed you on all of that."

"Oh yeah, and then some." I found myself laughing as I realized that the man sitting in front of me was one of those agents I'd lose, and occasionally give the finger while doing so. "There's no hard feelings, are there?" I asked, a little guarded.

He laughed. Watching me like a kid on Christmas morning ogling his favorite gift, just dying to take it outside for a spin. "No way," he said. "It's meetings like this that make the long car rides where we'd follow you out into the sticks worth it. I wanted to meet you first, sort of ease you into this slowly. I figured you might get a little raised up if you walked into a room full of guys scrutinizing every inch of you."

In order to avoid coming off like too much of a fool, I apologized for my finger-flipping antics, and I also explained why I'd dressed like a Hollywood pimp. "I don't want anyone to think I'm showboating or anything like that," I said. "This is the way that I normally dress to fit in with my colleagues. If I were to leave my house in a baseball cap, sunglasses, windbreaker, a pair of dungarees, and someone *was* following me, it would get back to Tony very quickly."

Tim assured me there was no need to explain myself. "We're all psyched to have you on our team.... Well, maybe one of them has a little beef, but he kinda has a good reason to." This time he was laughing hard, as if at some inside joke.

"Well, can you give me a heads-up so when I meet whoever this guy is it's not too uncomfortable and I know what I'm walking into?"

He laughed again, threw his hands up like it was out of his control. "It's nothing. So, like I said, I wanted to meet you first, having worked this case the longest. From here we're going to a satellite office we have out in the country. We'll debrief you there and see how we can start working together. We'll take two cars, if we lose each other I'll be on the phone. Did you lock in that number I called you from?"

"No, I have it memorized," I said.

"Excellent. From now on you'll have to memorize everything. I'm sure Chris explained to you the scrutiny you're going to be under with Tony."

I could only hope that all this guy's federal friends were as on top of their jobs as Tim was.

I followed his pickup truck and forty-five minutes later we arrived in a desolate wooded area in central San Diego

County—Ramona, California. There were old copper and silver mines, miles and miles of horse and cattle farms, stately wine vineyards that suddenly melded into avocado and citrus orchards, the air held a sweet aroma that, when combined with the lush colors of the indigenous flora, gave the whole ride a surrealistic feeling, and it was stunning. I couldn't stop smiling. In fact, I hadn't smiled like that since my son Mathew was born, and before that my other three children. The metaphor was not lost on me; I was moving from a bleak career of being indebted to the scariest man I'd ever come in contact with into a new life.

We headed into the valley's foothills that fed us into the base of the Laguna Mountains, from which we drove skyward for another fifteen minutes. I understood why the feds would choose this location: It was relatively close to the Mexican border, surrounded on two sides with mountainous terrain, so secluded that it would be impossible for anyone to follow you without being noticed.

We crawled on a dirt road up a mountain until it seemed impossible to drive any farther, as we were blocked by a stand of soaring white pine and cypress trees. But there, we turned off onto what I can only describe as a deer path with outcroppings of rock and heavy moss. A path that, without question, was not designed to be driven on with a Mercedes 500 SEL. Finally, at the end of this ever-tapering path we came upon the first signs of life—locked gates of chain-link fencing and a sign in big red block letters that read: "PRIVATE PROPERTY, KEEP OUT," indicating to the most adventurous and curious of hikers, *don't even think about going beyond this point.*

Tim got out, unlocked the gates, and drove in as I followed.

Once we were beyond the gate, he got out and locked it back up, giving me a smile and thumbs-up as he passed my car again.

We continued driving on this deer path now tightly walled in on both sides with more thickets of pine trees and cypresses that somehow formed a canopy overhead, making it impossible to see below, even from a low hovering helicopter. I wondered if that was purposeful.

Suddenly there was a small clearing off in the distance and there it was, the federal joint task force I'd been the prime enemy of for the past two years.

I was expecting to come upon a grand old hunting lodge with stone walls and towering stone chimneys, pine beams, and a majestic A-frame slate roof, perched beside a mountain, but I was greeted by a ratty single-width trailer home; a step above would be the equivalent of a planning shack on any low-end construction site in the country. The only modern appendage it held was an impressive radar-type dish on its roof with about five other antennas of varying sizes.

The inside of this fabricated office was a step or two above its exterior. Three grim-faced men, each wearing his own pained expression of discomfort, sat in different corners of this barely sixty-square-foot room. Their "workstations" were makeshift desks that were built into the walls with two-by-fours and plywood. They sat in wooden banker chairs that seemed to have been liberated off a set from a '40s noir film, which explained their pained expressions. They turned to the door simultaneously, stopped whatever it was that they were doing, and looked at me in stunned silence, the way a child would upon turning a corner in an aquarium and unexpectedly coming face-to-face with a shark.

Computers and walkie–talkie banks lined another entire wall with a large computer screen displaying dazzling real-time visuals of the city, something I'd never seen before. *Man, are they ahead of the curve*, I thought. The real question was, with all this high-tech gadgetry, why hadn't they caught us?

At each man's workstation were family photos, personalized coffee mugs, framed awards—the usual office clutter that is collected over an extended period of time. Wanted photos were hurriedly tacked to the walls.

A chill ran through me when I noticed the photos, pinned right in the center of the most prominent wall: grainy-to-high-resolution shots of every crewmember in my organization, displayed in a pyramid fashion. Tony was at the top, Hector just below, and then me, a clean shot sitting on a bench at Venice Beach, California. It scared the shit out of me because I remembered the exact day it was taken and who I was meeting there, another client from Los Angeles who owned a string of strip clubs. The crazy thing was, had whoever it was that took this photo stayed with the subject I met there, which I'm sure that person did, they would have seen that within fifteen minutes of that meeting he was handed six kilos of cocaine by one of my couriers. That's when it really hit home how close I was playing it to the edge.

Below my photo was an array of most of the men and women who had ever worked for me. When I saw that, it was like I had to absorb all over again how solidly they had me within their sights. They were only biding their time. To the side of my happy family tree were the beginnings of another pyramid, quite bare in proportion to our organization, with only two photos side by side, Eliseo and Abel Beltrán, the murderous heads of one of the largest Mexican cartels to date. This group of federal agents had been trying to bridge a connection between my organization and the entire Beltrán Cartel, and then blow that bridge to smithereens. Now, they finally could.

Tim introduced me. "Gentlemen, say hello to Roman, our newest asset."

A shorter man with upturned happy eyes, an unruly beard, long wildly curly black hair with flecks of gray, whom I'd soon find out was a retired Navy SEAL, stood up to shake my hand. He was a bundle of energy. "Welcome, Roman. I'm Mike Capella, DEA San Diego field office. Nice to finally meet you!" He started to laugh, turning to another man who was now lounging back in his squeaky chair, feet on the desk, toothpick sticking out of his mouth. He was about six feet tall with brushed-back black hair and not a strand out of place. He appeared to be a workout junkie as his arms were the size of a normal man's thighs. He glared at Mike, flipping up his middle finger. Mike turned back to me and said, "That ray of sunshine over there is…"

Before Mike finished the introduction the man said, "I'm Pete Davis, U.S. Customs." He moved close to me; he was not smiling, and yet he wasn't trying to intimidate me. He continued, "Do I look at all familiar to you?" It seemed as though they were all in on this inside joke and that maybe I was the punch line. Wouldn't be the first time for me, having had Tony as a boss. I would later learn that Pete had been one of the agents tasked with tailing Tony and me, and one day when I must have spotted someone following me, I raced away so quickly that Pete got in a wreck.

Al Harding stood up and grabbed my hand to shake it as he introduced himself. He was about my height, a little over five feet, ten inches, early forties, with an angular face and short-cropped black hair. He said, "Nice to finally meet you in person. Now that we got that out of the way, let me get down to business. Right now you're our only priority—your family's safety as well as yours is paramount to us. We are well aware of the danger you're in. You should remember that, too. But above all, you should remember that this is your shot to redeem yourself. You mess this up, you're not getting another."

I nodded my head, all of the butterflies in my stomach suddenly disappearing. All of these men seemed really professional and sincerely interested in what I had to offer them. They didn't know it yet, but I was going to build them a bridge that would lead them not just into the Beltrán Cartel, but also into the belly of their even more ruthless rivals, the brutal, infamous Fuentes Cartel.

Undercover

The four agents sat listening around me as I broke down my whole life for them, the way I had for Chris in Utah. I'd given them everything I'd been a part of for the past ten-plus years. Safe houses, organizational protocol, names of all our workers here in the United States, Mexico, and farther south. They'd had a large case file on us, but nothing compared to the nuggets of actionable intelligence I was giving them now. Our routes, their own gaps in security, how we were getting the drugs across the border, and, most important, all of the safe houses in Detroit, California, and New York where Tony kept his cache of drugs, weapons, and *money* he always claimed he didn't have on hand. As I previously explained, Tony was the tightest and cheapest man on the planet. I knew he had a war chest of money stashed in New York, so when the time came—*and it would*—he'd be able to buy his way out of the most egregious bails.

I gave them all the details about how we operated with the Beltrán Cartel: who was getting the drugs, grow fields, plantations, jungle cook houses, "soup kitchens"—the locations where their workers, some as young as ten years old, would disintegrate bodies in hundred-gallon drums filled with hydro-chloric acid or simply dismember a torture victim and bury the remains in a mass grave. Unfortunately, there were many soup kitchens in Mexico—and the fact that I'd contributed to their prevalence was one of the hardest things I had to—will always have to—live with.

I gave them the Beltráns' organizational hierarchy from the lowliest couriers up to the analysts and lawyers who supported the brothers. As I talked, one of the agents checked the mini tape recorder twice to make sure it was working properly.

When I finished, Tim quietly stood up, moved to a desk, and unlocked a battered black metal box, pulling out an envelope and handing it to me. There was still a pall of silence in the room as I'm sure the agents were suddenly realizing I was a game changer for them. I opened the envelope up and inside was $1,000 in cash; it was a good-faith payment for the information I'd given to Chris in Utah.

Tim said, "While you're working off your case, any seizure we make, whether it's cash or narcotics, based on information you give to us or any case you're working on directly, you'll receive 10 percent of whatever the street value is. That cash is just a taste of what's to come."

I reiterated to Tim and the rest of the men in the room exactly what I'd told Chris—that I just wanted to work off my case and get out of this shitty life forever.

We talked about potential ways of getting to Tony and then working our way into the Beltráns' organization. I knew getting to Tony would be easier than getting me into an actual buy with the Beltrán brothers, though I didn't voice that opinion; however, if anyone could come up with a tangible way in with my help, it was these guys because they had money, time, and, most importantly, the unwavering will to decimate the Beltráns' multibillion-dollar organization.

We wrapped up and my overall impression of this first meet exceeded all of my expectations. I knew that I'd made the best decision of my life by flipping and working with these men. For the first time in years I felt alive, capable, armed not with one of the Glocks Tony kept stashed at his safe houses, but with a real purpose.

It was after ten in the evening when I returned home. I noticed all of the lights were off in the house, save for our bedroom, which meant the kids were asleep, our nanny had left for the evening, and Inez and I could be all alone. I couldn't wait to tell her about the meeting. I was certain she'd been waiting in subdued horror for me to call—I hadn't been able to do so all day because the agents told me to refrain from using any burners or the new phone they handed to me, except to reach them, and only then with specific instructions. Tony had PIs, computer whizzes, and cell phone techies on his payroll, so it wouldn't be a stretch to think he might be able to listen in on one of my calls

The new phone was a direct link to any one of the team members, all with aliases, as well as a stored emergency number to the San Diego field office operations desk (F.O.D.) of the DEA. If someone were to find the phone—Tony, for instance—and call any of the numbers saved on it, including the F.O.D., the person on the other line would seem like an old friend of mine and play along. After a minute or so they'd call the person out on the other end, saying, "Hey, wait a second, this isn't Roman. Who are you? Did he lose his phone again? Guy's always losing shit!" This would alert them that I might be in trouble. If I were calling in a normal situation, they'd speak in the same conversational tone until I read out my code name, *C. S. 96* (Confidential Source 1996, 96 being the year I was starting my undercover work), which I'd been given that evening.

When the agents were calling me, and began talking in friendly conversation, I'd read out my code to verify that it was me on the other end and I was free and clear to talk—or if I wasn't, I'd continue the casual banter. As arduous as it might have seemed, this protocol could *never* be breached. It was a matter of life and death.

Inez had come out to meet me at our doorstep, and she buried her head in my chest. She let go, right there for all the neighbors to see. No one other than the two of us existed in the world at that moment. I suppose it was the finality of it all, or so she hoped, years and years of pent-up anxiety, a feeling of betrayal and probably rage at what our lives had descended into.

For the first time that I could remember, she had full faith in me. But I also knew that if I were to ever go back on my word, she would without question leave me, and maybe some fear inside her that Tony's game would seduce me again added to the intensity she was feeling.

Later that night Inez was lying on the bed holding a pillow tightly against her chest. She was watching me run her bath in our master bathroom. She said, "What about Tony? What if he finds out about today? He'll kill you, Roman. He'll kill you."

She had a point. Even with all my planning with the agents,

I sometimes feared what could happen if things went sideways. I explained how much Tony *did* frighten me, but that if I lived in fear of him I'd never escape his toxic pull. We talked about everything that had happened to us until it felt like there was nothing else to say.

Would he know that I'd given him up the moment his stash houses were raided? That's what Inez was convinced of, but I wasn't so sure.

I explained that Tony and Hector were both stealing from each other—and ever since the Beltrán brothers had confronted us, we knew about Hector's skimming, so it seemed likely Tony's suspicions would lie with the man. Yes, Tony had also been skimming off the top without Hector knowing it, and if Hector found out there would be a minor war between those two, and Hector might be angry enough to plunder Tony's stash houses himself or tip the police off out of spite and have them do it.

I wasn't in the clear, but I did have some cover.

Inez sat silently, looking intensely into my eyes. I could tell she was trying to gauge how sincere I was or if I were simply telling her what she wanted to hear. She knew me well enough to know I'd try, but she also knew how I was never much good at hiding my feelings from her. She wrapped her arms around me in relief. "Roman, I've been so worried, you have no idea. Please promise me you're going to take precautions, promise me you'll be safe!"

I kissed her gently. Nothing would come between us again. We were safe, and I was almost out of this life for good.

She continued nervously, "And these men, you trust them with our lives?"

It was a very good question. I knew they had the wherewithal to protect me, but what I didn't know was how much
they would invest in it. The best way that I could protect myself
was to prove my value to them.

It was late, after eleven at night, when we were escorted by two
customs agents through their base of operations at the San
Diego border crossing. They seemed annoyed to be pulled off
their cushy jobs watching video feeds from the dozens of cameras on the causeway. I'd never been inside the gigantic facility
before, though had passed by it many times wondering what
went on inside. The irony of my actually being invited into
this building without first being shackled in handcuffs was not
lost on me.

We moved through a large enclosed walkway similar in
fashion to the Jetway tunnel between the airport gate and the
actual plane.

All the while walking through this sarcophagus-like passage, I was starting to sweat, concerned with where they were
leading me. What if it was all bullshit? What if there was a
double-cross at play? Was Tony trying to get me jacked by
the feds on a false tip the Beltráns planted to try to get *him*
jacked by the feds? If so, there could be nothing inside those
tires but air. I was nervous, and the embarrassment I'd feel was
insurmountable. However, I looked back upon my early days
in Tony's operation when I was a smuggler, and channeled that
demeanor. Always look in control; you're meant to be there.

I pushed the potential clusterfuck this might turn into out
of my mind and moved with purpose and determination.

We reached a door at the far end of the tunnel and one

of the agents entered the code into its keypad. A small indicator light went from blinking red to steady green. The customs agent twisted its wide metal handle and the door opened with a *whoosh*, like an airlock being released. We were on the outside.

Facing the five of us was a garage the size of two football stadiums, filled with a massive display of every moving vehicle known to man. From waterborne vehicles to airborne, there was an array of helicopters, boats of all sizes, yachts to Jet Skis. There was, from my quick estimation, about ten what appeared to be submarines—yes, as in underwater submarines! Beyond that there were thousands of cars of every shape and model. And all I had to go on was that the car was a black Nissan Sentra, a little beat up.

All four men turned to look at me as if I'd suddenly received a battlefield promotion from lowly private to general. I was definitely in way over my head, but what I did have that could potentially narrow down this hunt was the *alleged* date that this particular car was jacked on, carrying *alleged* cocaine in its tires—something, by the way, I'd never heard of before, and I'd been doing this a long time. How do you get kilos or bricks of cocaine, twenty in total, into tires filled with combustible air? I pulled out my little notebook and gave the customs agent the date Tony had given me. The agent checked it against a manifest, a crease deepening on his forehead. There was no black Nissan Sentra on the list of impounded vehicles.

I said in as assertive a voice as I could muster, not easy under the present circumstances, that it was a midsize car that looks like a Nissan Sentra. "Remember, this one will have damage."

The customs agent looked at the manifest one last time and pointed toward the area that corresponded with the date in question.

We split up and began our search, shining our flashlights from car to car. There were rows and rows of them, each of us checking a section. After every half hour that passed with no hits on the car, my nerves frayed a little more. It wasn't the pure embarrassment of failing to come through for my new colleagues that worried me most but what Al Harding had said during our first meet at the base in Ramona: I had to prove to these guys that I was worthy or else they'd leave me like the agents who had dropped Raul. And where would I retreat to if I couldn't work off my case? Where would that leave my family?

I was thinking of all of this, my last nerve just about fried, when I heard one of the customs agents call out with a touch of pessimism, "Guys, I think I might've found something!"

My heart started racing, *please God, please let this be the car.* We pounced on the vehicle simultaneously, and sure enough it wasn't a black Nissan Sentra, but a black Nissan Altima.

One of the customs agents radioed for a tow truck to meet us at the location. That was the longest five minutes of my life. I could see that Harding and Dowling were sweaty, dirty, exhausted, and embarrassed for bringing these two guys out into this potential nest of nothingness. What was even worse, not once did either of my teammates look at me, I'm sure for fear of revealing how they really felt: *twenty kilos in car tires of all places? Why did we ever listen to this extremely imaginative bonehead?*

The largest tow truck I've ever seen pulled up. I was feeling unsteady on my feet, my nerves all but beaten down, my body dehydrated and fatigued. A short, heavy civilian driver, about thirty-five, wearing dirty coveralls and a San Diego Chargers ski cap despite the humid ninety-degree air, jumped out of the cab like Field Marshal Rommel alighting from a Panzer tank and teeming with excitement. He pulled a pair of dirty beige leather gloves off his belt with an imperious tug that bordered on comical. "All righty, fellas," he said, "whatta we got tonight? Guns, drugs? A body welded into the undercarriage? I *did* bring my blowtorches this time."

Again the four men looked to me for direction. I moved to the driver who was now also focused on me through hyper-intense eyes as if I were sending him on a secret mission that would potentially end the war or his life. I pointed to the rear tires. "We need to remove both of them, then release the air and pull them from their rims." The driver did as told without any further questions or attempts at humor. The two customs guys, assuming their work was complete, found a nearby pickup truck, released its rear hatch, lit up cigarettes, and chatted like they were at a tailgate party.

Tim and Al stood rigidly, arms folded, watching the driver move between an industrial jack and a hydraulic lug remover at breakneck speed. He had both tires flattened and the wheels off the car in less than three minutes. He impressively carried both of them to his truck, which was equipped with a tire remover. As he placed the first one on the machine's pedestal I slowly slunk backward, leaning on a car. I pulled my handkerchief out, swabbing the sweat off my face and neck. The driver jammed a jack in between the rubber and the rim, turning the mechanism on, and within ten seconds I heard him pop the tire off the rim.

Tim Dowling snapped rather loudly at the poor unsuspecting driver, "Back away." He and Al both aimed their flashlights into the interior of the tire, then Al frantically ran his hands around the inside. He looked at Tim as if he were delivering a death notice, and they then both turned to me stone-faced, a look I never wanted to see from them again.

I was almost ready to leave, but out of desperation I asked the driver to look at the other rear tire. When the next didn't work, Al's and Tim's shoulders drooped in defeat. I felt the pit widen in my stomach. There was a moment of complete silence; even the chatty customs guys now just sat on the back of the nearby pickup, staring. "Okay, okay!" I said. "He must've gotten the wrong info on the tires, must be the front two, pull those off." I knew at that point that I'd been screwed— Tony had caught on to me; what made me think I could fool him?—but I needed to buy some time and figure out my next move.

The driver moved to the front of the car with a little less Rommel in his step. This time when he'd rested the tires on the tire pedestal, I moved in close. I wrapped my arms around myself tightly, watching the man jam the tire iron between the rubber of the tire and its steel rim. He clicked the mechanism on and it wobbled to life. After what seemed like an eternity I finally heard that familiar pop. The tire was loose. Nothing came free from within! *SHIT!* I thought to myself, *NO!* Neither Tim nor Al even expressed interest in looking at it.

I ran forward, flashlight aimed on that damnable tire's innards. I looked inside while furiously banging the outside of the tire hoping, actually pleading with the gods for the packages to miraculously appear, shooting out from within the black hole like a slot machine paying out—DING! DING! DING! TRIP GOLD BARS—*your payout sir, twenty kilos!*

Nothing! And worse, no familiar packaging on its interior, just more of the same—black rubber.

I froze, caught up in a swirling typhoon of embarrassment and dejection. I wasn't giving up, because this was just too inconceivable. I ran my hand inside the tire just as Al Harding had done, and to my surprise it didn't feel like the smooth innards of a tire, it was rough.

Odd, I thought.

As I ran my hand along circumference inside, the *whole* interior of the tire felt rough with gaps in between.

Okay, okay, promising!

No one came near that tire, all expecting the same results. A symphony of silence ensued as they all watched the schmuck who had been taken by the bigger kids on the block, the schmuck who wouldn't admit defeat under any circumstances, who would actually try and *will* those kilos to be inside that black hole.

The agents and customs guys looked away like embarrassed parents.

And then—suddenly—I came across the tiniest of clues; it felt like a thin rubber flap about an inch in width and diameter.

Please tell me this IS NOT an irregular Taiwanese tire, PLEASE!

I started breathing harder, faster, could this be something, anything?

I pulled on it as hard as I could and whatever it was gave a bit, then one more tug freed something lose in my grip. I couldn't believe it!

Holy shit; I turned to Harding and Dowling, my face must've read—JACKPOT!

I pulled and continued pulling, feeling an epoxy-like bond snapping this thing in my hand away from the inside of the tire. There it was, a long thin black rubber package, sticky on one side to hold it in place.

This was something I'd never seen before, but it was ingenious. The sudden realization hit me that the customs people were about to encounter a lot more trouble than they had the hour before.

The package resembled a money belt, though there were no zippers or straps, and inside it was stuffed with pure cocaine.

Al and Tim stood in stunned silence.

We pulled out thirty-nine more "money belts," a perfect way to describe them because those odd-looking pieces of rubber were worth a hell of a lot of money once they were unloaded and processed, twenty kilos in all.

The two customs agents were suddenly our best friends, whipping out a camera to take photos of the unusual booty, the six of us holding onto all forty packages in every pose imaginable.

Before we packed up to head back to the base, one of the customs guys said, "Holy shit!" We all turned to look at him; he was aiming his flashlight at the manifest, staring at it with a look that was filled with both exaltation and horror at the same time.

I said, "What? What's wrong?"

He looked up at all of us and said, "This car was slated for auction tomorrow morning at 9:00 A.M."

There was a collective silence, and then we all broke out laughing one last time.

Can you imagine the expression on the poor man or woman's face that purchased the vehicle if they went in to change the tires and the skillfully packed cocaine was found? How do you explain that to your local mechanic—let alone the cops or dozens of federal agents suddenly surrounding you at the local Pep Boys?

That night was one I was certain to never forget because it marked the beginning of something special. My excitement in pulling that small load of cocaine out of those tires gave me more spirited elation than anything I'd ever done.

I'd brought tractor-trailers of cocaine, literally tons of it, on one single-haul into the United States and felt no rush— just guilt for the harm I did to people and fear for my family. But finally being on the other end of that business was like being reborn.

It was time to take Tony out of the picture for good. And now I had my bona fides to get the manpower I'd need to do so. We were on our way to organizing some of the biggest busts in the history of the DEA.

Before we headed back to our base in Ramona, I used a pay phone to call Inez. I'd made a promise to her that before and after we did this operation—or moved forward on any operation—I'd call her to let her know what we were about to do, and she'd say a prayer for me.

I told her what happened, and I just couldn't help myself: I began to cry because, as I told her, the whole experience was like a second baptism for me. I felt like a different man, as if so many more weights had suddenly been lifted off my shoulders. I told her I was safe and that I loved her.

Inez began crying as well. We were two blubbering adults marveling at the fact that I'd just stolen twenty kilos of cocaine from some of the most dangerous men on the planet. "It took some time to find your way," she told me, "but you did. You can help in this ugly fight. And as happy as I am, I'm happier for you, baby."

Walking back to the unmarked vehicle, I felt incredible euphoria, combined with the oddest feeling, like some sort of immutable déjà vu, that I'd done this before. I've always believed that before we are born we are all predestined in life to do certain things, and it's our job to find out what those are. I felt as if I'd finally found mine.

The next target in my sights was Tony Geneste, the man who'd come to me when things were bad so many years ago with an idea to make money in running drugs. It was time to tear to the ground those bridges that had ever connected me to this business, that had wrought nothing but havoc on my life and so many others.

The Demise of Tony Loco Tony

The next morning, all the team members—including me, now a full-fledged band member of the Alliance Task Force, aptly named for the pairing of two agencies, Customs and DEA—were to meet at the base in Ramona at 10 A.M. sharp.

On this trip I decided to drive my Range Rover up that steep craggy mountain trail. I was still very cognizant of any tails that might be on my ass, so after forty-five minutes of circuitous maneuvering, doubling back and then returning to my house, I parked my Mercedes in the circular driveway fronting my home. I then went through my house into the enclosed backyard, into the pool house, and out a back door that led to a six-and-a-half-foot retaining wall separating my property and my adjacent neighbor's property. I scaled and hopped over the wall, no easy task in a pair of TOD's driving loafers, a silk shirt, and thin gabardine pants. I then furtively made it to the adjacent street, finally driving off in my Range Rover, which I had previously parked there in the middle of the night. I was pretty certain I was clean, though I would remain vigilant.

I got to the base with fifteen minutes to spare and, surprisingly, the men were already at their usual workstations.

The first thing I noticed was the large whiteboard I'd requested from Harding the night before. There it was, now, covering up the rogue's gallery photo array of me living my life, unaware of the feds watching me.

Upon seeing me enter, Harding, Dowling, and Capella jumped from their banker chairs to greet me, cheering as if I'd just driven in the winning run of the World Series.

It turned out that we'd pulled more powder than any Alliance mission in two years. The team was ready for our next move.

I didn't waste any time. I stood in front of the whiteboard and arranged the men in a semicircle around me so I could lay on them one of the biggest multi-state, multi-agency seizures they would ever make, and all in one very coordinated swoop. We were going to need the cooperation of multiple law enforcement agencies, both federal and local, as well as judges, cops, and agents in four different states, one law enforcement–unfriendly European country, and a Caribbean island with very lenient banking standards. The agents asked me question after question, and when I'd finally satisfied them, we all decided we were in.

I hadn't heard from Tony, Hector, or Raul in almost a week, which seemed unusual, especially after Tony's *emotional breakthrough* phone call to me.

But I couldn't think about them all day and night. Instead, I recorded what I'd learned about Tony and his organization in the book I'd been keeping for years, recording all the details about how we pulled off our crimes, as if knowing that someday I'd flip. Whenever I uncovered a new piece of information on Tony, Hector, or any of the key players in the Beltrán organization, it went into that book. Call it insurance, call it payback, call it a way out.

Collected in the book's pages were the addresses for every one of Tony's safe houses, for his secret club in Washington Heights, his bank account numbers where he secretly hid the bulk of his very substantial holdings; some were offshore and some were in friend and family names.

I produced the book for the men and I explained, "Guys, as good as last night's rip was, this next one is going to blow all of you away, including your bosses and probably their bosses."

Tim Dowling laughed, "Well, Roman, you really don't know our bosses." The rest of the men started to laugh, even Pete Davis.

I laughed along. "Inside this book I have every one of Tony's safe houses where he has been stockpiling drugs, guns, and a lot of money for years."

I noticed all of the men sit up, eyes waiting for more. "Now the issue is they're in places scattered around the country—San Diego, Los Angeles, Detroit, New York, Long Island, and in some cities there are more than one or even two locations—and the minute he knows a spot has been hit, he has contingency plans for the caretakers to move the material to other spots, some of which I might not know about. So to pull this off, we need to hit all of his spots at the same time."

Tim and Al stared at each other for a long moment. I could see that in his mind Capella was already hitting the spots in California himself. He actually looked high, eyes suddenly glazed over with anticipation.

Tim said, "Roman, what exactly are we talking about?"

I didn't understand the question.

Al said, "What he means is how much material are we talking?"

I thought about this, even though I had been thinking about it for a long time. I knew, pretty much to the penny, what Tony had skimmed because it was my job to know how much material we brought in, how much we sold, how much we owed back to the Beltráns, how much we owed to all our workers, and what he owed back to Hector and myself. And invariably, for the past ten years, he was skimming from Hector and me between 10 and 20 percent of both the drugs *and* the money passing through us. I never said anything because this was Tony's business that *he* started. If anyone should've noticed and said something it was Hector. I hadn't realized until that day we were all locked in a hotel room with the Beltráns that Hector was skimming too, and that was why he managed to keep so quiet about Tony's antics.

I told Al we'd be looking at between a million to two million dollars in each spot if we busted Tony. Now that could be all cash or a combination of cash, uncut hard drugs, plus a lot of marijuana. Some spots might be all coke, heroin, or weed. How he decided which spots hold the material versus the cash or both together I didn't know.

It wouldn't be easy to round up all Tony's inventory. In fact, getting in the houses safely would be nothing short of impossible. Tony always had a crew of men on hand who he had supplied with weapons. And I'm not talking pistols, I'm talking heavy, military-grade artillery. If he entrusted this amount of material to someone and they didn't die fighting for it, they would surely end up dead once they'd delivered the news to him that they'd gotten ripped.

"We get the point," Al said.

All the men were pinned back in their chairs, thinking about the meaning of a $16 million haul. I thought about what we'd find on top of all of that: a cache of weapons I'd seen with my own eyes that were surely tied to multiple homicides, closing out even more cases.

No one was smiling, which I hoped was because they were anticipating all the moving parts that were needed with an operation like this one, but also the danger they were placing other cops and agents in. The worst part about it was that our team would lose tactical control everywhere outside of California.

I never doubted it would be worth it, though. Not with the suffering and dying of the consumers of Tony's goods, his dozens of girlfriends and mules—often the same women—the murders he'd piled up in the course of a ruthless, drug-fueled life. And now taking Tony out would be necessary for my own family's protection.

I had to stay on point with these guys because my life truly depended on these men taking this rip seriously. I said, "There's more—"

Mike Capella laughed, cutting me off. "Of course there is. Please enlighten us!"

I flipped to one of the pages in my book, turned to the whiteboard, and wrote six bank account numbers, along with bank names and the names of the people assigned to those accounts—all of them guardians for one person: Tony Geneste. Next to each account I wrote a number, added together a sum of $42 million, Tony's little nest egg or "get-the-fuck-out-of-the-country money."

In the hands of a very street-smart killer, $42 million was more dangerous than any weapon. He would know how to disappear for good, and from wherever he was he could have others disappear without lifting a finger to do anything, not dial a phone or tap a keyboard. Knowing where he was and where his money was stashed, that was power. And as long as those safe houses remained I knew Tony was somewhere in the continental United States. Losing him was a totally unacceptable scenario from where I was sitting.

I turned back around and I could see the realization forming in each man's eyes. I said, "Yes, all Tony's. The accounts with his name are offshore accounts, one in the Caymans that is linked to a bank in Geneva. The others are friends and family, dummy or dupe accounts, we call them 'Muldoons.'"

Mike Capella, for a change, asked quietly, "Should we ask how you got that information?"

I quickly answered, "No. But they check out—that I'm certain of."

Mike continued, "Crime sure does pay, huh, boys?" He laughed. "Until now."

Tim Dowling said with a big smile he couldn't conceal, "Well, it certainly has been an interesting couple of days." He thought a moment then continued, "Roman, if all of these spots are a hit-in-one rip, don't you think he's going to know you were the one who gave them up?"

I told him the same thing I had said to Inez: "Tony has no idea I know about these spots, nor does he know that I'm aware he's been skimming. So what would be my motive for taking out what essentially were my own spots?"

Then Harding asked, "Well, how did he justify money coming back to you short when it came time to pay you for your…" He had trouble finishing the question. I suppose there was still that awkward chasm between me and these battle-hardened agents. Who was I to be asking them to risk their lives? Did they fear I was a scummy drug dealer looking to beat the system? In a lot of ways I was the very epitome of everything going to shit in this country they were born and raised in. Deep inside I knew I wasn't their equal—not even close. But I wanted to be regarded as a partner. I knew it was going to take a long time and a lot of scores before I'd be looked at that way.

I explained how Tony got away with coming up short again and again. He had a million excuses, unforeseen contingencies he was forced to pay—he had to bribe someone or there was always extra security he had to pay for. He didn't seem to realize how my attention to detail—what had helped his operation run so well—would never allow me to overlook his thievery.

Davis asked, in as close to a civil tone as he could, "Is that why you're here, your motivation—revenge? To fuck Tony for fucking you over all these years?"

"No. Revenge doesn't fit into it, not the type of revenge that question implies anyway. I don't want to overcomplicate this, but money has nothing to do with this." I said I was doing this because I never should've been in this business to begin with, to find some redemption for everything wrong I'd done in the past ten years, for all the people I'd directly and indirectly hurt by bringing in so much filth into this country.

Tim Dowling said, "Okay, so what are we waiting for? Let's hammer out a plan of action and let's get this son of a bitch."

Capella laughed, "Well, it's about time, boss. I was actually starting to think you was going soft on us."

Tim smiled and pointed to the board. "Not at those prices I'm not."

I wrote out all of the addresses, escape routes, and, to the best of my knowledge, where the money and drugs were stashed in these apartments and homes. The planning then shifted to manpower. They had to choose the best men in these states that could work quickly, had exemplary careers, were beyond suspicion of any type of wrongdoing and without even the hint of corruptibility, but men who could also carry out this mission with precise timing and skill.

The next piece of business was to get the local agents, police departments, and district attorneys to draw up warrants based on my information, whose authentication in the minor seizure the night before would go a long way. Without that seizure, Tim explained to me, the district attorneys would never allow a first timer to coordinate such a large undertaking.

The good news was that all four men had worked in each of the cities containing Tony's safe houses at one point in their careers and they still had excellent contacts within the local DEA offices, customs, and police departments. They each divided and conquered. Whichever agent had the better contacts in each city, that was their responsibility; they pulled the men together, got the DA's office onboard and up to speed while disseminating the information on the spots I'd given to them, as well as having those ADAs find a judge who would sign off on multiple no-knock warrants—warrants that would allow these men to breach the premises or building with rams or even low-grade explosives to get into the more fortified locations.

It was decided that in New York they'd only use local detectives because the NYPD had the largest working police department in the country with narcotics or organized crime units built primarily for takedowns like this one.

Detroit would be garrisoned by DEA and Customs, Los Angeles and San Diego by DEA and local detectives working hand in hand in joint federal task forces. The plans were being formed.

When I left Tony's organization, I'd vowed to not just leave the drug pusher's life. I was going to burn the path behind me.

I prepared and detailed everything for Capella and called him back in twenty minutes. What I gave him was something no one knew I had up to this point, something that would, if coordinated properly, bury Tony even before any of these spots were hit.

I'd talked with Tony recently and found out that one of our tractor-trailers was heading to New York with close to a thousand pounds of marijuana. Once in New York, the driver would make stops at several safe houses, drop off a certain amount of the load at each one, pick up cash owed, and move on to the next location and so on till the driver had delivered all the weed, secured all the money, and would then head back to San Diego to drop it off at the safe house we called *the bank*. I even had this driver's telephone number—I was, after all, his boss.

The beauty about this was that the driver could be followed state to state, because he was driving my routes, rest stops, even motels if he chose to stop. He'd get handed off between state police at each state line until he finally made it to New York. The whole time, his phone would be tapped, and we would hear him plan his every move. Once inside New York City, the

NYPD—led by a first grade detective named Richie Fagan, who had organized some of the force's biggest busts—would take control, allowing the driver to make his first delivery and pickup.

And that's when the driver would get jacked and the spot would get taken out. Afterward, when he needed to make one call, I'm quite sure Richie, who knew the driver's phone was tapped, was going to be lenient: he could make as many calls as he liked.

Tony's safe houses were an assortment of spots that together paid tribute to the transient life he led and the damage he did to those who came into contact with him. One spot was an apartment on a tree-lined block in the northern Bronx. Tony kept a safe inside a wall behind a rather expensive Picasso he bartered in exchange for cash owed to him. Tony knew nothing about art, and when he was thinking of just whacking the poor fool offering the painting as a barter, I'd held Tony off until I had it authenticated. (Since it was worth three times what the man owed to Tony, I was able to talk him down from murder.) Tony also had a safe house on the Upper West Side of Manhattan with spectacular views of the Hudson River; the apartment itself was stunning and in a landmark building. The keeper of this location was just another one of the Fellini-esque troops of oddballs that surrounded Tony's life. Her name was Heidi. Tony would also use her spot to store coke or heroin for the many clients we had in New York City. At the moment I knew she was sitting on two hundred pounds of weed and at least ten kilos of coke, two kilos of pure heroin, and $500,000 in cash she owed Tony. Tony and I had discussed me organizing a trip to bring it all back to San Diego just before my arrest in Utah.

The third safe house was in the Corona section of Queens on Roosevelt Avenue, a Colombian enclave where Tony moved a lot of cocaine and marijuana. In a three-story building, this safe house consisted of two railroad apartments situated above a bogus travel agency, which was a front for a very real money-laundering operation, with money being wired from this location all around the world, supposedly for tourists.

Tony lent the two apartments to Colombians who lived there rent-free in exchange for receiving drug shipments at all hours of the night and doing most of the breakdown and packaging. The sad thing about these two apartments was they were inhabited by two *families*—husbands, wives, and a gaggle of kids, who I'm sure, when there was an overload of material, were utilized to help with the "family business." These kids ranged in age from six to thirteen. They were quiet families, never fought, stayed below the radar, and were very loyal to Tony. Exactly what he needed to facilitate the sales in the state and adjoining states.

The last stash house was in Medford, on Long Island's south shore, about a forty-minute drive from New York City.

Medford was Tony's Italian connection, or his wiseguy/ Mafiosi connects. The home belonged to some capo in one of New York's five crime families, a man I'd never met. This was one of Tony's private clients, of which I never saw a dollar of the profits, though I did know he was making a fortune with the New York wiseguys.

Tony had all the nationalities covered; he wasn't prejudiced or racist when it came to picking his associates, though he did have a favorite color—*green.*

This Italian client lived in a mansion that doubled as a horse farm situated on dozens of acres of land. Getting him the drugs was easy because his property was gated and the home itself was not visible from any roads or highways, so we'd just drive up to the large front gates, announce ourselves, the gates would whir open, and we'd drive to one of the barns where we'd store the product and would be gone without meeting anyone from the house. This very private capo then had his workers transport the weed, coke, or heroin into the neighborhoods of Long Island or boroughs of the city in horse trailers. It was an ingenious way of moving dope around the city. What cop is going to root through hay and horse shit looking for dope?

Tony often stayed at the house, and if we were lucky enough that Tony was in New York at the time of these raids, if he wasn't at his Bronx condo entertaining his harem of young twenty-somethings, the chances were good he'd be at the horse farm.

There were many other locations on that list. In California alone there were four spots, one in Chula Vista, just south of San Diego, that was our first location to drop off drugs brought in from Mexico. Not in the house itself, but in a warehouse we owned through a cut-out company that was close by the property. It's where the transport vehicles, mostly trucks, would unload and store the tonnage of product we'd bring in. This warehouse was also used to house the many trucks and cars we'd use to ferry the drugs across the country, as well as to cut up the parcels into more manageable loads easier for traveling to our other safe houses. It was absolutely necessary to be in close proximity to our product once it reached American soil. Chula Vista was close to the border and the quicker we got the bulk loads off the road the better. But this house was special for one reason—the Beltrán brothers rendezvoused with us there every month to collect the money we owed. To please and impress them, we didn't just hire a famous Spanish designer to help decorate the mansion's interior, we also built an exact replica of the Trevi Fountain.

There were also two spots in Koreatown, a house where we also packaged the material and directly across the street a duplex condo where Tony stayed when he wasn't in the Inland Empire with Maria or in the Chula Vista *"Roman Castillo."*

Last on the list was the rather spacious home Tony shared with Maria and their two children, which was used for cutting, storing, and packaging, and counting all of the money flooding in every week. I'd sometimes be the one organizing the money—tallying the profits, dividing out money for our workers and the Beltráns, for days on end.

There were days, before we were able to transport the cash out of the house, when its rooms were jammed so tight from floor to ceiling with cash there was literally nowhere to move.

The safe house in Detroit was in a Spanish section of the city, manned by a cousin of Tony's named Carmelo. The location was another three-story structure, the first floor an excellent taqueria, a family place where many of the neighborhood folks would eat, including the local cops, and a great cover for us. Here we used refrigerated trucks to move the dope in, packaged in every variety of food container you could imagine. We walked the dope and weed right through the front door, regardless of how many men in blue were eating the delicious enchiladas.

All the properties were now being monitored, our law enforcement partners across the country waiting for the moment to strike.

Operation Clean House

It took two days for "Operation Clean House" to gel. The NYPD OCID (Organized Crime Investigation Division) detectives had to move fast because my driver was heading out in *three* days at 6:00 A.M. on a run to New York. He'd be transporting a thousand pounds of weed stashed in the back of a tractor-trailer carrying ball bearings. On his return trip he was to bring back $3 million in cash from his various stops at our safe houses.

Richie Fagan, an NYPD detective who seemed to have seen it all, took control of the organization, coordinating the operational plans of the takedown with the various law enforcement components in Detroit, San Diego, Los Angeles, and San Diego's Inland Empire. He then organized, in coordination with each city's tactical aviation units, multiple flyovers of the safe houses in order to photograph them. The objective was to locate potential ways in and out, but also to analyze anything that looked suspicious around the locations, anomalies that could be perceived from the air, like nearby subway tunnels or cars parked in close proximity for prolonged periods of time that might be used to facilitate escape or evade capture or that might contain well-armed men for an added layer of security—employed by the caretakers on their dime, as none of them wanted to find themselves in the impossible position of explaining to Tony how they were ripped off of millions of dollars in cash and drugs and yet remained still alive.

So it began—a four-day odyssey of unparalleled anxiety, dread, and fear of the unknown.

As planned, my best driver and courier, Pedro, left promptly at 6:00 A.M. on the planned morning. Like many of his past runs, it would take him four days and some odd hours, all depending on the traffic patterns, to get within New York City's limits. We expected him to arrive about 12:00 P.M. or thereabouts. In the meantime, warrants were secured for every location while three teams of cops and agents watched the spots in every city around the clock to make certain that no product was *suddenly* moved.

A net now hung above, just waiting for the "go signal"—"*Impact*"—to be transmitted to so many point-to-point radios across three different states. Once that tight net of American justice was dropped, Tony would be one of the many prizes caught up in its inescapable webbing. If not—if something went wrong and he remained at large—my days left on God's green Earth would be numbered.

For an agonizing four days, we didn't see Tony, and I was starting to wonder if he'd been tipped off. There were many ways that cops or agents could've inadvertently given away this information. For instance, the telephone game: One cop tells a buddy about the raid over a few beers and a game of darts, and that friend tells another buddy who doesn't realize the significance of the case and he might quizzically ask one of his CIs, or street stools, if they had heard anything about this *big raid about to happen* in his or her hood. That CI, who might be double-dealing, or looking to curry favor with one of these caretakers or a friend of the caretaker, might know about the spots and tip them off. Another scenario could be as simple as two cops talking at a local gin mill that might not be so *aboveboard* and are overheard talking about the upcoming hit. With so many people planning the bust, the possibility of a leak kept me up at night.

I stayed in my house the entire time, the company phone glued to my hand as I counted down the hours until the operation.

I slept downstairs in my family room, well-fortified with water, guns, and ammunition, though sleep isn't really a proper description. Catnaps is closer to reality and they lasted all of about twenty minutes at a clip, and then I'd be on guard for another few hours, dozing for another twenty minutes to a half hour. It was a continuous battle of sleep versus vigilance. The yin versus yang my life had become.

On the third night, with barely ten hours of sleep in all, I could no longer keep my eyes open. I remember being for a time suspended in that wondrous, precious space between consciousness and sleep, completely aware of the magic your totally relaxed mind and exhausted body offer you.

I was there in that netherworld, numb, lifeless, floating on a velvety blanket of warm fragrant air. In the distance I heard the pulsating rhythmic sound of water cascading off a mountain cliff, sluicing through a slow-moving stream. I drifted closer and closer to this waterfall, floating—not on the glistening water, *but above it*. It was a magical experience. As I neared this waterfall I could feel its cool mist on my face, the air, abundant with sweet honeysuckle, and oddly, as I moved closer and closer to the falls, its pulsating rhythm drifted further and further away. I could feel I was very close to it now, spinning, riding on the pockets of air just above the roiling waters below me. The honeysuckle mixed with the clean aroma of ozone, and then I started rocking up and down, faster and faster.

I snapped up searching for my gun. It was gone—someone had removed it from my chest. I opened my eyes in a panic— and there he was, standing above me, alone.

"Tony?"

He was holding my Glock firmly, without the slightest tremor, indicating no remorse for what he was about to do, or what he had already done to me over the course of so many years. The gun was inches from my face, so close I could smell the oil I'd used to clean it not two hours before.

He spoke calmly, without animus. He said, "I knew you'd fuck me eventually, *puta*." He grinned.

How the hell did he get in? Where are the cops who were suppos-edly watching my house? Inez, the kids, are they all right? A million thoughts ran through my mind in the blink of an eye.

That's when I noticed his hands, covered in blood—*dried blood.*

The inside of my mouth flared with that familiar coppery taste of fear and dread; I felt my heart pounding in my ears, heard the blood rushing through my veins.

I tried to move but he jammed the big heavy Glock harder into my forehead, pushing me with all his might deeper into the cushions of the couch.

As he pulled the trigger, I kicked away, falling onto the thick carpet. I rolled over, quickly aligning my first shot at Tony, and then I'd take out the other hitter who had suddenly appeared in the room. My sweat-damp hands were shaking wildly, sweat stinging my eyes making it impossible to see clearly. I couldn't tell if the other man had a weapon, but I figured he'd have fired it if he did. I grabbed the Glock from where Tony had dropped it on the floor and began squeezing the trigger, and I heard my name clearly, someone was screaming, ROMAN! ROMAN! And through the sight of the gun I finally saw who I was face-to-face with.

Inez!

It took me about half a minute to return to consciousness and fully understand what I'd done. I was soaked in sweat, hyperventilating.

And then it all became clear to me. There was no one in the dimly lit great room other than Inez and me. She was wearing a bathrobe, crying, shaking uncontrollable at the foot of the couch. Her hands and arms covering her face and body in a defensive position as though she were waiting for the shot that would certainly kill her.

I looked at the gun still gripped tightly in my hand and slid it across the room as if it were a pit viper ready to strike. I could never keep one with us in our bedroom again.

For now, all I could do was cry.

The clock read 12:02 A.M. Just five minutes had elapsed since I'd fallen asleep in Inez's arms. Just a few more hours left until Tony's reckoning.

I called Mike and asked him to make sure my house was in fact being watched front and back.

Mike sympathized with me, hyperaware of the pathos in my voice. He calmly reaffirmed that there were three teams of battle-hardened ex-Delta operators and Navy SEALs well-hidden and with clear visuals to all points of entry into my house. "No one is getting in there, Roman, and if they try they'll be dead in seconds." He paused. "Listen, we all know what you and Inez are going through, but I promise you this will be over tomorrow. And understand this: We won't stop until we have this prick in cuffs. You have my word on that. He's never getting out, and if he does he'll be too damn old to piss straight. And trust me, Roman, I've found guys living in tree houses in the jungles of Guinea. There's nowhere on Earth this man can hide from us."

I thanked him for offering some reassurance.

"G'nite, partner," he said.

I snapped the phone shut, walked to our bedroom, and curled up beside Inez. Knowing that the house was being guarded gave me enough comfort to drift in and out of sleep.

My alarm woke me at 4:45 A.M., and I called Tim Dowling on my way to the office, as I'd been instructed to do. He told me that a car would break off and follow me to the location. There was no need for countersurveillance on this trip to Ramona; the follow car would determine if I had a tail. He also told me that another car would replace the unit following me to base in order to help keep Inez protected. If she left the house, two cars would follow her and one would remain on the house until they returned.

As I pulled into Ramona, agents across the country were taking their places, too. Al Harding, who was coordinating and monitoring the entire operation, was pacing nervously here with me, surrounded by four other DEA agents I hadn't met. They were there to make sure all the coms and computers were functioning properly and that all of Pedro's phone calls were being taped and that his every move was recorded based off of the cell tower information delivered from his phone. Mike, Pete, and Tim, along with ten other agents, were tasked with *"the bank"* in Riverside County and there were dozens of other men, both DEA and local joint task force detectives, at each safe house in California, all armed to the teeth just in case they were met with resistance.

No one had had eyes on Tony. In fact, it had been four days since we had last seen him. That made me extremely anxious.

We waited, listening to the officers following Pedro on Interstate 80, in New Jersey, heading east toward the George Washington Bridge. The three State Police detectives following since the Pennsylvania line were maintaining excellent visual contact.

As each minute passed, the urge to consider all the ways this operation could go violently, disastrously wrong seemed harder to suppress. I reminded myself that all of the safe houses in the three states were being monitored. Everyone was in place awaiting the go signal.

I did a lot of walking and soul searching in those tense hours waiting for something to happen, wondering where I'd be had I never gotten into the drug business, but also what would happen to me and my family if Tony escaped. He'd find us, without question, and I decided then and there that if it ever came to pass, I'd find him first.

I heard Richie Fagan's voice on the speakerphone as he set up in the Ramona basecamp. It was one o'clock in the afternoon, four in New York. Pedro had just driven over the George Washington Bridge and was heading toward Harlem River Drive South.

There were three units on the truck at a safe distance. If he did somehow recognize the tail and made a call alerting the caretakers to move everything out, every team would blow the doors off the spots and start the process of arrest and seizure.

Throughout the night Pedro had made a number of calls to the safe houses, explaining there was traffic in a number of states and he was running late. When he finally arrived at his first stop it was an unexpected one, one I knew nothing about. One of Tony's. How he hid it from me could only be explained one way: he'd just set it up.

This safe house was in DUMBO, Brooklyn, a former industrial zone that was transitioning into a high-end residential neighborhood, boasting incredible views of the East River, the Brooklyn and Manhattan Bridges, and Manhattan's financial district. Amidst DUMBO's bustling cobblestone streets was a nineteenth-century docking bay where Pedro was met by two forklifts.

The teams decided to hit this spot first before calling the go signal for all the other spots. Their logical reasoning was that they wanted Pedro to make a call and see who he'd alert first. Chances are that person would be, if not Tony, someone in close proximity to Tony, thus tightening the net and chances of getting Tony immediately. He was their main target and knowing where he was would make the operation easier and, above all else, safer. If Tony wasn't at any of the safe houses, "Impact" would begin.

Richie Fagan was at the Brooklyn drop-off point, and as soon as the back of the tractor-trailer was opened he and two dozen other cops swarmed it like a heard of wild buffalo.

This was the tensest part of the operation for me because I knew Pedro sometimes carried a weapon, even though he was trained by me and I had told him to never carry a firearm due to the added charge he'd receive if the truck was ever seized in a random police stop or raid. Yet I also knew that Tony insisted behind my back that Pedro, and many of our other drivers, carry a strap on these long hauls, *just in case.*

Pedro was a soft-spoken, twenty-three-year-old kid who came from a hardworking family living in Chihuahua, Mexico. He sent most of his money back to his family and their little cattle ranch. Pedro was not a killer, but like everyone under Tony's thumb he knew that if he didn't fight for the drugs, Tony would have no mercy.

I sat with my hands almost covering my ears as I heard the cops yelling commands at him, waiting for some cop to scream: *Shots fired! Man down.*

It was torturous. Then I heard they had everyone in the factory, including the driver, in custody and under arrest. Pedro wasn't able to make a call, so for now the mission was still compartmentalized. The detectives were now searching the trailer.

It took a while to unload the thirty-foot trailer using the forklifts, and to my utter surprise all they found were pallets and pallets of ball bearings.

Al looked at me nervously. He didn't say anything though I knew what he was thinking about the deep shit he'd be in if this wasn't, in fact, a drug run. The problem was I didn't know which trailer Pedro took—some of them had secret compartments built into them, others, depending on the content of the truck, contained the drugs within the boxes or packaging. But ball bearings were ball bearings, and it wasn't hard to decipher that's all that was inside that truck.

"Have the men measure the inside of the truck and then measure the outside," I told Al. If there was a discrepancy in the measurements that would mean a false wall was built inside.

I waited and waited, sweating through my pants, biting my nails down to their cuticles. Finally they came back to Al telling him there was a five-foot discrepancy from the inside versus the outside. I finally sat back, took a deep breath, and quietly advised Al to tear out the false wall.

Inside, they found a thousand pounds of marijuana and a million dollars in cash. That was money Tony hadn't told me about, but I was sure this was money he was transporting back to New York to hide it from Hector and me. I practically fist-pumped the air I was so happy. The thrill and risk of the operation was being rewarded more times over than I could have imagined.

The first part of Operation Clean House was complete; but now came the hard part, executing the other spots without any injuries to the cops and in the process bringing Tony to justice.

Richie Fagan, calculating as ever, allowed Pedro to make a call from his car and walked away to give Pedro a sense of privacy. Pedro did exactly what was expected: He called the Corona, Queens, location, told them he got hit and they needed to clean the spots. What Pedro didn't know was that his call was tapped and as soon as Richie heard it, he called the men at the location to hit that particular spot immediately. The detectives were inside within two minutes, and no one at that location made any other alert calls, so the other caretakers were still unaware of the raid.

The Corona spot yielded forty kilos of cocaine and $3 million in cash, along with a number of defaced firearms. Tony wasn't there, however. Assuming I was right in thinking that he was lying low in New York, I wasn't sure where else he could be.

It was closing in on 9 P.M., and that was when Richie Fagan broadcast the call sign "Impact."

It was on.

Every spot was hit simultaneously, from California to Detroit to New York City to Medford, Long Island.

And Medford, Long Island, was the charm.

The detectives hit the spot with speed and the unwieldy knowledge that they might be walking into their deaths. They burst through the large home's front and rear doors, guns in hand, screaming, "Everyone get down," and what they found there was *not* what anyone—including me—was expecting. There were fourteen women sitting around a giant TV, enjoying popcorn, soda, and beer, all watching the soap opera *Melrose Place*. Once I heard this, I knew Tony was in the building.

Melrose Place was Tony's favorite TV series, and he *never* missed an episode. He was obsessed with the series and on so many occasions would wax on for mind-numbing hours about all the characters, their story lines, who he wanted to fuck, and also who he wanted to kill off. Fourteen women and a new episode of his favorite soap is what Tony considered his ideal party.

Tony gave up quietly—no surprise there. Yes, he was a maniac, but he wasn't stupid. This was a battle he knew couldn't win—twenty heavily armed, badass New York City cops. I felt liberated and sorry only for the women who had to experience the fright this bust no doubt inspired.

All of the other spots were hit with no casualties on either side. Thanks to Detective Fagan's stellar coordination of the NYPD OCID unit and the planning of the men and women in the DEA and our partner police departments around the country, it was a flawlessly executed takedown.

The whole operation yielded close to $30 million in cash, just under a ton and a half of marijuana, sixty kilos of cocaine, twenty kilos of heroin, two hundred pounds of methamphetamine, and a combined total of thirty-six handguns, machine guns, and hunting rifles.

The NYPD Public Morals Division of the Organized Crime Control Bureau, whose main responsibility was taking out illegal after-hours clubs, gambling dens, prostitution rings, and the like, hit the illegal club Tony was running in Washington Heights. It was a place teeming with money and prostitutes, where scoring an eight-ball was as simple as flagging down a bartender and ordering it off the menu. It took the cops about forty minutes to cut through the iron door, but once they got in they went to work. Chain saws in hand, they tore the place apart.

In the pictures taken afterward, there was nothing left but broken wood, mangled furniture, ripped-out fixtures, cut pipes, cut wiring, broken glass, and open spaces where iron doors once stood. The apartment above the club netted twenty-five guests and security elements, all clambering up the ladder through the apartment's trapdoor only to be met with as many detectives just waiting for them. All of the security men and some of the guests were carrying firearms. They were all arrested and arraigned. Each would be spending time in "the tombs," Manhattan's 150-year-old granite detention center that resembled ancient Egyptian tombs, then be carted off to Rikers Island, New York City's violent and infamous jail, where perps were housed while awaiting trial, while others did short sentences and yet others waited to be transferred to state prisons.

Additionally, eighteen men were arrested in total in all of Tony's safe houses. Neither Hector nor Raul were amongst them. The fourteen women found with Tony were cut loose.

Richie Fagan relayed to the detectives who were holding Tony to transport him to the Manhattan DA's office before bringing him to central booking for processing. There, Richie would try to flip him, though I knew that was an act of futility.

I later learned that Richie excelled at flipping guys; in fact, he was not only the opener, but the closer as well, when the most hardened criminals or underworld gangsters were collared. He talked to them with respect, but also with the hard truths regarding the unwinnable circumstances they faced when sitting in their unenviable position. He'd slide photos of their daughters across the table to these men and say, "Twenty years away from this little girl, you're going to miss all the milestones in her life. She'll never forget the moments daddy was there for her—or wasn't. Soon she'll be dating, and without a man in the house to guide her...Well, do I really need to go there?" I'd soon get to see this firsthand, watch Richie grind the hardest guys to putty in his hands.

The problem Richie faced with Tony was that Tony was one man unto himself. He had children all over the place but no love for them. And since the friends and close family he did have were all enmeshed in the drug business, talking to Richie could only put them at risk. It was a hardscrabble rule of the drug business—and one Tony knew better than anyone—that if you talk about the trade or people you had worked with, every one of your blood relatives, friends, even acquaintances could be eviscerated. Only after every one of them were tortured and killed might the rat become the target.

*   *   *

The next day we all met at San Diego's field office at 9:00 A.M. to discuss all the after-action reports. The team leaders in every city were patched in via a conference line. I wanted to know what Tony was saying: What was his demeanor? Did he snap telling these detectives he knew who rolled on him? If so, I'd know he was trying to send me a message and that I'd need to do more to protect my family from him.

The detectives' work had only begun. The tasks now before us all were to determine who was who in the organization—something I could help with—and then the daunting challenge of trying to flip these guys upward, trying to help the detectives get an undercover into one of the Mexican cartels or at the very least get a man who could observe the cartel's actions from a trading partner's organization. It is a never-ending game of collecting intelligence, corroborating it, and disseminating it amongst the various agencies that help to keep drugs off our streets.

When asked if Tony talked, Richie said something interesting. He said that Tony actually looked defeated, almost like he had given up. He was a total gentleman with Richie, and after Richie brought him a sandwich, soda, and a pack of cigarettes, they launched a cordial interview. Every question was carefully thought out—not too hard, not too soft, easy ones at first—but Richie never made it anywhere. In fact, he struck out.

Tony said to him, "All due respect, detective, let me ask you a question. If you got caught doing something that jeopardized your job, your livelihood, a job you were born to do and loved with all of your heart, and your bosses came to you and told you, 'Hey, detective, we'll let you keep your job, but you have to give us all of your relatives to answer for your crimes and they'll be tortured and killed,' would you give them up? Would you do that to save your job?" What Tony wasn't thinking about, however, was the harm these people he was protecting had done. If your family hadn't done anything wrong, your job as an informant wasn't to jail them. It was to find bigger and bigger fish at the periphery of your one-time drug trading network, and by taking them off the streets, you forged a safer world for everyone else.

But Richie knew exactly what Tony was saying: he was not going to say a word about his work. Tony capped off the conversation by saying, "Listen, I appreciate you treating me fairly, but the longer I'm in here the more suspect I become, because if you don't think that the boss of all my bosses doesn't know the exact time I was brought here as opposed straight to lockup, you're wrong. The longer I spend in this room, the easier it will be for them to assume I'm talking to you. So I'd appreciate it if you could wrap this up and let me get to the booking process so there can be no misunderstandings with my people."

Richie could've kept Tony at the DA's office all night if he wanted, solidifying the man's demise. But Richie's street currency was that of an excellent cop, and beyond that he was a truly decent human being. He agreed with Tony's logic and got him out of the building and into booking in less than ten minutes. He also made a show of the fact that Tony didn't talk. "This was a tough cookie," he said to the cops stationed in central booking. "Don't bother bringing him to the DA's to talk."

In the end, Tony received seventeen years without the chance of parole on a plea bargain deal. Tony wouldn't be out in the street till he was well into his late sixties, and that's only if he were a model prisoner, which I knew he would not be. A team of forensic accountants was analyzing his bank accounts, and already his overseas accounts were frozen. The State Department would be called in and they'd barter and deal with the foreign entities that were the holders of his millions. Tony would never see a dime of that money, and once the accountants figured out who the powers of attorney on his stateside accounts were, those lawyers would be arrested and those accounts forfeited, too. Tony would be broke.

After hearing there were warrants out for his arrest, Hector did what he had to do: he fled. Now that his friend, bodyguard, and benefactor was behind bars, there was no one who could protect him from the Beltrán brothers, who were no doubt eager to collect the $2 million he owed them. Hector would stay underground for as long as he could survive, and as long as he was still outside I had to remain vigilant.

I worked a deal out with my guys to keep Raul out on the street. He was small time and meant nothing to anyone other than me. If he got caught outside in a buy-and-bust operation or was caught with anything illegal, he was told he was going away for a very long time and could end up in the very prison where Tony was housed, which would probably be a death sentence.

It was put on record that I, too, was arrested and sent away to an undisclosed prison. I still had more of my case to work off, but for the time being I would lay low. Word would hopefully get back to the Beltráns that both Tony and I were locked up in a major sting. But would the Beltráns believe it? Only time would tell.

II
The Cartel

An Unexpected Gift

Hector was wanted. Wanted by the Beltráns for the egregious amount of money he personally owed to them. Wanted by several law enforcement agencies all clamoring to catch him in order to claim partial credit for the huge arrests and seizures just procured. I wondered who would get him first.

I never wondered if he'd manage to elude us. He couldn't. Hector was no Tony—he was no planner, no negotiator. Tony was the brain and the killer, and now Hector was on his own, a man fucked six ways from Sunday.

But his situation gave me my own reasons to worry. I was the next in line on Tony's sinking skiff—I was the only other one in the room with the Beltrán brothers not already in prison. Thankfully the Beltráns didn't know where I lived. But how hard could it be for them to find me?

So, naturally, I was seeing all sorts of things in my rearview mirror. Now and then a helicopter hovered over my property at dawn and again at dusk. Was it really possible these visitors could all just be delusions of my paranoia?

Without a doubt the potential killers out there who had me in their scopes were growing in number by the hour. With Tony's demise and with Hector underground, he had to know I set the whole takedown up—who else would have the information to do it? But the newest concern I had to endure was a caravan of Mexican special forces–type psychos, activated by the Beltrán brothers, to snatch me off the street—or worse, out of my bed, family included. I saw movement and surveillance wherever I went. I also went to great lengths to teach Inez how to use the Mossberg "street sweeper" shotgun I now made her keep in close proximity when she was home alone. Was she happy learning how to skeet shoot? Hell no, but she knew this was just another wrinkle she'd have to endure in the line of work I was pursuing as I worked off my case.

It's hard not to be paranoid, of course, knowing the hitters the Beltráns had. They weren't the type of guys you see— not until you're in some abandoned factory in Juarez, Mexico, hanging upside down, four Michelin tires fit snugly around your midsection, waking up to gasoline being poured over your head and a guy tossing a lighter from hand to hand.

One morning in one of those tense days not long after the bust, I was pulling out of my driveway, swiveling my head in all directions to see if anyone was parked in a nearby car, tracking me, and all looked clear, but just as I made it to the corner, a head popped out from behind an old telephone pole. Raul, the only person I knew skinny enough to be completely obscured by a telephone pole and one of the very last people I ever expected to see again.

I was stunned. Was this a trap set up by Hector, to lull me

into some kill box? Had Raul found out that I'd told Tony he was talking to the feds and come here for revenge? I put the car in gear, one foot barely touching the brake, the other foot hovering above the gas pedal. If I saw him pull a weapon, I was ready to mow him down.

That's when I saw his face, creased with worry, his eyes scared to death. I could see that this was no trap.

We eyed each other for a few more seconds before he cautiously approached. He held out his hands, indicating to me that he was clean, and then he lifted up his shirt, and twirled around like a ballerina, showing me he had nothing strapped to him.

I lowered the window a crack.

"There's any number of hitters out here looking to air you the fuck out," I said. "You do know that all of our spots got taken out by the cops, don't you?"

He went stiff.

"So what do you want? And by the way, not cool coming here because if someone is following you, you just brought them to me and my family's doorstep."

He dropped his head like a scolded child. He said quietly, "Listen, Roma, we need to talk, and being out here in the open I don't think is very good tactics."

I laughed. In a way I was grateful to this bonehead for finally giving me the escape route from my dangerous life that I'd for years been looking for, but I could certainly never reveal that. "Not good tactics? No, driving the wrong way into oncoming traffic on some superhighway median surrounded by cop cars, that's not good tactics!"

"We...we need to talk. I'm shelved, can't even get 'hold a

my bro Hector. And I need your help. You're the only one I trust with this."

"You can't get ahold of Hector because he's wanted by the feds and probably hiding in Greenland."

I told him to get in—it was dangerous to talk here. When he was settled, I stomped on the gas.

I shot onto the interstate, checking my mirrors for tails. After about a mile, I turned into the emergency vehicle turn-about and, not stopping, I crossed it and started in the other direction, barely missing getting squashed by a parade of cars with understandably pissed-off drivers who had nearly braked to a stop to let in the madman who'd barreled into their lane.

Throughout this insane maneuver, I was sweating more than I'd ever thought was possible and Raul was shrieking in the pitch of an eight-year-old girl.

Now, finally, I could calm myself. No one had followed us, and if anyone who had me within sight was crazy enough to try it, I'd spot them as I coasted away.

I looked at my watch. "You got two minutes," I told Raul. "Make it count or so help me God I'm tossing you out of this car right here."

"Wait a minute. You don't think I was the one who rolled on the spots, do you? I didn't even know where's they was, and you know that!"

I told him I didn't know shit, that all I knew was that I had a lawyer on retainer just waiting for the feds and that it had cost me a fortune to make bail. I was rough on this skinny guy. I needed to keep him on the defensive, because harmless as he seemed, if he sat back and thought about the situation for one second, he might realize how few people there were who could have given up our organization and how neatly I, just weeks after our arrest in Utah, fit the description of someone who might.

"Two minutes," I said again.

He began nodding as if with passion. "Okay, two minutes, two minutes. You got it, *primo*. And by the way, what I've got is going to help you pay for that lawyer of yours."

The traffic on the street thinned and I began to speed aimlessly, as if to advertise my boredom.

"But there's one thing I need from you," he said. "I need money, money to get out of here. But where I'm a get money without the boys to hook me up?"

I couldn't believe him. His bad driving had led to my arrest—what he must have thought was one of the most upsetting events in my lavish life—and he wanted to ask *me* for money? I laughed.

"I'm all out of charity, Raul. That little stunt you pulled back in Utah could've gotten us both clipped." He frowned and began to apologize, and I realized this was my chance to crank up the heat on Raul in case Tony had sent him to test my loyalty. I needed to show that all was well between Tony and me. "To roll on me and tell Tony *I* was the one who flipped," I said, shaking my head. "You're lucky I don't just kill you now to save you from the torture he's is going to inflict on your sorry ass." I glanced at my watch. "You've got forty-five seconds by the way."

Now he was desperate, grabbing handfuls of his greasy hair like a child in the middle of a tantrum. He hadn't told Tony anything, hadn't so much as spoken with the man since the trip to Michigan was busted. He was begging me to believe him.

I did, but him giving me up to Hector was my bigger fear. I

pressed him. "I know you didn't tell Tony, you told *Hector*, you rat fuck, and Hector told Tony to save your dumb ass."

"Roman, man, that's not true!" His eyes were glistening with tears, and for the first time I felt a pang of guilt for what I was putting him through. This wild-eyed but innocent man was never a match for substances he got involved in—and all the unsteady figures they attracted.

"You know what I told Hector? I told him that I tried to get outt'a there by giving the cops something that would show them I was cooperative and maybe they'd let us both out, that maybe they'd think I'd cooperate later too, but once I was out they'd never see my ass again cause I'm in the wind."

I stared into his scared eyes. Yes, he was a notorious, routine liar—all junkies are—but what he was saying didn't sound like something he could've come up with on his own, and if this were a trap I'd be dead already. It began to make sense now. Hector came up with the story telling Tony I flipped, not Raul; this would buy Hector time to take the heat off of Raul. But what Hector didn't anticipate was that Tony, above anyone else, trusted me. My loyalty had been tested for years and not once had I faltered—I was too afraid of what Tony would do to me and my family.

Tony had underestimated the hell he put me through—put all of us through—and how desperately I'd been searching for a way out.

I asked Raul point-blank what he wanted from me.

He said, "Okay. I know you think I'ma fuckup an' all, but I'm gonna show you that you're wrong about that. I have a plan that will pay for your bail and help get each of us enough money to disappear for a while: I got a line on some Mexican family in Nasty City who's got a lotta cocaine to move. They supposedly sitting on like a ton a shit they need to get rid of. And my boy tell me it's a direct line to Fuentes."

I looked at Raul the way I would look at a boy who said he'd spotted a werewolf. It just didn't seem plausible that anyone from the Fuentes Cartel would look twice at a junkie like Raul, let alone talk any type of drug business with him. Had Raul told me that both Beltrán brothers had suddenly recognized the genius in him and decided to have him replace Tony in the distribution operation, I might have been just as inclined to believe him.

"The Fuentes coca, you say. As in *Queen of Hearts, Lord of the Sky* cocaine?" I looked at my watch, "Okay, I gave you an extra minute and a half." I reached over to open the door and he grabbed hold of my wrist in one last desperate plea. He must've noticed the storm gathering in my eyes because he let go instantaneously.

"Listen, Rome! The woman's name is Sylvia. I met her son—he knows I'm with Tony and you, and he knows Hector, but he's a kid, like maybe eighteen, if that, and he seem a little nervous. He asked if I could set up a meet with you."

We looked at each other, and I swallowed. Maybe I had this situation all wrong. "I knew how pissed off you were," Raul said, "so I reached out to my brother but he gone. I can't go to Tony cause that mafucka locked up"—he made a quick sign of the cross—"so that's why I thought I come to you. Rome, there's money in this, and the kid asked for you."

They would only have asked for me—and not Tony or Hector—if it had been broadcast all over the street that Tony got taken down.

I looked into Raul's eyes, and I saw a man equal parts desperate and dangerous. There was a coldness in him, a fearfulness that made me realize that he knew he was risking everything, and he was really ready to risk all that and more for a big score.

Here it was: my second undercover case. It was also the first time the guilt and pain associated with taking drug traders off the street really hit me. I never doubted that it would be the right thing to get Raul out of this dirty game—for the people his work would harm and also for him—but somehow, in a way that was never possible with Tony Loco Tony, it was hard not to feel sorry for this guy.

I cleared my throat. "Okay, Raul. What did you tell this kid?"

It was as if he were on Death Row and I had just told him that the governor had commuted his sentence and he was going free on some technicality. He closed his eyes and exhaled deeply. He said that if I made the connect, he'd tell the kid's mother, this Sylvia, the matriarch of the crew is what he called her. I told him I could make the connect.

Whatever operation this was that Raul had stumbled upon, I needed to take it out from the top. "Sylvia's the one I need to meet," I said. "When can you set that up?"

"Listen," he said, "just a heads-up: They into some weird shit, like that Santeria voodoo shit them crazy Mexicans and Cubanos fuck with. I could tell 'cause I seen dudes with the same tattoos, that Santa Muerte shit, back when I was in jail in Havana."

This sealed it for me. The Fuentes, like many of the other cartels in Mexico, did in fact practice a form of Santeria that appropriated aspects of other religions and the occult. Tony and I had heard they'd indoctrinate their drivers, all pious to begin with, in elaborate rituals, sometimes using human sacrifices said to provide them with superhuman powers before sending them on deliveries or more dangerous border crossings. These drivers would actually believe that, after drinking another man's blood or eating his heart, they had mystical powers and were able to become invisible, or at least impervious to arrest. Of course, many of these drivers met ends as quick and tragic as the people they'd slaughtered and cannibalized.

The next step: I had to be 100 percent sure that the Fuentes did not know about the recent disintegration of my entire organization. "Where are they?" I asked.

"Here in San Diego, near Ysidro border." Raul pulled out a sliver of paper and handed it to me. It was an address in National City. I had the urge to drive there that second and scope out the property of the matriarch, try to somehow conquer the house that would come to haunt my dreams. But that could be suicidal, and my colleagues at Alliance would never forgive me for going without warning them, no matter how well it turned out.

"How much are they sitting on?"

They had as much as we wanted. Raul said he wasn't bullshitting me. I'd heard *that* from him before, but I'd never been so convinced he was serious. They literally had tons.

It was conceivable. A ton—2,000 pounds—is a lot of powder, but if this family was hooked up with the Fuentes, a ton was a drop in the bucket.

"And if they're so heavy, how come they don't have their own networks set up here already?" I asked. "Why are they giving us, a crew they don't even know who's clearly working with their competition, the Beltráns, this great opportunity?"

It turned out that the kid's brother-in-law had all the connections in the states and got pinched by the feds. All their usual clients ran from them, thinking maybe they cooperated or something. They feared that one of their buyers set up the husband, so they didn't much want to deal with their old distributors, either. They needed new buyers to get rid of their excess product, and, in Raul's words, they knew I was the shit.

The paranoia associated with this business is astounding, and I understood exactly what this family was going through. A few short weeks ago I was in something like their position, and now Tony and Hector had the pleasure of sitting on that hot seat—one in prison, the other in hiding God knows where.

"And what if they've flipped—the husband got pinched and they're working with the feds now?" I had to ask the question. It'd be suspicious if I didn't.

Raul answered openly: "Well, I don't know, you might be right, Rome. But ain't it something you could figure out?"

I started up my car and pulled out, and Raul relaxed in the seat for the first time. He started fiddling with the windows, up and down, playing with the air vents, changing the radio stations. He was now back in his own world, on his very own asteroid flying through space without a care. His childlike curiosity never ceased to amaze me, and that's why I suppose I had a soft spot for him. He was like a confused little waif lost in a forest of evil. Raul was not cut out for this work, and rather than recognizing this and committing him to a long-term addiction treatment facility, his asshole brother Hector enabled Raul as he continued to build out his empire.

If all the stars aligned and this family was in fact who Raul purported them to be, I was going to make sure that he got credit for the initial tip. Maybe this case would be the beginning of a new life for him.

But before bringing this tip to Ramona, I'd need to be certain it was based in truth. I needed to put eyes on these people.

I parked about a block away from the "Nasty City" home with a clear view of the front and side of the property. I opened up the blinds of the rear tinted window so that I could see out but no one could see in. I flipped one of the captain's chairs around and grabbed my binoculars.

The ranch-style home was at the end of a ratty block. It was in a declining part of the National City neighborhood, and most of the homes reflected the neighborhood's struggles. Cracked sidewalks, junked cars on patchy lawns, old indoor furniture on many of the porches, sneakers tossed over telephone lines, graffiti spray-painted on the sides of some of the homes. But there was one house in particular that stood out from the rest, and it was the house I was there to watch.

It was in no better shape than any of these other homes, but this home was like a fortress. A newly constructed eight-foot-high metal fence protected the commodious lot the house stood on. It had an electric gate that rolled open to expose a double-space car park on the side of the home, its cement driveway lined with weed-filled cracks. There was a small dirt patch out front that at one time must've been the home's garden or lawn, now scattered with children's toys. These folks weren't renting this home for its aesthetic beauty, nor were they interested in landscaping, paint, or, as far as I could decipher through my binoculars, the décor inside. But the most telling detail that made this property stand out from all of those around it was the security system—the high-end cameras built into the two sides of the house, above its front door, and perched in a tree with a clear vantage of the street.

I staked out the property for three days, at different times and from different locations away from the viewfinders of these cameras. An older woman of about sixty came and went without any regularity, always in her three-year-old Mercedes and always in the company of a man, about forty, who looked Arabic. I assumed this woman was Sylvia, the one Raul had called the family matriarch. The man could have been her driver.

I watched the teenager who had approached Raul leave in the mornings around ten and return at four every afternoon. Could he have had a job? On very rare occasions, a beautiful woman with a dark olive complexion, high cheekbones, and straight jet-black hair would sit in the alley and watch a toddler as he played with the toys on the lawn. She was always dressed in very high-end clothing and wore tasteful, understated jewelry. This woman did not fit in this neighborhood—at all. In fact, she looked tired, as if discouraged by her circumstances.

In my training as an undercover informant, I'd come to understand that in surveillance work what you don't see happening is often more telling than what you do. On this block chock-full of gangbangers hanging out on their porches and in cars double-parked in the street, radios blaring, I couldn't help but notice how no one so much as said a word to this beautiful woman or even looked in her direction. Clearly, she was tied to the matriarch, and everybody knew it. And, as I'd come to learn, the matriarch was terrifying.

The next day I went to Ramona and explained the situation to Tim Dowling. I needed to get the Alliance Group onboard with the takedown and to confirm that another team wasn't already onto this family. Tim made a number of calls and confirmed they weren't already being watched.

Eventually, he gave me the green light to move ahead, but I could tell he was nervous about me going out on my own for the first time. If something happened to me, the finger would be pointed at him.

I, on the other hand, didn't lack faith that I could ensnare these drug runners. Meeting families like this one had been the core of my existence for the past ten years—my ability to procure new buyers and sellers was part of what made Tony's operation what it was: one of the biggest smuggling outfits in the United States.

Tim was also obliged to ask if I needed or wanted a *"ghost"* to follow me, an agent to watch my back. That was the last thing I wanted, especially in light of this family's current predicament. They were going to be very raised up and suspect of me from the outset. If they felt at all threatened, this deal was going away, and they might leave me with a bullet in my head.

I told Tim a ghost would be more of a liability than anything. The thing about first meets is that they're always a game, two dogs sniffing at each other. What I had going for me was my pedigree—they were looking for a reliable source to sell to. They wouldn't kill me on our first meet. What would be the point?

I smiled. "No," I said. "They'll wait until I bring them a duffel bag full of hundreds...and *then* they'll kill me."

Tim suppressed a laugh. "It's time for you to start thinking of relocating," he said.

I nodded. "I'm bringing it up to Inez. Even though the Beltráns don't know where I live, I realize that a good PI can find me. Believe me, I don't like the fact that after what happened, Tony might get word to someone to get to me at my home."

I don't know whether it was my insistence on not having a ghost or my frankness about the fear I felt for my family, but Tim decided to finally let me in on a secret he'd been keeping from me. "We have people watching your house," he said. I'd never see them, but they'd be there. "I would have told you, but I knew you'd worry that it would raise up Inez and frankly we don't have a choice about this."

It was time to earn my keep, knock down the case pending against me, and move with my family on to a new safer, quieter life.

Raul called the teenager, telling him I was interested. Our meeting was to take place at the National City home that next afternoon. I was nervous about bringing Raul—imagining what Sylvia or whoever was running this operation would think of our 130-pound crackhead connection—but what choice did I have?

Raul would have to be tossed under the bus.

Queen of Hearts,
Lord of the Sky

I nez was helping me pick out my outfit and jewelry for the meet. Raul had coordinated with the teenager, and I was to discuss our potential deal with Sylvia in their home. Inez seemed at first apprehensive about the operation, but she knew I was in my element. She picked out a charcoal pin-stripe Brooks Brothers suit with wide lapels and a pair of black leather Gucci shoes.

Everything in this business is predicated on first impressions, and I had to find a way to impress the hell out of these people in spite of Raul. I had to drip money because they would check everything from my belt, to my money clip, to my keychain, and the clothing had to be in concordance with my legend as the Beltráns' American distributor.

I was prepared. Beyond my $4000 suit and accessorized clothing, I was wearing my Platinum Daytona Rolex, a platinum pinky ring that held a flawless three-carat diamond, a solid gold link bracelet, and, in a nod to these very *pious* Mexicans, a solid gold rosary with a garish three-inch cross bathed in diamonds. I left this last piece of jewelry partially hidden just below the third button of my shirt.

This whole meet was a charade, a game of cat and mouse. If I came on too strong, I risked belittling them; if I came on too soft, then maybe I wasn't as solvent as they'd expect. Attention to detail and analyzing the way the beautiful woman at the bunker dressed helped me decide on my level of physical deception.

Inez looked me up and down and smiled. "You're either an international man of intrigue," she said, "or you're a drug dealer.... Just don't ever wear this outfit to meetings with the PTA."

We hugged, and she brushed the lint from my arm. She told me I wasn't the same person I was last month. The truth was, I *did* feel transformed. No longer did I live in fear of Tony's next temper tantrum or the fallout from Hector's lavish lifestyle. My fears were of another kind. Yet I felt more confident than ever because I knew there were now men behind me who would actually lay down their lives for me.

"I always have faith in you," Inez said. "You will call me before and after?"

I promised I would, and we kissed one last time.

Raul and I rendezvoused at an amusement park in National City. He twirled, proud of his new look. I'd asked him to dress up, which apparently meant to him throwing a suit jacket two sizes too big over his black t-shirt and ratty jeans.

Driving to the house, I set the ground rules. Raul was there only to introduce me to this woman Sylvia, or to whoever meets us out front. Once we were in, I was to do all the talking. He was to find an excuse to step out and leave us to negotiate.

He looked crestfallen. "But, Rome, man, I'm the dude who set this up. Won't it look funny if I just walk away?"

"No, in fact it'll look exactly how it should look. Listen, Raul, these people know who I am. They also know Tony and your brother, but they don't really know you. And they're already raised up about this meeting." It was no secret that Raul got high, and even though it broke my heart to tell him, I said that if they thought my partner had a drug problem, they might call the whole thing off.

He dropped his head, and I wondered if the realization at how his life turned out—the realization that he had already squandered so many of the opportunities he'd ever be given—was hitting home.

"I get it," he said.

He pulled down the vanity mirror and looked at himself long and hard. He rubbed his balled-up fists into his cheeks to try and add some color to his normal gray pallor. When that didn't work, he began slapping his face—hard—and he continued to do so until I grabbed his arm to stop him.

"You look fine, Raul. Please don't overthink this. We're two friends, you and I, acquaintances of your brother, who is my partner. If they ask anything about Tony, you tell them you haven't seen him, that you're just my driver. And tell them I keep you in the dark about these things to keep you safe."

He nodded. "I'm gonna let you do your thing, Roma."

I didn't want to tell him this, but I felt I had to: "Call me 'Roman,' always the full name." Roma suggested a deeper relationship.

I pulled in front of the sliding electric gates, which rolled open before us. I parked behind two Mercedes, older but in decent enough shape to suggest some money. Before we got out of the car I grabbed Raul's leg and looked at him one last time. I covered my mouth with my hand as I assumed that those cameras were working overtime zooming into my face at that exact moment and said, "We cool, brother?"

He smiled at me as if nothing had transpired. "I'm going to let you do your thing, Roman." He enunciated perfectly. No street slang, no Ebonics or whatever dialect it was that he sometimes spoke. It was as if a ventriloquist had hopped into the backseat.

The front door to the house opened and the teenager who introduced himself as Estefan stepped out. We both reached him at the same time and he quickly shook Raul's hand then mine vigorously. "It's a real honor to meet you, Mister Roman," he said in a thick Mexican accent. "Thank you for seeing my family today."

I chuckled. "Listen, Estefan, the only people that call me Mister Roman are my wife and kids. You can call me Roman."

He didn't seem to get the joke and nodded quickly, then led us into the house. For the first time on a mission I could feel sweat run down my back. I wondered if I'd made a mistake not to bring a gun, though I knew deep down how disrespectful—and potentially dangerous—that would have been. When I pitched the operation to Tim, I was certain this family would never lay a hand on me in this first meeting. Now I wondered what I could do if I was wrong, and the horrifying truth was nothing: I'd be trapped.

The inside of the house was no different than the outside,

other than the horrendous color schemes on every wall: lime green, yellow, lavender, and blue. The parlor area I entered was cluttered with furniture that looked like it fell off a truck from the 1960s, plastic slipcovers included. Colored glass lamps hung from the ceiling strung by thick brown chains. There were plastic flowers and crucifixes everywhere.

The woman I recognized as Sylvia stepped into the room wearing a colorful Fendi dress that wouldn't have been sexy no matter who was wearing it. On Sylvia, the dress was especially far from the mark, if that was in fact her aim. We locked eyes, and I felt the oddest chill run through me, as if she was trying to reach into my soul, devour my secrets, learn all of my tells.

I gave her the warmest smile I could manage and told her how nice it was to meet her.

Her face was so tightly nipped and tucked that it appeared ready to split up the sides had her smile widened any further.

In an accent like her son's, Sylvia told me the pleasure was hers. "I've heard a lot of good things about you," she said. Only when she let go of my hand did she finally notice my sidekick. "And you are?"

Thankfully Estefan jumped in; I guess he was as worried about Raul as I was. In Spanish he said, "He's Roman's partner, Raul." He explained the connection to Hector and lowered his voice. "He won't be involved with you and Roman—just here for the introduction."

Sylvia shot her son an evil look, then quickly regrouped, turned back to Raul, and gave him her hand. The moment Raul touched it, she quickly pulled it back. She looked at me without saying a word, and her glare said everything.

Raul picked up his cue and cleared his throat. "Okay, I'm

going to let you do your thing, Roman." Raul then did something that shocked me. He pointed to the couch and in a perfect Mexican dialect asked Sylvia, "Ma'am, would it be okay if I sat on one of the couches or if you'd like I can sit in the car outside?"

Sylvia thought about this for more than a moment. Then, in a half-hearted gesture, she pointed to the couch and then whispered something to Estefan, who took a seat on one end.

I followed Sylvia through a large foyer. As we were walking she said, "A man like you, why are you involved with...with the vermin you just walked in here with?"

It was the question I dreaded more than any other, because even though I was prepared for it, even though I'd wake at night thinking about it, I couldn't come up with a convincing answer. My nerves ran cold. Before I could second-guess myself, I gave her the answer I'd prepared. I needed to keep him on because he was my partner's brother. He was misguided, but harmless and above all else loyal. And we, like everybody else, needed to get around. He was our driver.

I let out a resigned sigh, and scanned the room Sylvia had led us to. She caught me staring at a Jesus statuette hanging precipitously over the fireplace. "Listen," I said, "I'd be as skeptical as you had you brought him to me during a first meet of what hopefully will turn out to be many meetings, because I've heard some good things about you and our mutual cousins down south."

She stopped walking and looked me directly in the eyes. She nodded her head and then wrapped her arm around my waist.

That's when I knew she was mine.

"There are some interesting people I think you'll be happy to meet," she said. When she smiled, there was heat attached to it, like she was coming on to me with her big cappuccino-colored eyes. Though I was terrified at the way she was sizing me up, I did my best to smile right back. Let her fantasize all she wanted if that was going to get me to the next level of business. I had a case to work off.

We entered a rather large dining room, and its centerpiece was a massive mahogany table covered with the most extravagant plate settings, soup bowls, wine goblets, and fine antique silverware I'd ever seen. It was as if they were expecting the Queen of England.

The vaulted ceiling and candelabras of all shapes and sizes crowding the room gave it a gothic feel. I was impressed at how well it pulled off the look Sylvia had attempted. That's when I realized that the room was lit entirely by candlelight and the abundance of candles had raised its temperature by at least ten degrees. At exactly the moment in which I needed to meet her partners and project composure, I found myself pulling out my handkerchief to swab the sweat from my neck and face.

Yes, I was hot, but for the first time that day I was also truly terrified. Everyone in the drug trade knew the stories of the Fuentes family's cannibalism, about the powers they told their workers it granted them, about the time they'd cut a man's bleeding heart from his chest and passed it around the table. And sweating through my pants in this isolated room in the middle of Sylvia's house—under what looked like a coat of arms depicting hooded men carrying long sickles covered in blood—I wondered if I'd been wrong to think I had Sylvia in my palm. If she chose to have me killed here, no sign would emerge from the house that anything was amiss, nothing to tip off my colleagues stationed outside—not until it was too late.

A large-screen television was playing a Mexican soccer game. At the end of the enormous table three men sat mesmerized by the game, barely acknowledging Sylvia and me. She waited for a moment and when they did not turn to us she began banging fork to plate. The men jumped, then turned. They seemed to startle when they saw me sitting next to her at the head of the table.

Sylvia introduced me to the men. Her husband, Miguel, was a quiet man in in his late sixties, with a squat build and eyes that bulged slightly as if the result of a thyroid condition. The others were Robbie (who was wearing a flashy purple suit), Miguel's nephew, and Joaquin, whose relation I didn't gather. I asked Robbie who he was wearing, and we talked fashion. Outwardly, he seemed obliging. Did he notice, I wondered, how whenever I tried to laugh, my voice caught?

They didn't bring up the purpose of this meeting, and at first I followed their lead. Aside from not getting killed, my objective for the day was to assess all of these men—and Sylvia—to confirm whether she indeed or one of them was the head of this bizarre, powerful clan. Once I knew my target, I was confident I could finish the job.

But as the soccer game rolled into the final quarter and the five of us continued to make small talk, I could tell I needed to make the first push.

"Again, it's nice to meet you gentlemen," I said. "You know I work with Tony and Hector." I noticed Miguel and Robbie lock eyes. There was the slightest unspoken communication. "We've been together," I continued, "since 1985, and—"

That's when Robbie cut me off. "All due respect, Roman," he said, "but let's wait until we're all seated at the table before we talk business."

I nodded in agreement.

Sylvia walked in carrying plates of food, followed by the stunning woman I'd seen sitting in the front yard, who was also carrying plates.

Soon, we were all tearing into the food.

It was too quiet. All I could think about was how slowly this meeting was progressing. I wondered what my ghosts outside were thinking. Tim had convinced me I needed to let them follow me, but what could they see—or do—from outside? Would they call this off and bust into the house if I didn't emerge?

I tried to loosen the family up. "I have to ask," I said. "Do you light all these candles and candelabras every night before your dinner or just for special occasions like this evening?"

At first there was silence. Then Robbie started to laugh. Eventually, Sylvia and Joaquin followed suit. Miguel, I'd decided, was a hopeless case.

"No, it's for special guests," Sylvia said, composing herself.

The man beside her suggested they enter the twentieth century and turn on some lights.

"Has anyone ever been wounded at one of these dinner parties?" I asked. "Any clothing catch on fire, maybe a bouffant shoot up in flames?"

Sylvia continued laughing. "Roman, I promise you the next time we have dinner here, no more candles. How's that sound?"

I flashed her the most radiant smile I could. Inside, it felt like a grimace. "So now that we're all here," I said, "I was wondering if we could talk about the potential of us doing business together."

Sylvia lost her smile. She said, "Well, considering we reached out to you, maybe why not let us tell you why we had Estefan search you out."

I nodded my head. "Of course."

Sylvia directed the conversation. It seemed true that she was the matriarch of this organization. She certainly had the courage and silver tongue for it. "We know who you are and what your organization here in America is capable of," she said. "We also know you're involved with the Beltrán brothers," she paused for a second, "who our connection in Mexico sometimes doesn't see eye to eye with, and that's why we are reaching out to you to see if that might be a problem."

I clasped my hands on the table as if to mull this over. I said that whether I could work with them would depend on what type of business arrangement they were talking about. "Though I have to say I've heard very good things about you," I added. "Otherwise I would not be sitting here with you."

Sylvia asked, "And what did this due diligence tell you?"

"Your son-in-law, Savior, was arrested in what appeared to be a sting operation led by the DEA. I learned that your clients—"

"Someone gave him up," Joaquin cut me off. He was almost standing out of his chair. "Someone in a rival organization. Someone we will visit soon."

My blood ran cold. Was I here because they were fishing for information? Had Estefan used Raul to get me inside this fortress? This looked like a much more dangerous situation than a first meet of buyers in which I said they'd never kill me.

"All due respect," I said, my voice as firm as I could muster, "but are you suggesting that me or *any* of my people have *anything* to do with Savior's arrest?"

Joaquin answered back quickly, angering even further. "I'm not suggesting that, I'm making a statement. Someone rolled over to the cops on him, but I can assure you if we did think you had something to do with it, you would not be sitting here enjoying our hospitality."

Now Robbie, who had previously been enjoying the soccer game, rested his hands on the table. It was his turn to speak. "Roman, we do not know how the police got to him, but they did. It was highly unusual, because as tight as your organization is, I can assure you ours is just as tight. So no. That is not the reason you are here. You are here because we cannot trust anyone. And though we have never met you or your partners, Tony and Hector, we do know a lot about *you* personally. We know that you've been in business with the brothers for many years and other than the occasional seizure, which unfortunately is a hazard we all have to endure, you've escaped incarceration for many years. And the drivers who have been arrested, as far as we can tell, have been taken care of financially and have not spoken to the police. To us that means loyalty and good business acumen."

Impossible as it seemed, they did not know about Tony's arrest. But they could learn about it any day. I had to make this deal happen as quickly as possible.

"So what can I do for you?" I asked.

Sylvia was about to step in when Miguel cleared his throat

and held up a hand to speak. He spoke just above a whisper, so low, in fact, I had to lean in to hear him clearly. He said, "We're not sure yet. But as you can imagine we can't trust anyone in our organization, nor can we trust any of our clients because someone gave up my son to the police."

Joaquin clapped his hands loudly like they were going to hit something if he didn't put them to work. "This is all fucking bullshit," he said. "No one in our fucking organization gave us up. It was a competitor." When he said the word "competitor" he unconsciously gestured toward me with a hand. Here was the real Joaquin.

I took the expensive dinner napkin off my lap, tossed it onto the table, and stood up as if I was about to tell my hosts that the meeting was over. In a black market trade in which it's protocol to defend yourself against such an accusatory statement, it was the only move I had.

Miguel slammed a large hand down on the table. Everyone in the room, me included, froze. Joaquin sat back in his chair, red-faced, and listened.

Calmly, Miguel asked me to please excuse the little tantrum. "We're not here to make stupid accusations," he added.

I shot Joaquin a look of piss and vinegar.

So why were we here? Miguel told me that they had excess material. They knew I was already set up with the brothers, but perhaps we could work out a better deal, one that remained between all of us at the table.

The irony of the situation was one you just couldn't make up. They were in the exact same position as Tony and Hector just a few weeks before—consigned a lot of cocaine that they had to sell because they couldn't trust anyone, not their clients and no one in their organization. All of us lived in the same maze of deception.

You see, once the cartel hands you material, whether it's a gram bag or a ton of cocaine, it's yours, you now own it, and you have a certain number of days to pay for it. If you don't get them their money on the agreed day, there are no negotiations—someone dies. Another week without paying—someone else dies. And so on and so on until the note is paid in full or the entirety of the organization and their family members are completely eradicated.

These are hard and fast rules and they're in place to keep order. Losing the note on a ton of cocaine is meaningless to the *padrinos* of the cartels, so if a whole organization of dealers is wiped out and the *padrinos* don't get their money back they won't shed any tears. The lesson all the other dealers learn from that bloodletting is worth a hell of a lot more than the loss in paper. Everyone understands the rules, and everyone abides by the rules—unless of course you find yourself in the unenviable position of Miguel, sitting on a lot of cocaine and needing a guy like me who he could trust.

Now there were many other organizations out there, but I was certain they came to me because of our reputation of being fair and, above all else, honest. We could be trusted. But then again there was too much money and lives at stake so they had to be 100 percent sure I was the man they could trust, essentially with the lives of every soul inside that room. Because if I decided to take their gack and run, especially in light of the knowledge I now had—if they couldn't sell the material, there would be no retribution against me or my family members—they'd all be dead.

The teenager came down from upstairs and reported that Raul had gone home on the bus. I was relieved that it seemed he hadn't caused any stir, and that now the risk of that was gone.

"What kind of deal are we talking?" I said.

Miguel had done his homework. "You're paying roughly seventeen thousand per brick from the brothers. If this all works out, and you buy from us in volume, we're willing to give you every brick for fifteen and we're willing to give it to you on consignment, which shows our level of trust."

It was a very generous offer. "When you say volume, what are we talking?" I asked.

He returned the answer quickly. Fifty keys and up every week would be fifteen thousand a kilo. Any orders smaller than that would be sixteen thousand a brick. "We both know you're not going to get a better deal than that…anywhere."

I nodded my head again, pretending to think over the economics. The breezy way that we were ignoring—or pretending to ignore—the bloodshed this deal would set into motion reminded me of all the pain I'd caused while working in the drug trade and why we so badly needed "narcs" like my new colleagues fighting drug violence across the nation. The bloody fallout of a deal like this would be inevitable because if I were truly going to change Tony's and my relationship with the Beltráns, they would find out why. Every person in the room continued to eat their dinner knowing that bodies might pile up on both sides of the Rio Grande because of what we were doing here.

I counted to ten seconds, then said, "Those numbers are very generous and the brothers could never match them. And I'm pretty certain my partners are going to feel the same way. But I'm sure you understand that this is a very delicate situation."

Miguel countered, "This is a very competitive business. People on our end of the business are always looking for cheaper product. It's a very," he paused to find the right word in English, "*transient* business. Organizations always moving from one cousin to the next. You don't actually think they'd risk going to war here in the United States over losing one distributor, do you?"

He seemed to be a convincing liar. If he didn't think the Beltráns would kill to keep us—or in retribution for losing us—he had no idea how much Tony and I had been pushing.

Fortunately, none of that mattered. Miguel had just solved the conundrum I was faced with, and if he was stupid enough to believe his lie, or think that I was stupid enough to believe it, who was I to challenge him?

I smiled and said, "I need to talk with my partners first. How much time do you need before I give you an answer?"

Miguel stared at me long and hard. I suddenly felt all eyes on me. Did I miss something? Answer too quickly?

Miguel broke his odd stare and nodded his head. He then looked at Sylvia, who tilted her head. There were so many possible meanings to that simple head tilt—she didn't trust me or she thought it was a bad idea or what did they have to lose?

Miguel said he'd get back to me on the date. He stood up slowly, indicating the meeting was over. We shook hands. Then I shook hands with the rest of the family.

Before I turned to walk out I noticed Lourdes, the beautiful woman from the front yard, staring at me, this time not looking away. She looked like she was in despair. I felt even sadder for her, and even worse for her little boy.

That night I got a call from Raul, his voice shaking wildly. "Something happened," he said.

"Did you say anything to Estefan that might jeopardize the meeting? What'd you tell the kid?"

"No, no. I was only in there with him for a few minutes before it happened and I left. I got a little bored and told the kid I needed to take a pee. He pointed to a bathroom down the hall, near the dining room you were all sitting at." He hesitated.

I was starting to get impatient. "What's the problem, Raul? Talk to me."

He snapped back at me, a first. "Give me a *second*, man." I could hear him breathing.

"Did you see the tattoo," he said, "on that tight-faced lady's neck, the right side?"

I thought about the question. "I was to her left side during dinner," I said, "and her hair—no, a scarf—was covering her neck."

"Well, I didn't see no scarf, Roman. No, man, there were two of them both joined together, which is not good. One was the Queen of Hearts."

I was confused. "So she likes to play cards, or she sees herself as some love queen?"

"Don't you know what that represents? That's the brand of the Fuentes Cartel."

He was right—every cartel had a brand to let buyers know where it came from—but that didn't freak me out.

"Well, yeah, we knew she was dealing with Fuentes. They pretty much told me so inside."

That's when Raul reminded me that not just anyone can get that tattoo—only blood-related Fuentes family members, the shot callers and killers for the organization.

I considered this piece of information he'd suddenly dropped in my lap. Sylvia was more than just a dealer, and they were more than a mere distribution arm of the Fuentes clan.

"That's not all," Raul said.

"What'd she have a swastika tattoo on her left tit?"

"Worse," he said, "she also had a tattoo joined to the Queen of Hearts. La Santa Muerte, mother of death. You know, the skeleton in the black robe wearing a crown of roses."

I'd heard of the Mexican drug gangs giving homage to the Priestess of Death. She was an icon based in black magic and Santeria whom they prayed to and offered money and even human sacrifices in exchange for a clean hit or safe passage.

Raul said, "That means she's a practicer, she's the priestess of death . . . You know, I don't know if I want to be involved with these people."

If he would truly step aside and I could stop worrying about him getting in the way, it'd be a big break for the case.

I told him that if he was worried over this he didn't need to do anything. He had set this up, so if I made a deal with them I'd break a piece off the profits for him.

"That's fine," he said, but his voice still sounded shaky.

I had trouble falling asleep that night, but for the first time in months it wasn't because of worry; it was because of excitement. If I could swing a deal with this family, buying small loads at first, fifty keys a week, and after gaining their trust hit them up for one big score, I would finally have my ticket to a more fulfilling life, protected by the police. Not only would I be out from under my trafficking charge, I would have proven that if given the opportunity, I could be the CI trusted to take down the most embedded operators and bring in the biggest hauls along the way.

The Setup

I arrived at Ramona at nine, an hour earlier than we'd agreed, and as usual everyone was already there. I couldn't wait to tell them about the opportunity we had to get straight to the head of the Fuentes Cartel. It was something they'd never accomplish otherwise, not without an unknowing source. To get an unknowing source like I had in Sylvia, one who worked directly with the Fuentes and a blood relative to boot, was a once-in-a-very-lucky-lifetime feat.

I walked into the office trailer and these agents were buried in their typical mounds of paper. I wondered how many other *mes* they were working with simultaneously. After the meeting with Sylvia, I felt like a superstar. But now I felt like just a number—C.S. 96.

Tim Dowling swiveled to face me. "So, Roman, you said you had a line on something big. Let's have it."

"Yes," I said. "Let's get it on the books. I think you're going to like it."

I used the whiteboard to write down all the information I'd committed to memory. The address, what everyone was wearing, the ins and outs of the house, whether I saw any guns or drugs at the location, each person's name and demeanor, and how the hierarchy of the organization ran, as I saw it. Conversations we had, even suspicious looks and glances amongst themselves. I gave them everything.

The room was quiet.

Then Pete Davis, ever the skeptic, started chuckling. "You guys come at us all the time with stories like this. Let me ask you something: was Pablo Escobar there as well?" He clapped his hands and laughed louder and harder this time. "Do you know how many CIs try to bullshit us every day? Guys that have been in the program a long time."

It always took a lot to convince that guy—and sometimes I've wondered if he was planted there by the other agents as some sort of psychological lie detector, some sort of "bad cop" game only they understood. Unlike before the bust of Tony's operation, Davis seemed to have some allies today. No one quite believed what I was telling them.

As disgusted and as exhausted as I was, I knew they still had a hard time understanding the level to which I had lifted Tony's operation and how committed I was to trying to do some good after being embedded with a violent man in a violent job for so many years. I wasn't going down without one last fight. I had to plead my case and hope they'd see through all of their failures or near misses over the years and finally just fucking trust me.

"Listen, guys, do you think I want to be stuck up this mountain for two years pulling a few keys a month just to keep your bosses happy with some consistent volume? I told you guys when I came in here that I was going to get you serious scores, and so far I have. I also said that if something is legit it means I've done my work and it will turn out to be a legit lead. And this is as legit a lead as I'd ever come across. These people are acting so rashly because they are truly desperate. This is about self-preservation: If this family does not sell the dope they've consigned for, they're all dead. They can't trust anyone in their organization and they can't trust any of their clients out in the street, not until they plug up the hole."

"Why you, Roman? There are plenty other dealers out there," Al said.

"Distributors like the kind of person I was are essentially the American arms of the cartels. And people talk. The cartels all know who, for lack of a better description, the good guys are and who the bad guys are. They know Tony's the enforcer, that I'm the guy who keeps the wheels moving. Are there many like me? No, but there are some, and if I don't take this deal and work with them ASAP, these people are going to move to the next guy like me quickly because they're running out of time."

I waited. Mike Capella was, of course, smiling. I suspected he was down the moment I mentioned fifty keys a week. Slowly Al and Tim both nodded their heads. As far as I was concerned that was three out of four—a unanimous decision.

Tim said, "Okay, Roman. But you can't run this alone. With something like this, we need another man with you. For corroboration and for sight and sound."

I thought about that. Inez's van, already installed with an aftermarket surveillance system, would be the perfect vehicle to do the deal in.

"That's fine, but they're going to vet whoever I bring with me," I said. "They're going to ask for a valid license, even passports, and they'll be thorough. I assume you know that the cartels all have ex–Federales men on their payroll."

Tim nodded. "Not a problem." He looked at Davis, and after a long beat he smiled. "Don't worry, you're not the u/c." Then he looked at Mike Capella.

And that was it. Mike Capella was to become Joey "Bing" Boningo, my New York–Detroit mob connect, an alias he used before that if backtracked to some New York or Detroit heavyweights in the drug community would actually be verifiable. He was known there as a serious player—and even better, he'd never been burnt.

Al looked at me sidelong. "So what's the next move, Roman?"

"We wait for them to contact me. They're what we call in the business *motivated sellers*."

Inez came outside. She stood in front of me, blocking the sun, and when I opened my eyes there she was—in full clown regalia—makeup and all. It was hard to decipher her face behind all that white makeup, the overaccentuated red smiley mouth and arched red eyebrows, the big, curly red wig, and, of course, the rubber red nose. Had I bumped into her in the street, I might smile, apologize, and be on my way.

Her long red shoes and enormous sequined blue pantsuit hung impossibly from her limbs.

Inez twirled like a little girl showing off her first communion dress. "So, how do I look?"

I laughed. "Like a sexually confused clown."

"What are you talking about? It took me a week to find

this outfit and the makeup. Two hundred fifty bucks at a theatrical store."

"The kids are gonna love it," I conceded. "So what time does this extravaganza take place and what time does your performance begin?"

She looked at her fake watch that was the size of a saucer, "Half past the cow and a quarter to his cajones. Otherwise known as *now*."

She stood up and started to back away. "I'm going across the street now and you're coming over, yes? They're expecting you."

I was not looking forward to flipping burgers with my overly curious neighbors—telling them how "the construction business" was going. Owing to my Jaguar, I had to say I was making a killing. I needed the neighbors to buy into the life I'd first convinced them of years ago: that I owned a construction company that built homes from San Diego to San Francisco. That I'd also recently divested into moving frozen food to the East Coast with refrigerated trucks I'd purchased, which technically wasn't a lie, though it wasn't exactly meat and potatoes that I was moving. On occasion I'd bring home one of the trucks to keep up appearances, telling them I was slowly phasing out of the construction business

"Yes, Bozo. I'll be there for your first set."

"Earlier," she said, "You're not going to make me hang out there alone all night in this outfit." Again she looked at the fake watch, which was actually a pretty funny gesture to slip into conversation. "I'll give you exactly thirty minutes and then I'm coming over. And you don't want an angry clown after you."

After she left, I dozed off in my chaise; I woke after only twenty minutes, but when I did, I felt groggy, my eyes red and dry. I blinked them open, expecting to see Inez, arms folded, tapping that gigantic shoe waiting to escort me across the street.

But the shadow cast was larger than that of one person; in fact, there were three people standing in front of me.

I sat up quickly, and when my eyes were finally accustomed to the light, Miguel, Robbie, and Joaquin were standing in front of my chair. They weren't smiling, just staring. My chest felt like my heart was seizing. Had my tradecraft gotten this sloppy or was I just trying to beat someone who was out of my league? I wondered if they'd followed me up the hill to the Ramona base, too.

Were they here because they found out Tony was locked up? The situation had spun fully out of control. I had no idea what they knew about me and what they didn't.

I swallowed. "I was expecting you guys yesterday," I said, as if unfazed, "maybe even sooner."

"Nice neighborhood." Miguel looked at the pool and the spectacular vineyards trailing down deep into the wine valley beyond my property, the gardens and rose trellises, the bougainvillea that covered the roof of the pool house. He studied the pool house, then me again.

My throat felt like it was closing up. I could only think about Inez and the children. I had to get these men out of here before she came home. Even though I put my family unfairly at risk for every day of the ten long years that I was in the drug trade, I'd never before—aside from the neighborhood pop-in from Raul that launched this case—had my work darken our doorstep.

I needed to get near a gun in case this was the worst-case scenario, but my gun was in the pool house.

"Do we have a place where we might be able to speak quietly?" Miguel asked. "Undisturbed?"

I looked at my watch. "There's a birthday party for our neighbor's kids across the street, so I don't have much time. Had I known you guys were coming tonight, I'd have changed my plans. Can we meet, say, in an hour? I only need to make an appearance there."

Miguel wasn't listening. Instead, he walked confidently to the pool house.

"Business takes precedence over pleasure, no?" Miguel said in his wispy, ominous voice. At least he had picked the room where my weapon was stashed.

I couldn't believe that after all Inez and I had poured into our family, after I'd finally had the chance to work to disavow my sins and make our streets safer, our lives could end with a tug on Miguel's gun.

I did my best to retain my composure. I gestured to the couches that were in front of the glass doors to the pool house. Inez would see their backs, hopefully she'd see me standing in front of them talking. I could signal her not to come in. Years ago we'd devised a method of nonverbal and verbal communication. If I said anything that seemed out of the ordinary she would know to make up an excuse that she had to leave, take the kids, and go. But we'd never imagined what she would do if that happened in our home.

They took a seat on the couches, and I maneuvered to the side of the couch that had a secret flap in which I'd put my gun.

Miguel didn't waste any time. "We want to work with you, but we need to know a few things."

Though I'd keep myself on point around these dangerous and cagey men until I understood the situation, I started to relax.

"First of all," Miguel said, "what did your partners say— did they agree to this? Second, can you guarantee us fifty plus a week? Third, we'll need to know how and where the material is going, and four, who your couriers are. They need to be checked out."

It seemed like a strong close. I wanted to make this deal as big as I possibly could. "This is good news," I said, but I sighed audibly. "It's not a great week for us, actually, but it's a very good time for this deal. One of our shipments, a very big one, was confiscated. The courier has been taken care of financially and his family is being paid, and he's got the best representation money can buy, so we're not at risk." He looked down, either pensive or disgusted. "I'm telling you this," I said, "to be as transparent as I'd hope you would be with me. That's how I want us to begin working, no bullshit."

Miguel contemplated a bit. "And why is that, what did you say, really good timing?"

Joaquin, without asking if he could smoke, pulled out a torpedo cigar, bit off the tip, and spat it onto the tiled floor. My blood boiled, and I focused every ounce of my energy on breathing deeply. Then I saw, on the floor to the right side of my couch, an ashtray. I casually reached down, quickly pulling on the Velcro of the secret flap until it was open, came up with the ashtray, and walked it over to Joaquin. Before handing it to him, I made a big gesture of picking up the wet gob of the cigar tip and dropping it into the ashtray.

He took it from me without looking at me or saying a word.

I sat back down, crossed my legs casually, and after a silent count to five answered Miguel. "Now is good timing because Tony and Hector, my partners, want to lay low for a while. I don't. This hit was a lucky car stop by some bumfuck townie, no organized takedown. Even better, Tony relayed to the brothers we were shutting business down for a while just to make sure we weren't hot."

All three men looked at one another, nodding their heads in agreement. First hurdle complete.

"And the movement of the material, the weight?" Miguel asked.

"We can easily do fifty a week, that's not a problem; in fact we'll probably double that after you get comfortable with how things are run..."

He quickly asked, "And how are these packages run?"

I smiled, not glibly because that would reveal cockiness. No, I had to exude confidence in a way to evoke pride in the work I'd until recently been doing and getting away with for the past decade, save for my little excursion through America's most fortified state, friggin' Utah.

"I move my material through a cut-out company I own. Refrigerated trucks. We have legitimate contracts on the East Coast that buy frozen food from me. Half these trucks are filled with the legitimate food, the other half is our material that is boxed up in the same packages and boxes the frozen food is. We've never been hit using *this* method of transportation."

I was pleased at how the conversation was going but still

terrified for my family. I needed to wrap this up before they returned. "Listen," I told Miguel. "I'm a money maker." I moved my hand in a grand gesture around the room and property. "I like what I have, and I live a very comfortable life under the radar and free of suspicion. I want to make money with you. And I don't like to stay still; I always expand."

For the first time I saw the slightest positive reaction from Miguel: He actually smiled. It was only an inkling, perhaps more of a grin, but it was there.

Miguel slapped his hands gently across his knees and said, "Okay, let's meet this courier. If he turns out as good and as clean as you say he is, then we have a deal. Let's say tomorrow. You know the IHOP near my home?"

I needed to speed this up. "Know it well. Say 10:30, that good for you guys?"

For the first time Joaquin opened his mouth. "In the morning, yes? We want to move on this quickly."

Miguel slowly turned to the dandy and gave him a look that could stop a clock. It reminded me of the scene in the classic 1972 gangster film *The Godfather*, when Sonny talked out of turn during a meeting.

"Yes, tomorrow 10:30 A.M. Let's meet in the parking lot."

Miguel agreed, he stood up, and that's when it happened. It was like a fiery asteroid shot out of the sky and crashed through the roof of the pool house: my beautiful wife "Bozo" was happily skipping toward us; her eyes were not on mine but on the backs of the three men now standing and blocking my eye line with hers. She stopped skipping, but continued walking toward the pool house.

It was a horror I'd dreamed so many times, acted out in real life.

In a whisper, I told the men that she didn't know the business I was in, to follow my lead.

Inez cautiously slid open the glass doors, and in unison the men turned to see who was walking in and what in the hell I was talking about. Regardless of the face paint, I could see the immediate terror in her eyes once she saw the faces and outfits of these men.

I needed to undo this situation at all costs, to go back in time and unravel the knot of choices that had led here.

"Guys, this is my wife, Inez. Honey, I know I'm late to the party but these gentlemen are in the frozen food business and we're discussing the possibility of taking on their trucking needs." I moved to her and hugged her.

She joked about her attire. "I'm usually only this dressed up on special occasions, wherever I can get the work. Kids are *big* tippers."

Inez laughed and I noticed Miguel smiling at her.

Each man shook her hand, tentatively, as if startled by the clown ensemble.

Miguel seemed to be the most taken by the surprise visit. "A pleasure to meet you," he said. "You must forgive us for the intrusion. We were all together today, which is unusual as we're all traveling so much, so we decided to stop by unannounced. Obviously terrible manners. Please let me make it up to you; I must invite you and Roman to my home for dinner."

Inez accepted the offer as gracefully as she could given the circumstances.

Miguel laughed again. "So, Roman, see you tomorrow at 10:30."

"Ten thirty it is."

The three turned and walked out as quietly as they'd come in.

We watched them leave through the side, and once that gate was closed Inez gave me a hard-eyed glare I'd never seen before.

The tears followed, cascading from her eyes, smearing the makeup she'd applied for hours with such joy. I rushed to her, grabbing her up in my arms; she was now sobbing and shaking uncontrollably. I sat her down on the couch.

"How could you bring them to our home? How could you do this to us? They know where we live!" she said while trying to catch her breath. "That old man—his eyes, his eyes…" She sobbed louder and louder. "I should have never let myself—my family—get caught up in this business."

For years I'd wondered how Inez controlled her anger over the line of work I'd gone into, no matter what financial benefits it brought my family. She expressed disapproval at times, whenever drug-related violence was in the news, for instance, but she never lost her temper over it in front of me. Now, I saw that the emotions had been lying within her, dormant for all the years the situation had seemed out of her control.

We sat there, me holding onto her, her indifferent to my touch, immovable. She wasn't looking for solace or comfort from me but rather trying to come to terms with what just happened. Her sobbing stopped and she suddenly went quiet, again hiding from me the feelings she'd buried for so long. Had I lost my one chance to prove to Inez that my new line of work would be better for us, freer of the shadows of men like Tony and Hector?

What could I say to her? I had no excuse for what I'd let happen. Beyond my irresponsibility in slipping up in my countersurveillance procedures, I had also ignored this inner storm gathering because I was in my own self-absorbed world of money, money, and more money. Inez's apparent self-loathing was all predicated behind my horrendous life choices. She had worked years of night school to become a brilliant physician's assistant, and in spite of me was close to realizing her dream. And still I had dragged her into this murky abyss where her safety was severely in danger.

I watched her as she walked mechanically into our house. I knew I was running out of time. She was alone—in dealing with her own demons and in dealing with this reckless man she somehow loved. Only now did I realize how low I'd brought her, how devalued she must've felt, all of the wealth she was surrounded in taken off the backs of the poor and destitute, the very people she counseled and treated as an inner-city physician's assistant. She wanted to end the treadmill of despair she saw every day, and when she looked at her husband she must have for so many years seen a man turning that treadmill forever up.

I sat there in the dark pool house, and the same feeling that I'd felt while sitting in the giant quad in Sevier County jail came over me.

I had to focus on the first challenge before me. Right now, I had to make this one big score to finish working my case off and get away from this life. Once I showed Inez the good I could do, I hoped that I could begin earning her trust back. If I lost her, I'd simply die. But more important, I wanted her to take her rightful place in life. To be proud of what she'd accomplished, to understand that I was no longer the problem but possibly a solution to this chaos I'd been a part of for so long.

I ran to one of my other "hides" in the pool house, a safe built into a false wall next to the fireplace, keyed it open, pulled up the tile, and grabbed the company phone. I dialed Tim Dowling; he picked up on the first ring.

I fed in my code to alert him. I went on a ten-minute tirade about what had happened.

"Roman, you need to calm down," he said. "Of course they were going to find out where you lived. I'm sure they had five different teams stationed on different blocks, all with radios to communicate in order to follow you back home that night." This was the first time I'd realized that being a source was not going to be a walk in the park. There were serious ramifications to doing the job I had so easily thrown myself into.

"Roman, let me ask you a question. Had these been two new business partners looking to buy from you, wouldn't you do the exact same thing?"

He was right. I'd follow them for weeks, and if they seemed clean I'd send out some of our people to ask about them.

I told Tim about the meet tomorrow, and he patched a three-way call in with Mike Capella to discuss it. Mike seemed jacked up and ready to play. We agreed on one safety rule: While I was alone with Sylvia's family, if anything seemed out of the ordinary, I'd slip away, telling them I needed to use the restroom. When I had privacy, I'd call in the cavalry. Davis, Tim, and Al Harding would be close by in case anything went wrong.

Tim said, "Roman, you've got to get them inside your

van to make you the offer. Once we have that offer on tape we'll at least have the first charge of conspiracy to sell a controlled substance, which will enable us to get a trap up on their phones and covert communications up in that house of horrors." Tim cleared his throat. "The most important thing is that you tell them that you bought the van from Boningo. Work it in somehow."

I didn't get it. "What does it matter who I got the van from?"

I was happy to learn that it mattered because my colleagues were thinking about my future as an undercover. We needed them to think it was Joey's van because if the operation succeeded, all of us would appear to get collared except Joey Bing. If they were caught talking on camera in *my* van, they'd assume I'd filmed them. But if I bought it from Bing, well then, that's plausible enough for them to believe I got caught up in this sting as well. He installed all the listening devices and cameras pre-sale to trap me and whomever I was dealing with.

"Any questions?" Tim said. "Roman, you okay? Any reservations or nerves about this at all, now's the time to speak."

I answered no.

But the truth was my nerves were fraying, and I did have one big reservation. Not about the operation, but about my family. The question of how exactly—and how much—the feds were going to protect us had begun to weigh on me.

When I got back home after the meeting with Tim and Mike, I noticed that the bedroom door was closed, which meant *off limits*—Inez needed space. I was not about to step into her only sanctuary after what had happened tonight. I went across the street, apologizing to my neighbors for missing so much of the party.

Later, I got the kids squared away for the evening and put them to bed.

Then I slipped into bed. Inez was snoring deeply, no doubt making sense of her life's decision in some far-off dream world. I prayed that she would choose to stay with me—even if the career I was now looking to have as an informant came with its own risks. I hoped that my work with the DEA helped her forgive me for the ten years I'd spent with Tony.

There was no use pretending to sleep any longer, so I got up, grabbed my gun from the fireplace safe, left Inez a note that I was using the van and would be back this afternoon, and I left.

I wondered how many eyes were on me as I pulled out of the neighborhood. What time had they gotten there to put eyes on my house, or had they never left? It was a dreadful feeling knowing we were under surveillance throughout the night by men without souls, men that took sport in killing in the most gruesome ways. Worse still than the thought of one following me was the thought that some would remain stationed at my house in case anything went wrong at this meeting. Images of returning home to a bloody crime scene made to look like a burglary gone horribly wrong descended on me. Electrical synapses fired with these horrible images, an orgy of blood and dismemberment. They were like the murder photos I'd viewed in the Sevier County lockup, though the brutal images I saw now were of my wife, ravaged, cycling in front of me as if on a Kodachrome slide projector.

I had to shake this off. I needed to gain control of my emotions, compartmentalize them somehow, bury them in a part of my unconscious, and lock them away till this was over and done with. If I was going to survive these next few days, or however long it took to wrap this case up, I'd have to become two different people, because the moment I cross-pollinated these two lives, I was going to make a mistake that had no good ending.

I had three and a half hours to kill and I had to assume there were a number of hitters following me, communicating my every move. I didn't try to shake them or scope them out. What would be the point? I knew they were out there, that my own team was watching them, and that soon enough they'd be hiding from us.

The night before I'd timed down to the second the series of things I now embarked upon again.

I went to the local diner for takeout: I ordered a coffee and buttered roll, picked up the newspaper, paid for everything, then headed back to the van. I parked and casually strolled into a local park with stunning views of a manmade lake filled with swans and ducks and surrounded by magnificent indigenous trees. The severely clear blue sky above was filled with more swans, starlings, and sparrows. Anyone following me was watching a man of leisure, comfortable in his very expensive clothing and jewelry, as he goes about his day. I took my time eating and reading every page of that newspaper. Finished and satisfied, I slowly walked around the park, never once using my phone. I wanted to show them that I was living a good life. That if they wanted to, they could join me.

I continued on with the most mundane chores I could think of. I went to my tailor, paid for the dry cleaning, and slowly and meticulously hung the expensive clothing on one of the hooks inside the van. I drove to the local Quick Lube and had my oil changed. I wondered how those tracking me were doing, all crowded into their smoke-filled jalopies.

After about forty-five minutes of reading every magazine available, I was ready. I drove to IHOP.

To my surprise the parking lot was fairly empty. I searched the entire lot for any suspicious vehicles, or any of the vehicles I'd spied at Miguel's house while surveilling it—nothing. I checked my watch, twenty-seven minutes after ten; they had three minutes to get there.

Were they spooked? And if they were, was Inez safe?

I needed to calm myself down. I reasoned they were being cautious, as I would be if the circumstances were in the reverse. They must be waiting and watching me to see if I'd brought anyone along to do exactly what they were doing to me. I had, of course, but my guys had been set up and hiding for more than five hours.

And then I saw it—the big black BMW 750, one of the cars at Miguel's home. It pulled slowly into the lot, avoiding the potholes carved out in the entranceway. The windows were so tinted that I couldn't see who was in the car. As predicted they rolled directly in front of my family-friendly van, even though I hadn't told them I'd be driving it.

I covered my mouth as if I were rubbing the bridge of my nose and in a clear voice spoke into the hidden audio recorder the time, car make, plate number, and once the doors to the BMW swung open, who had made the party. It was Miguel, Robbie, and Joaquin.

Miguel was dressed in the identical clothing he wore at our last meeting. Robbie switched it up, wearing off-the-rack brand names and a nice pair of Italian driving loafers. Joaquin wore a steel gray t-shirt underneath what seemed to be a deep ocean blue sharkskin suit and turquoise alligator boots. If Tony ever started a clothing line, Joaquin looked like he'd be the spokesman.

I purposely slipped out of the front seat, stepping into the rear cabin and exiting from the side doors of the van, sure to leave them wide open for all to see.

The men slammed their doors shut and approached. I waited.

"This is quite a step down from your other extravagant choices, no?" Miguel asked. Then he saw the inside and smiled. "*Dios mio*," he said.

The other two men stepped to his side and peeked in; I could tell even Joaquin was impressed.

"It's got an extra gas tank, too," I said. "Just hit the auxiliary gas button and you can go almost 600 miles without stopping." I tried to keep them focused on the shine and glitter. "The van was a gift, believe it or not, from my boy Joey Bing," I continued. "The courier you're going to meet if the prick is on time. The guy isn't punctual, but make him a little dough and you'll find he's a very generous dude."

I told them a story about how he'd gotten me the van after I had my third child—it was really for my wife and kids, but I love to play with it and use it for work, given how understated it is on the outside. "Say you're a cop: Are you going to take the time to stop this soccer-mom van, or someone in say," I hesitated, looked around the near empty parking lot, finally landing on the pretty 750 drug dealer whip they rolled up in, "that car, for instance?"

Robbie gave a halfhearted nod of his head.

"So where is your partner?" Miguel asked. "Time is money and a luxury we have very little of left, *sabe*?"

I checked my watch. "If Bing was the marrying kind of guy," I said, "he'd be late at his own wedding. But he knows this is an important deal. We just have to be a little patient."

I realized the mistake I'd made the second I'd said it. I hadn't discussed Bing's legend in depth with him or the supporting agents. After mentioning the origins of the van, I should have steered the conversation from my partner as quickly as I could. All he had to do was walk in with a wedding band on and I was fucked.

I slid the van door all the way open. "You guys want to look at all the bells and whistles? These things are a blast when you have time to kill."

Miguel stuck his head in, as did Robbie. Joaquin was preoccupied with the time and where and when my partner was coming. Neither of the men wanted to step into the van first.

So I led the way. I knew their words would be picked up and recorded standing this close to the van, but I wanted it on video, crystal clear for the jury these men would face. I pointed to the two captain's chairs in direct line of sight of the cameras, and they took their seats. Joaquin decided to stand outside the van. No part of him seemed to suspect that once "Bing" got to the set, Joaquin would be joining us inside, whether he wanted to or not, for a ride to the station.

I made small talk about all the aftermarket toys, but I could tell they were starting to get impatient. As if on cue, I heard the rumble of what sounded like a muscle car from the '70s. A fire-engine red Ferrari convertible was making its way toward the van. In a precise maneuver, its driver downshifted and peeled into a perfect U-turn parallel park, stopping just feet from Joaquin, and out walked Joey Bing.

It took him a moment to regain muscular coordination, but Joaquin eventually had the wherewithal to pull open his shiny jacket to reveal the .45-caliber automatic tucked in his waistband.

Without missing a beat, Mike, who had changed his appearance so drastically that I'd have walked right past him on the street, reached under his front seat and in a nonconfrontational way smiled while pulling out a suppressed MAC-10 machine gun with extended clip. "Hey, you got yours and I got mine," he said. He held it loosely in his hand, fingering the trigger. As Joaquin pulled his jacket shut again, Mike slid his weapon under the car sear, swapping it for a canvas bag. Mike's transformation was astounding. He was wearing expensive black Persol sunglasses; his thick black hair greased back into a tight ponytail. His form-fitting t-shirt revealed muscles as well as sleeves of tattoos down his arms that I hadn't noticed before. I checked for a wedding band, and thankfully there was none.

"Bing, my man!" I said. "Late as usual!"

Mike got to the door of the van, standing side-by-side with Joaquin and waiting for him to enter. "Well, we gonna stand out here all day in this Mexican standoff," he asked, "or are we going to talk business?"

Mike could be very persuasive, and he had raised our optics by tenfold: he looked exactly the part of a dealer that Miguel could identify with. Only later would I learn that Mike was up half the night before this going over photos of known associates of the Fuentes Cartel.

Joaquin looked at Miguel, who tilted his head for him to enter the van. Mike followed him in, sliding the door shut. He took up a bench seat next to me holding onto a bulky weekender bag.

I grabbed him playfully by the shoulder and introduced him like an old friend.

Mike shook each man's hand quickly. He was playing an act easy to follow—super excited to show me what was in the bag but also to show these men that they were inconsequential to the already huge business enterprise we were running, aloof without being disrespectful.

Mike looked at me and then to the men in the van, then back to me in nonverbal communication: *Is it safe to proceed?* I nodded. "They're cool, Bing."

He smiled and unzipped the bag, pulling it apart wide enough so that every man saw what was in it—piles of street money—mostly twenties wrapped in thick purple rubber bands, the kind that bind broccoli or celery stalks together. I saw in Miguel's eyes a glazed look of greed that I'd seen thousands of times before and, in the two decades of informant work that I had embarked upon, would see thousands of times again.

I pulled the bag from Mike, zipped it up, and tossed it to the rear of the van like it was par for the course. "Great work, Bing. We'll whack it up tonight." I looked at Miguel and continued. "Sorry about the delay. Let's talk turkey, brother."

To our complete surprise Miguel did not ask for any paperwork from Mike. Instead, he simply told Mike it was nice to meet him and that I'd said he moves the material in frozen packages.

Mike became serious and thoughtful suddenly, outlining

the distribution operation. "We have a warehouse of refrigerated trucks with real manifests so if we're stopped the paperwork is legit at the weigh stations across the..." Mike stopped and looked at me. "You did explain how this is run, yes?"

"He did, he did," Miguel said. "What I'm interested to know is..." he searched for the right wording in English, "in these trucks, say one truck for instance, how many bricks can you load without going over your, you know, the load when weighed?" It was a question from someone who had done his homework—every truck after a certain amount of miles traveled on highways had to be checked in at weigh stations for a multitude of reasons, and the weight had to match the manifest on the trucks. Many carriers tried to double their loads, increasing their profits, but if caught they'd be heavily fined and the drivers could lose their classed-up trucking licenses, basically ending their courier careers. Was I underestimating Miguel in thinking Bing and I could fool him?

Mike explained that weight wasn't the issue for him. His trucks could physically carry as much as ten thousand pounds of goods—and he had the permits to carry that much—but he couldn't have a truck loaded up with nine thousand pounds of product and a thousand pounds of frozen food. "We need to distribute properly because these guys *do* root around in these trucks occasionally. It's usually at a ratio of four to one food versus material."

"How many trucks do you have?" Miguel asked. When Mike told him—fifty—I could see him working out the math in his head.

I studied Miguel's partners, who were letting him run the conversation. Joaquin seemed happy to become part of the furniture, but for some reason I felt Robbie was the man at the head of the table ready to stop Miguel at a moment's notice from continuing the conversation.

"Okay," Miguel said. "Can you take fifty or more from us this week and we'll see how it goes?" Now he was looking at Mike, no doubt gauging chain of command. Mike was smart enough not to answer. He sat back, stared at Miguel, and then, like the loyal soldier and friend, looked to me for the answer.

"Sure," I said in a calm voice. "Let's start with fifty this week, and if you like the way we do business, we'll see where this can go."

We negotiated the terms, much of them the same ones Tony had with the Beltrán brothers: If we got hit and couldn't produce the money, we would need to bring them the paperwork from the arrest.

Miguel shook my hand and added, "Oh, one last thing, and the most important thing we haven't even discussed."

Here it comes, I thought. Mike's passport or license or blood samples.

"We give you the first load, say, on Monday," he continued. "How long do you need before you pay us back for that load?"

"Well, our deal with the brothers has always been one month; that's standard on consignment," I said.

There was a sudden drop in temperature in the van. Gone were the smiles. Miguel sat back in the chair as if he'd just heard the bank in Paraguay where he kept all his money went under and they had no insurance to cover the losses. He was stunned.

"What's wrong, Miguel?" I asked.

There was a long silence. "Why do you think I came to

you with my business with such reasonable numbers?" he said. "Why do you think we're giving you people we don't know a lot of coca on *consignment*, a sign of trust, yes?" Once he'd begun, he couldn't stop his momentum. "What did you think this was just a gift because we heard you were a nice guy?" He began shaking his head no. "We came to you because you're solvent and have the cash flow to move the material quicker. You know our situation and you insult me like this. What the fuck is that all about?"

His eyes bulged, and an angry vein snaked, throbbing, over the top of his forehead.

I had to walk this back delicately without looking too anxious not to blow the deal. So I told him I was sorry if I offended him. "I'm not a pig, Miguel, and I realize these prices are the best we're going to get. And the fact you trust us without any cash up front, well, what can I say? I just assumed you needed reliable distribution until you plugged up the leak in your organization."

He shot up in his chair now, pointing his finger at me and raising his voice even louder. "Yes, there's that but we have loads that we owe the Fuenteses and we're running out of fucking time. If you can't do a quicker return, then we're forced to go elsewhere." His finger still pointed at me. He was almost panting. I was grateful that he'd given me so much information: He had just implicated the Fuentes Cartel on camera. In that instant, I knew for certain that this dangerous trio of drug pushers would be behind bars soon, and the Fuentes Cartel would find themselves with one less major client. I was so ecstatic and relieved that I worried there was a crazed and suspicious smile plastered across my face.

"Okay," I said, sitting back in my chair now. "Let's stop tap dancing around this fucking elephant in the room. You have a backload you have to get rid of, and we have the means of moving a lot more than fifty a week and you know that. Tell me how much you're sitting on and what your expiration date is on the cocaine." I wanted to use the word *cocaine* as opposed to bricks or product or material because I knew in a court of law, depending on how good their lawyers were and how inept the jury was, those lawyers would have them believing we were talking frozen peas and carrots.

Robbie tapped Miguel gently on the knee. In Spanish he told him to calm down lest he have a stroke. He laughed down the tension in the van. "Okay, we need to get rid of 220 kilos in a month," he said, "paid back in full."

"So why are we doing fifty here and fifty there? I don't understand," I said.

It was a matter of trust, it turned out. They needed to know we had the capacity, that we could do the first run and return the money in two weeks. After that they'd up the quantities.

Now, if this were real life and I was dealing with my organization, we could easily distribute and sell 220 kilos in a month, but I did not know if the government could come up with that kind of buy money when it came time to pay—that is, if they were willing to go further to get the whole 220, a very nice score for a small team of four. This time I looked at Mike because I knew he understood exactly what my dilemma was. "Well, well..." I stammered, and then I saw he was nodding his head.

It was the best news he could have given me. If I could pull the whole 220 in one score I knew it'd be enough to send me home free, away from these dangerous men and onto the business of repairing my personal life.

"Okay," I said, "we'll get you the eight hundred back two weeks after taking possession of the bricks." I wondered if I'd just handled the situation so awkwardly as to make them suspicious.

Miguel sat back in the chair, pulling a handkerchief out of his pocket and swabbing his neck and face much the way I'd done at his dinner party.

They all stood, and only Robbie shook hands with Mike and me. He said, "I'm sure we'll be in touch."

Miguel and Joaquin left the van without as much as a good-bye. I had a feeling I'd not be seeing them until we were all in handcuffs together on some daisy chain at the San Diego office of the Drug Enforcement Agency.

Bait and Switch

Mike and I shut the doors to the van then waited till they drove out of the lot and were at least five blocks away before we celebrated. God, did we feel lucky.

"How'd you get those tattoos on so fast?" I asked him. "And where'd you get that fine-ass ride?"

"C'mon, bro, this isn't the grapefruit league. This is the United States government we're dealing with!"

We hugged each other. We were acting like two high school jocks that had, hitting three-pointers in a matter of seconds, just brought our team into the finals. We hadn't won the championship yet—at any moment Miguel and Joaquin could get spooked or be killed by a Fuentes operative or find out about Tony—but man, did we feel close to winning it all.

We need to be careful now not to tip these dealers off. Tim had asked me not to head back up to Ramona—to stand down completely until I got that call from them. They were likely keeping an eye on me.

The feeling that knowledge inspired—that whatever you do to stop your work from ever crossing over into your family life, and you do *everything* you can—is perhaps the darkest one that I would learn you must learn to endure in CI work. You find yourself taking extraordinary measures—renting studio apartments with front and back entrances just to be able to quickly run through them to a car waiting in the rear, spending nights on the highway trying to shake the dark sedan behind you that you're convinced is holding the drug smuggler's grunt, rather than a tired parent on the way home from work. But no matter what you do, that fear always lingers.

I reached into a plastic compartment that held the DVD player/recorder and popped out the disk, handing it to Mike. We knew where it went from here. Soon, we were going to nab these guys. In the long term, we were going to grab hold of the ladder, keep climbing, taking out the bad actors in the drug trade one by one until we were at the very top of the pyramid.

I watched as Joey Bing left the van, morphing ever so slightly back into Mike Capella. Gone was the big swagger as he loped into his car. I suppose it was the adrenaline crash he was now dealing with. I could see now that undercover work is a series of extreme highs and really low lows. In a way, the work is an addiction, too—often incredibly stimulating, and sometimes better than sex.

Slowly, I made my way to my house. I wondered if Inez and the kids would be there. Recently, she'd gotten understandably frustrated with how much this case had taken over my life.

It was excruciating knowing that as hard as I was trying to turn my life around I might have waited too long. Yes, Inez had stayed with me through the thick and the thin of marriage, but were the dangers of my new work finally going too far? Was she unable to leave me while I was at my most vulnerable, adhering to those wedding vows, or grateful, understanding the pressure I was under all those years ago when I first agreed to smuggle a load for Tony to make money so that we weren't evicted from our apartment? She knew that I was as vehemently opposed to drugs as she was, and that if I didn't make that first mule run all of us—including two little children, one with special needs—had nowhere to go. Inez could never look for help from her mother, who could barely survive herself. I wondered if perhaps she felt complicit in my criminal activity, having allowed me to continue in the life after she found out about it. Turning a blind eye because I told her *this was the last score, the last run.* I could see the troubled look that took over her every time the phone rang, as if she were afraid to pick it up for fear of who or what terrible news was on the other end.

When I pulled up to the house, all the cars were there. I dropped my head on the steering wheel, exhaling loudly and thanking the Lord. Please, Lord, let her not be waiting inside, bags already packed, to give me the consolation of saying good-bye to her and the children.

The only light in the house emanated from the large stone fireplace in our family room. Inez's back was to me when I entered the great room of the house. She was sitting in a rocking chair, staring into the crackling fire as she cradled and fed our infant son. I quietly moved to her, hoping not to disturb this most beautiful moment, a moment I wanted to remember forever. She gently rocked back and forth and I noticed his little throat moving up and down rhythmically. They were both at peace, floating harmoniously on a cloud of oneness that can only be shared between mother and child.

I stared at the two of them for what could've been a minute or could've been ten, I was so transfixed. Then Inez breathed in deeply and exhaled gently as if she'd received the same nourishment and love as our baby had. She stood and carefully moved past me without saying a word. I heard her pad quietly upstairs.

Later, that night, we had the conversation by the flickering fire.

"Roman, I've loved you from the moment I first saw you," she said. Her voice was soft, warm, but what she was saying made me cringe at what I could feel coming. "I knew I wanted to spend the rest of my life with you. I knew the moment I laid eyes on you that this is the boy who will turn into the man that I will be with for the rest of my life. This is the boy who will become a man and be the father of my children. He's going to take care of our family and do whatever it takes to keep us all happy and loved. I've loved you for almost half of my life." She cleared her throat. "Right now, I fear for you. And I fear for myself, knowing what it would be like to lose you. If something did happen to you it would destroy me, and I'm not sure I could go on. We have a family that needs not only me but you, too."

I had a lump in my throat. I knew if I spoke I'd start blubbering, and Inez needed me to be as strong for her as she had been for me. I moved to her, sat next to her on the couch, and I pulled her into my arms. I looked into her eyes and I nodded.

We kissed each other gently. She said, "You know I can't live here any longer knowing that those people know where we live. Every time I hear a noise, I think someone is in the house. And I'm alone here, Roman, with the kids."

I nodded my head. "We'll start packing up tomorrow. We'll put the house on the market tomorrow as well. No signs outside, we'll do it quietly with a real estate agent. In the meantime we'll put whatever we don't need in storage and rent a place far from here where you'll be safe."

She nodded in agreement and smiled; we kissed again.

There could be no surprises like yesterday ever again. I was going to make sure of it.

My cell phone buzzed underneath the pillow where I always kept it. This wasn't the company phone but my personal cell phone, the number that Miguel and friends had. I was woken from a dead sleep as soon as I heard the voice on the other end: "Roman, c'mon, man, you can't make any money in bed. If you're serious about our last conversation you have exactly forty-five minutes to meet me at the 7-Eleven on National Boulevard—you know the one I'm talking about?" He sounded like he'd already run six miles, had his Wheaties, finished reading all the newspapers, and was ready to take on the world.

I nodded, even though he couldn't see me, still not fully awake.

"Roman, are you there? You've got forty-four minutes and thirty seconds. You're not there, then I'll assume you're not serious about doing business with us and we're moving on."

"Yeah, um, yes, yes, I know the 7-Eleven, but, guy, you literally woke me from a sound sleep—can I get a little cushion on that time?"

"No."

And the line went dead.

The 7-Eleven he was talking about was in National City

not far from their home. I'd made sales there in the past on a number of occasions with some old solid clients, but I tried to steer clear of this neighborhood because it was as gnarly a place as you'd want to find yourself stranded without a gun or backup. To get there it would take me at least thirty minutes and that's assuming traffic was light.

I called Tim Dowling, who didn't answer, and left a voice mail telling him where I was headed. I had no choice but to do this on my own.

What the purpose of this meeting was eluded me. I laid my burner down on my bathroom counter and for whatever reason placed the company phone in the pocket of my pajamas as I began moving my ass into gear.

No time to shower, I cleaned up the best I could, picked up the phone that was on the counter, and was out of the house with exactly thirty minutes left to get there.

As I was driving, bending every traffic law as much as I could possibly justify, I realized that in my haste to leave my home I forgot to pull the company phone from the pocket of my pajamas and that was a big problem because it was a new burner the team did not have the number for. So once Tim got word of this early morning meet via my voice mail, he'd have no way to contact me or me to contact him just in case shit went sideways. I had lost my only chance of having backup.

As I swung my high-riding Range Rover off the interstate cloverleaf, the all-terrain vehicle lifted on two wheels, and I had to pull the wheel hard to the left, trying to displace the weight of the vehicle against the sharp right turn. The car slammed back onto all four tires, and I lost control, spinning into an intersection where—thank God—there was no oncoming traffic in either lane.

In the California Highway Patrol car that I spotted sitting in the nearby 7-Eleven parking lot, precariously close to the BMW that I knew the drug pushers were parked in, I saw the two uniformed officers shaking their heads.

I decided to go to them rather than have them come to me. I drove into the 7-Eleven holding up my hand to them completely embarrassed and then swung into one of the parking spots.

Over the cruiser's loudspeaker the wannabe comedian cop said, "Driver, you been out all night partying, or are you just waking up still half asleep? Put the vehicle in park, stay in your vehicle, open the driver-side window, turn the ignition off, and place both your hands outside the window where we can see them. If you need me to repeat that slower or in any other languages, just wave your hand up and down like a bird, don't worry, we'll see." I heard his partner giggle before the car mic was clicked off.

Not this again, I thought as memories of Sevier County, Utah, washed over me.

I wasn't worried about getting in trouble with the cops. I was worried that I'd spooked my associates in the BMW. I was waiting for them to pull out, leaving me stranded with this uniformed comedy duo, thus taking with them the sale and the deal of the century—this was going to be impossible to explain to the team. However, the BMW did not leave. I suppose they wanted to watch the comedy show that was about to unfold. I could hear a dance song emanating from the BMW's high-fidelity speakers.

I imagined they were having a ball watching me get pulled from my car, performing all sorts of sobriety tests for this ball-breaking team of cops. They had me counting backward from one hundred, finger to nose while standing on one leg, reciting the alphabet *backward* from Z, which I couldn't do stone-cold sober on my best day.

The cops, after having their civil servant fun for the day, took pity on me after I explained I was heading up north to try and get to my sister before she had her first baby; I, of course, being the godfather. And I desperately needed coffee for the long trip. They gave me a spirited warning telling me to drive safe unless I wanted to be referred to as "Uncle Jell-O legs" for the rest of my life. They actually patted me on the back, congratulating me, and were on their way.

A good legend and the power of persuasion have never let me down. And I still rely on them for my life every day.

As the cops left the lot, I had to make a play of going into the 7-Eleven for one of their Big Gulps of the day just in case they were still watching me. As I passed the BMW I winked at the driver, indicating I'd be right out.

I was expecting all three stooges again, and man, was I surprised. It was Robbie without Miguel or Joaquin.

Robbie was with a young, handsome, well-dressed man about twenty years old who bore a striking resemblance to him—his son. Robbie was the true connect to the Fuentes. He had been in control the whole time and we would later learn that he was here in the United States to solve the mess that Miguel had apparently fallen into.

I entered the rear of the BMW. Robbie wasn't even trying to suppress his laughter at the scene that had just played out in front of him. He looked at his son and said, "Hey, Junior, that was like a real-life episode of *Cops*. Man, I was waiting for them to toss your car; they found a gun in there we wouldn't be having this conversation." He jerked his thumb toward the young man next to him. "This is my son, Junior."

"Yeah, that was fucking hilarious," I said sarcastically. I looked at the kid in the front seat, stuck my hand out, and said, "I'm Roman Caribe. Nice to meet you. I hope you didn't find that as funny as your father did."

The kid just stared at my hand then looked to his father, who nodded his head in approval. Only then did the obedient mini kingpin shake my hand.

This case just kept getting darker and darker. First I'd been confronted with the reality of Lourdes, the young mother present during the first meeting which in any court of law could be construed into some conspiracy charge, her little son likely entering the system as mommy and daddy were probably undocumented. It was a never-ending hamster wheel of despair that I was so glad to be off, though I couldn't help but be saddened over the oppressive bureaucracy and foster home hell that that boy was going to have to go through because of this operation.

Robbie got right down to business. "Okay, I like the way you handled yourself with those *pincha* imbeciles. I trust you so our deal stays the same, but I don't want that *familia idiota* to know the extent of our business." Robbie reached around and shook my hand. "First of all, welcome to the family. My family."

"Which idiot family are you referring to?"

"Who do you think? How do you say…" He turned to Junior and asked in Spanish, "What's that cartoon character you called him, the one with the big…?" Robbie used both his hands cupping them around his eyes indicating eyeglasses.

Junior said, "Mister Magoo."

"And let's not forget that other one, Joaquin. Him I have no description for. That one makes my blood boil, odd piece a work that one."

Junior gave the description for his dad, "*Puta*,"

"Ahhh, yes, no doubt, son." Robbie laughed.

This was a very different man than the one I'd observed these past few days. He was much more confident, with a grotesque sense of humor. I didn't want to look confused but rather allow him to believe I knew who was who all along.

"I was waiting for you to reach out," I said.

"Yes, I figured you knew, but I had to let those busted valises play their little games. They're trying to make connects here and they can't put two pesos together. Though Sylvia is a lovely woman, she is not going to save that bumfuck husband of hers or that *puta* Joaquin from running our business into the ground. That's why I came at you and not your partner Tony—or no, his fat pig of a partner Hector."

I smiled.

"No offense," he said. "You know…" He sighed a deep, long sigh. "How do I put this?" he said. "We know all about his little escapade with the brothers. It was nice of Tony to cover the debt, but I'm not so forgiving. So you're the one I'm going to deal with. Not Tony, and definitely not Hector." He lost his smile, mood darkening, "You have a problem with that?"

I wondered if perhaps he'd heard about the takedown of Tony, and that was why he'd called me tonight in a panic—if this was possibly his way of trapping me in a lie.

I said I didn't have a problem. I had no choice but to play along.

He continued, "Tony is a loose cannon who's going to get you arrested or killed. And Hector, that fucking greedy fool, he's going to get you arrested or killed if he's not killed first. Do you want to sit on the deck of this sinking ship waiting for the band to drown around you, or are you going to move out on your own and instead of taking a cut of the profit keep all the profit for yourself?" He nodded his head thoughtfully, while lowering his voice, capping off his sales pitch. "I think you have been waiting for me to come along and help you make these decisions for a very long time."

He stared at me, an all-knowing ear-to-ear grin revealing a row of blindingly white teeth.

Robbie was aggressive, smart, and one hell of a pitchman. But if I agreed too easily I'd come off as suspiciously unafraid of Tony, who I was now convinced Robbie still believed was in business and who was a ferocious killing machine.

"What you're asking is problematic," I said. "But I agree with you that it may be the best course. We've been having issues, Tony and me. It's time I moved on." I was trying to give myself a bit of an opening in case it was revealed that Tony was locked up and Hector was underground.

Robbie and I negotiated the deal: He wouldn't ever have to deal with anyone but me, and the same losses policy applied— if we lost anything distributing the product, it was still on us to pay it back.

"I plan on giving you a lot of weight," Robbie said. "After this 220 there are tons I can get you. The question is, are you solvent enough to cover a lost ton of coca?"

I smiled. "Robbie," I said. "You've seen my house."

"Okay," he said. "Now that whole business with sixty here, sixty there is all bullshit. I'm going to give you the whole 220 consignment. Pretty fucking trusting gesture, yes?"

"Absolutely," I said.

"Good." He clapped his hands excitedly. "Why not jump in your car and follow me? I want to show you something I think you're going to like, a surprise. No, no, no, I know you're going to like this. Right, Junior?" Junior nodded unenthusiastically.

I stared at Robbie. Where else could this conversation and meeting take us? All he had to do was give me a day, time, and location to pick up the cocaine and we'd be done. But I couldn't say no. Was it possible he found out and this was all one big act and was now lulling me into a kill box? Wherever he was taking me, at least I would be able to call Tim from my personal phone in the car and let him know where I was heading. I'd leave the phone on speaker and give him my direct coordinates so he could get someone close to me.

"I'll follow you," I said. "But if I lose you, where are we going?" I was thinking quickly to try and gain the upper hand and at least find out the exact location, though I was certain Tim had received the voice message and was fanning out teams all over San Diego to find me.

"Don't lose me," Robbie said without hesitation or emotion. "Oh, and I'd like my son to ride with you." He smiled. "Just in case you get lost."

His uncannily quiet son and I stepped out of the car and trudged to the Range Rover; I felt like I was walking to the gallows.

Junior didn't say much for the duration of the drive. Either daddy had taught him well or there was something seriously wrong with this kid. After about fifteen minutes of trying idle conversation while also trying to glean some information out of him as to where we were headed, I finally gave up.

I remained vigilant throughout, checking to see if we had picked up any tails. We hadn't, but that didn't mean there weren't a dozen hitters waiting for me wherever in the hell we were headed. I also wondered if my quiet passenger was strapped, just in case I decided to make a detour or use my phone. My biggest fear, as it would always be from this case forward, was that the criminals somehow found out I had flipped and was helping to develop a case against them. Cartel members are smart and devious—they don't let you know the garrote is around your neck until you have trouble breathing and your shirt is covered in arterial spray.

We rolled onto the 101 heading north for at least an hour and then onto the 10 for another forty minutes, finally ending up in Ontario, California.

The town consisted of prefab homes, moderately maintained trailer parks, outdoor malls, motorcycle gangs hanging out in front of dive bars, and a lot of dairy farms. Nice enough, though hardly the place I would search out to raise my kids.

The destination we arrived at was another unimpressive little house on a corner lot. *These people like corner properties,* I thought. I followed Robbie through a very narrow driveway that was barely able to accommodate the BMW, let alone my wider Range Rover. I carefully followed Robbie to the end of the driveway where a large three-car garage stood in stark contrast to the tiny house. It took up most of what would've been a decent-sized yard.

There was just enough space in the back to park our cars. Robbie jumped out of his car and Junior quickly followed.

Without saying anything, Robbie vaulted the back steps of the house, produced a key ring, and began to unlock a series of deadbolts on the heavily fortified iron door. He couldn't get in there fast enough, couldn't get *me* in there fast enough. He swung the door in and it creaked. I felt like a character in some B horror film. Where inside this house would I find the man in a rain slicker and a hockey mask?

Robbie stood in the doorframe waiting for me to join him. He was smiling. All the while Junior stood behind me, a little too close for comfort.

I started sweating, mentally running through every scenario I could think of for how they might've found me out—but there was none, so I had no choice except to walk into this dwelling over a hundred miles away from backup.

This is the part of being a confidential informant, or an undercover agent for that matter, that without question is tormenting: the walk out on the high-rope into the unknown, not knowing if your cover has been blown. Taking me out would be easy and if they planned on that, Robbie and mini-me would be in Mexico days before my body was found, if it ever was.

The Mexican cartels were masters at disappearing bodies for good. And wanting me to disappear would explain why he called me at 6:45 in the morning to tell me I had forty-five minutes to meet him, making it impossible for me to mobilize any of my people or the cops.

Though I'd taken to arming myself with a pocket knife since being banned from carrying guns, I foolishly hadn't even done that on this morning. This was supposed to be a simple meet-and-greet in a public place, and I'd had to boogie out of my house with zero minutes to spare.

There was nothing I could do to escape this, as the last thing I wanted was to show fear. I'd let Robbie corner me. I flashed him a big smile and said, "A two-hour tour, this surprise better be a good one."

Robbie said, "Oh, don't worry, you'll be surprised."

Not the words I wanted to hear. I walked up the steps.

Robbie backed his way into the house like a real estate broker excited to show the newlyweds their new digs. I cautiously followed him in, still trying to look as cool and collected as I could.

Once inside my blood ran cold.

The house was completely empty. No furniture, pictures on the wall, utensils, nothing. Dust mites swirled in the air and cobwebs were collecting everywhere.

The downstairs of this tiny home was an open layout where you could see the entire first floor. The kitchen separated the living room with a small ugly Formica island. There was absolutely nothing in this empty space that indicated anyone lived here, let alone visited, the perfect place to whack someone.

The first thing I did was look for anything I could use as a weapon. Without furniture, though, the hunt was fruitless.

WHAM!

Mini-me slammed the backdoor closed and I almost jumped out of my Guccis. I spun on him, hands raised. When he saw me in that absurd defensive position, he smiled.

"Are you fucking kidding me?" I yelled. "That's how people get fucking shot." I hoped with that statement they would assume I was strapped.

I peered into the living room to see if there were any spots someone would be hiding and also to look for the most clear-cut harbinger of death—plastic drop cloths on the floors.

Robbie jauntily made his way into the living room, waving me in to follow. I did *slowly*, all too cognizant of Junior bringing up the rear. Once we were in the smallish, empty living room, Robbie pointed to a half-opened door and directed me to go inside.

I stood in the middle of the room not moving, trying to look bored and impatient. I said, "After you, this is *your* surprise. Why spoil all your fun?"

I scanned the room quickly. The front door was as heavily fortified as the back door and keys were needed to open the locks from the inside. I'd never seen a house lock rigged that way before, and to say it was a bad sign would be an understatement. There was a window directly to my left that revealed a desolate side street. I figured with a full-on running leap I might be able to crash through, but I might just as easily fudge it, end up breaking my spinal cord and being shot to death execution-style by a cartel family member. That was the only plan of escape I could come up with.

Robbie shrugged as if to say, *okay, suit yourself,* and he moved to the door, pushing on it lightly so it swung open. The room was bare of furniture and dark behind thick blankets duct-taped over the windows. Stacked haphazardly throughout were moving boxes.

Robbie maneuvered himself around a stack and pulled one open—*ta-daaaa!*

I could not believe what I was staring at. I instinctively took a step backward, blown away. Robbie dug his hand in and pulled out a loose kilo of cocaine. I noticed the stamp on it— *the Queen of Hearts.* This was real Fuentes-brand cocaine, and to have it still parceled together the way it was meant it was direct from the Fuentes' showroom. I'd found the top of the pyramid.

I was stunned because since meeting this entire clan, there was always this little voice in the back of my mind reminding how much I'd learned, as a distributor for Tony, that dealers loved to talk themselves or their positions up. All of them had a "connect" to the purest coke or heroin through their "uncles" or "cousins" south of the border.

Suddenly everything came into focus and all of my trepidations melted away. My eyes had adjusted to the lack of light in the room, and my senses came rushing back to me. I noticed the stale odor of mold and nicotine, even the smell of the old pine floors hit me all at once.

Robbie held up a kilo for me to hold, but there was no way I was going to touch one single package. The last thing I wanted were my fingerprints on that gack or anywhere inside this house.

Feigning excitement—not hard to do in that moment—I said, "Yeah, bro. I can see it. Holy shit! You're right, I am surprised. You are the fucking man!" I made a play to move away from him by looking inside the other boxes super excited, again not hard to pull off.

Another mental note: Remember the exact address because after we lock these guys up I'm sure one of the houses nearby, with a clear visual of this house, would be rented and a team of agents, cameras in hand, could identify people of interest in the drug war by looking at who came and went.

This snapped me out of the excitement of the moment, remembering my team. They were no doubt frantically searching for me right now. I was completely off the grid, in total violation of the mandate given to me by Tim Dowling on day one. Had a nosy neighbor caught sight of two very expensive cars rolling into the driveway of this obviously low-end abandoned house and decided to call the police I'd be in some seriously deep shit. Yes, I'd left a message with Tim, but I didn't tell him I was going to a stash house location where there would be mountains of cocaine worth $4 million, and that's $4 million just to me. Once all of that blow hit the streets in dimes and jumbos of crack cocaine, we're talking tens of millions of dollars.

Tim or the other teammates could easily conclude that I had lied about a simple meet-and-greet but my true motives were to go to the safe house and work out a separate deal with Robbie before we locked him up—a "double deal." I'd take half the kilos for myself then I coolly go back to my teammates and set Robbie up for the other half of the cocaine and roll him up. What could he tell them? "Hey, guys, by the way my partner here got away with a hundred or so kilos, you might want to check under his bed."

I was sure CIs had tried to pull this maneuver before, and the last thing I wanted was to be suspected of it. I had to get out of there immediately and call this in.

Robbie said, "Okay, it's all there. You fold down your seats, we stack them neatly and I bet we get every kilo in your fat-ass Jeep. Bring them to your warehouse or wherever it is you store them and we'll see each other in two weeks."

I was shocked at how carelessly this until-now cool character did business. In all my years I'd never seen kilos just tossed in the open like this without any security, as if they were paving blocks bought at the local home and garden emporium. It was borderline insane.

"Robbie, are you crazy? You expect me to just drive for two hours back to San Diego with 220 keys of pure coke in my car *and* out in the open? What do you think this is, TJ, where we can just hand a key off to the local cops and get an escort back to the safe house? This is Mickey Mouse, man. This isn't how I do business."

Robbie raised up immediately, stepping toward me. "Mickey Mouse? What is that, some kind of joke? I don't like fucking jokes like that." He kept coming.

I lifted up my hands, palms out, in deference to him. My back was to the living room and Junior was nowhere in my peripheral vision.

"No, no, no. All I'm saying is that if I took those keys and I got stopped by highway patrol or just some bored rookie, I'd be the biggest Mickey Mouse knucklehead in whatever police station I'd be locked up in. Not only am I looking at thirty years but also being the biggest idiot in the police station for driving a car in broad daylight with all that cocaine in it. No, man, we have to be smart about this. I need to call my partner and set this up properly. Taking it right now, for me, is just too dangerous."

Robbie asked calmly, "How long before you can make this happen?"

"I'll call Bing to set everything up."

Robbie nodded and then pointed at me. "Right now we have a deal." He jabbed a finger into the room. "That's yours, not mine. No backing out now. You keep your phone with you and we'll meet tomorrow. Early, *sabe*?"

"Understood," I said.

"We're moving the material out of here soon to Oxnard, do you know it? That's where we'll make the transfer."

Oxnard was another rough neighborhood about an hour and a half away from where we were that moment. Hector and Raul had lived there for a period of time and that made me a little anxious, especially because they had relatives there.

"You got it," I said.

Robbie nodded slowly, eyes fixed on mine. I knew there were a million scenarios playing out in his mind.

I told him that it meant a lot to me that he would do this, consignment on our first deal. It showed a true sign of respect for me and my business. I then wrapped my arm around his shoulder and laughed, "You and I, my man, are going to do some serious business together."

We shook hands once again, and then I moved to Junior, who was watching the whole charade of newfound friendship and patronage. I stuck out my hand and he took it this time without asking permission from big daddy.

Takedown

My heart was beating out of my chest. I'd never done "hard" drugs before, but the elation and high I was on must've been similar to a dude mainlining pure cocaine or methamphetamine. I was sweating, actually shaking; it's incredible what chemicals one's brain can produce to create this incredible natural rush.

I couldn't get out of there fast enough. I needed to call Tim immediately, but I wasn't thinking clearly because I was so hyped on adrenaline. I needed to put some space between Robbie and myself. I wondered who might be on some fixed post outside that house just waiting for me to leave and drop another tail on me. I made some surprise turns trying to make it look like I was lost. I stopped at a street sign looking up at it, though in reality doing a 360 of my surroundings to see if there was anyone following me. I found a large shopping mall and headed into its humongous parking lot, the easiest way to lose someone, hide, or to see if you're being tailed.

I waited till I knew I was clean, then I called Tim. He didn't sound happy.

I was too nervous to properly defend myself while getting

dressed down for the next five minutes. In his tirade he'd informed me that he had mobilized every agent and cop available to search out my Range Rover.

Once he calmed down and I was able to speak coherently, I finally informed him of what had occurred throughout the morning.

"Wait, wait," he asked. He chuckled, as if in disbelief." You actually *saw* all that dope?"

Knowing how the wheels of justice turn—very slowly—Tim and Al had their work cut out for them. We needed a warrant for the house, and a team to help us make the purchase.

Tim and Al had very little time to put a series of teams together from the DEA office in Oxnard and then have the Alliance Group liaise with them sometime that evening. The initial plan was to mobilize our team and any other agents he could grab up from the San Diego office, stay the night in a motel near, but not in, Oxnard, and everyone would stand down until I received the call where the meet was going to take place.

Tim told me to go home, pack a bag, and then meet him at the hotel once they knew where it was. Before we ended the call he sighed and said, "Listen, Roman, you did good today, but don't ever lose possession of that company phone again. And beyond that, why are you using an open line on a cell phone? That's just dumb and careless. Oh, and it would've been nice had you given us that number. What in the hell were you thinking?"

He was right about everything, and there was no defense or excuse. I'd been acting on pure adrenaline and desperation. Desperate to make sure this case wasn't blindsided by anyone's mistakes. Desperate to wrap this part of my life up and move on.

"Have you begun packing up to move?"

"No, but Inez and I have talked about it."

"You need to get her and the kids out now. This should've been done right after we rolled up Tony. Now it's a must. Have movers do all that. I'm sorry, man, but this is protocol. They know where you live and tomorrow after the arrest, whether you're collared with them or not, they're going to get suspicious. Your house is safe now, but these guys wouldn't hesitate killing federal agents to get to you..."

I called Inez on the drive home, and told her we needed to pack. She instantly understood the gravity of the situation. "We have to think of it as going on a trip," I said. "We have to tell ourselves that this is a vacation if we have any hope of convincing the kids."

She groaned.

"We can go wherever you want," I said.

She said, "Anywhere but Mexico."

We mobilized in a rather large and swanky hotel in a community called Camarillo in the heart of Ventura County, California, a couple of towns away from Oxnard and located exactly half the distance between Santa Barbara and Los Angeles.

Because this was technically a DEA case, Al Harding was the lead agent on this operation. For the command station, we used his suite, which consisted of two large bedrooms, a living room, and a kitchenette. It would also be used as the communications hub where everything that was said during the transaction would be heard through the wire Mike Capella would be wearing. There was also an adjoining room of the same size, where the overflow of agents, all here for the tactical meeting, were hanging out and catching up as some agents were brought in from San Diego's field office as well as customs agents and local detectives. It was a very boisterous locker-room environment. The only men I knew were my teammates and they were busy sharing old war stories with friends they hadn't seen in years.

The plan for me was easy—or it was supposed to be, anyway. Once I received the call, I'd tell Robbie that I needed about an hour and a half to get to the proposed location. Once we had knowledge of where the transaction was to take place, Al would have his agents, all in appropriate street clothes and driving their personal vehicles—from soccer mom vans to decade-old clunkers—as no one could look out of place, and they'd be positioned nearby "the set," or the drop-off point. Once I took control of the drugs, I was to drive, scrub myself clean of any tails, find a quiet out-of-the-way location, and park the car. Behind me, Al explained, "*if* everything goes according to plan"—the phrase didn't sit well with me—"a backup team that will be following you will pull up next to you and relieve you of all that cocaine, thus securing the proper chain of command." I'd be arrested, handcuffed, and brought into the DEA's office in Oxnard to be processed with Robbie, where I could keep an eye on him and be listening if he gave us any clues for how to reach further into the Fuentes clan.

I found myself sitting in a corner watching all these agents mingle. Mike sat next to me, popping open two cans of soda. He handed one to me and held his out for a toast. "You see all of this—this is all you, baby. After tomorrow—your first arrest—you're forever one of us. How's it feel to be on the other side of the law for a change?"

I took in all of the men who seemed like they were at a reunion party, none of whom seemed worried that tomorrow might turn into the gunfight at the O.K. Corral. I said, "It feels good, Mike, really good."

We tapped cans together and drank. "Let me ask you a question, Mike. It's something I've been meaning to ask you since the first day we met. How come you accepted me right from the jump? You know my background, you'd been on me for almost two years. And clearly some of your colleagues weren't so happy about working with me."

"I been doing this a long time, man. So long, in fact, my philosophy is this: We're all in a war and it's us against a much larger, stronger, and sometimes smarter army. If you're lucky enough to capture an opposing soldier who is holding a white flag giving up, you work with them. I know your story. We all do. You had that case beat out there in Utah but you said, 'Fuck it, I'm done and I'm joining the other army,' and with a big ass *bull's-eye* on your back. So what does that tell me? You're at least trying to do the right thing, help our soldiers win this thing. Why would anyone turn down help from a one-time enemy combatant who knows a hell of a lot more than we do about the force we're fighting?"

We tapped cans once again when Al Harding suddenly called everyone into the room. All of these cops and agents filed in, all eyes on him. Al looked at me and asked if I would stand up. I did, and he introduced me only as C. S. 96 and told the men that I would be making the initial pickup. I noticed the men whispering about me. The riddle of why I was there had been solved.

Al explained how Mike and I would make the deal and the takedown would then unfold.

It was just after midnight when I slipped into bed, far too jacked up to actually get any sleep. I called Inez and told her how the evening went. She was exhausted from packing and moving the kids to a hotel in Santa Monica and she fell asleep in the middle of our conversation. I listened to her breathing, that occasional snore that to this day she denies being afflicted with. I finally clicked the phone off and tried in vain to get some sleep myself.

I didn't know how early Robbie would call; it could be any time from the wee hours of the morning to early afternoon for all I knew. He was cagey and might try to rouse me early like he did the last time to keep me off balance or from mobilizing men at such an early hour. So sleep was out of the question.

My biggest fear was knowing that Robbie would never come to a meet like this alone. He'd have backup watching, just in case I decided to double-cross him by putting a bullet in his head and taking off with all that gack. So what would happen once I made off with the coke and they saw Robbie get taken down? They'd assume I was a part of it and come after me, shooting first and asking questions later.

That is all I thought about for the next five hours.

* * *

The phone rang, and I jumped up as if someone had kicked open my bedroom door with guns blazing.

"Hello?"

"Yo, my man, I almost hung up, thought you had second thoughts about our deal." Again Robbie sounded like he'd been up for hours, just raring to go.

"Really. Why would I do that? Are you kidding me? This is one of many, partner."

"*Bien, bien,*" he said. "Okay, so do you know Oxnard?"

I said, "Yes, know it well. What guy in our position doesn't know Oxnard?" I laughed.

"Good. How well do you know the area around it?"

"Same."

"*Bien,* you know a little town called Camarillo?"

I was now standing and my knees almost buckled. Of all the towns he picked, it was the place that *we picked* for the base of operations.

What happens if he's already in town, what happens if he's in the *same hotel* we are in? This was bad, very bad. As it was, there had to be at least ten DEA and customs agents, all looking the part, in this hotel; hell, half of them might be downstairs in the restaurant at this very moment talking up today's operation with Robbie sitting at the next table, sipping a mimosa in between bites of his eggs Benedict.

I leveled off my breathing. "Yes, beautiful town. I know it as well."

"Good, you know Santa Rosa Road?"

"Yes."

We agreed to meet at a McDonald's there. "Don't be late,"

he said. "We don't want to be sitting around with a carload of my finest product just waiting for some *Mickey Mouse* cop to nose around." He chuckled at his joke.

I laughed with him. "No, we don't. I'll be there on time. Don't you worry."

The line clicked dead.

He had said *"we,"* indicating more than one man with him. In the back of my mind I secretly hoped his wingman wasn't his son. I knew how this was going to go down—fast and violent, and someone could easily get hurt.

I grabbed the hotel phone and gave Al the details. He took it all in stride and told me to meet him in his room as soon as possible. He was going to mobilize the rest of the men to the room and call in the locals.

We all met in Al's room. None of the local agents looked thrilled to be there so early in the morning.

Mike was strapping on his "Kel" between his legs, a small-ish rectangular metal object about the size and width of two double-D batteries that would transmit our conversation to all the teams and back to the comm base here in Al's room. "Mexicans are very macho," he said, catching me staring at his uncomfortable-looking recording method. "If they're going to toss me, they ain't going nowhere near my cock, balls, or taint."

Most of the teams were gone before 9 A.M. Al made them all leave separately, through different exits and spaced in two-minute intervals.

The location was literally less than a mile away, so the

men had plenty of time to set up at their predetermined locations, all within a two-block area of the McDonald's. There were also two teams of undercover men and women whom I had not met, a smart move keeping their identities from me so I wouldn't subconsciously recognize them in the fast-food restaurant and stare. Their job was to enter the McDonald's at separate intervals, one couple at approximately five minutes before ten and then the second couple five minutes after ten. They'd order food; one couple would eat inside the restaurant, the second couple would order and move into the parking lot, sit in their car, and watch. If anything went wrong inside or outside, they were there as backup.

We were ready. My four teammates and I were the last to go. Tim placed his hand on my shoulder and said, "You've done this a million times before, I'm sure. The only difference now is that you have a battalion of professionals all watching your back. Just do what you would normally do in this situation. You take the packages and drive. Don't look back, just drive. The chase team is placed in two separate locations. If you go left, a team will wait to see if you're followed and then catch up to you. You'll only be out of their sight for thirty seconds so don't make any quick turns where they can't find you. Same scenario if you go right. As soon as you get in the car, speed dial me."

There was nothing left to say. Mike patted me on the shoulder, laughing, "C'mon, boys, this guy's done this more times than we have. He knows what to do."

I pulled into the McDonald's at 9:50. The parking lot was half full, though, and I didn't see Robbie's car, which didn't mean anything as he could've been driven there or taken a different vehicle.

I parked in the middle of the lot, where there was a space next to my car so he could pull in. If we were transferring from his car to mine, we could open the doors. We found a table inside the McDonald's and sat to wait for Robbie.

At 9:58 I looked up and Robbie was standing at the foot of our table. "May I sit down?" he asked.

"Yo, there's my boy!" I said, then stuck out my hand, which he shook. Mike also extended his hand and Robbie shook his as well and sat down, über comfortable in his own skin, just another day in paradise—*not for long*. "Everything cool?" I asked.

He nodded. "Did you hit any traffic on your way down?"

"We stayed in my apartment in LA," Mike said.

"Nice, you guys do a little partying last night? Hook up with any movie stars?"

I laughed. "Life's one big party for my man here. He's got a chick in every city."

"No, it ain't really like that," Mike said. "We were very low key last night. Business *always* before pleasure. Tonight, though, I got two honeys I'm meeting at the Roxy." He invited Robbie to join us and mocked me for being "handcuffed" by my marriage. "There's just too much tang out there, bro. I don't know how you do it." Mike tapped Robbie on the wrist. He was good, I thought—get close and personal with him, invade his space a little like old friends or new ones who will grow old and prosperous together. "You should think about it, Robbie. Trust me, you won't be disappointed."

Robbie was smiling now. "I just might take you up on that."

"So where is the package?" I asked quietly.

Robbie looked at me. "*Paciencia, paciencia,* brother. It's coming."

"You want something to eat or drink, a coffee, Egg McMuffin?" I asked.

I noticed his eyes were fixated on the parking lot when he didn't answer me. He looked at me. "Okay. So two weeks, drop off the money at Sylvia's. Go get the package."

I was totally confused, as was Mike. "Where is it?" I asked.

"Black Explorer, right next to your Rover. Keys are on the floor. Once you drop it off, bring the car back here. Don't worry, it's clean—you won't get stopped. Leave the doors unlocked and the keys under the mat. We'll pick it up later tonight. Oh, one thing, the count was short thirty, so it's only one-ninety, but trust me I'll make it up to you in two weeks. Okay, partner?"

I was looking at the Explorer that had magically appeared next to my car. If the team saw the SUV pull in, after hearing this conversation could they be tailing the dude that dropped it off? Probably not—that driver was probably as far as the 101 by now.

Robbie was smart, too smart, to have gone anywhere near that car with all that dope in it.

I feigned excitement. "Okay, *hermosa*, perfecto. Mike, you take the Rover and meet me at the warehouse." I stood up, "I let you two 'playas' talk about your conquests while I *go to work*. I'm sure I'll hear all about how many bitches you two slayed tomorrow. Have fun tonight, you crazy bastards." Over my shoulder I said, "Hey, Mike, no glove no love, child support is a bitch in this state!"

It was as if I was suddenly slapped in the face with a cold wet towel. A shiver ran down my spine as the cold reality of this potential life-threatening mistake hit me. Had he caught me calling Joey by the wrong name? I couldn't believe that I'd put my partner's life in jeopardy, that I'd made such an amateur and dangerous mistake.

I squeezed my eyes closed, then I turned back to see how Robbie reacted, not knowing what I'd find. Would he be glaring at me, wondering what I'd just said, or would he be slowly maneuvering to get to his gun before Mike got to his?

But he said nothing. He either hadn't caught the slip— which seemed hard to believe—or was simply very cool, playing it off like he hadn't heard and just waiting for the right moment to strike.

I walked to the car, trying to remain calm. I worried about what Mike and Robbie were discussing. There were no agents running into the McDonald's just yet.

I made my way closer to the SUV. Could this be it, could there really be 190 kilos of pure cocaine in this truck? I almost didn't believe it till I got to the rear of the truck.

I stopped walking, unable to fully comprehend what I was looking at.

Yes, there was 190 white bricks tossed inside the truck with the stamp *Queen of Hearts* on every package. But these bricks were in worse disarray than they had been at the safe house in Ontario.

They were thrown in with no order, not stacked and no tarp or blanket covering them, just a mountain of white bricks that a ten-year-old could spot had he walked by. How in the hell did they get it here without getting stopped, and what balls did it take for the driver of this car to make this delivery? This implied that Robbie's workers were dispensable to him. Now he would learn how dispensable he'd become to his own masters down south.

I did as I was told: got in the car, found the keys, and, while trying to sneak peeks at how Mike was faring, drove out of the parking lot. I was nervous, foremost because if I pulled up next to a cop car, all it would take was a glance into the rear of the truck and they'd see half of Colombia piled into a little mountain. Then they'd pull me over with very twitchy trigger fingers.

I rolled out of the lot and saw that Mike and Robbie were walking slowly in the opposite direction of the parking lot. Odd, I thought, but at least they were talking.

The light had turned yellow, but there was no way I was waiting at a dead red light. I totally disregarded what Al had asked me to do—I drove my friggin' ass off once I turned that corner. Why? Because if Robbie's backup was following me, they'd be stuck at that light, giving me some much-needed distance. I flipped on my company phone and got Al on the line. I asked nervously, "Al, did you see anyone take off after me?"

"Negative, the chase car has just made the turn and are coming up on your six," he said calmly.

He might have been calm but I was not, not even close. I continued blowing lights, making right turns, left turns, trying to scrub myself clean. I finally saw a desolate lot that was under construction. I barreled into a dirt encampment, skidding the car to a stop and kicking up dirt and smoke in the process. My eyes fixated on my rearview mirror, car in gear, foot on the brake, my other foot hovering over the gas pedal. If anyone other than a bunch of white dudes with short haircuts in minivans pulled into this construction site, I was slamming the gas pedal through the floor and hauling ass out of there, not stopping until I ran out of gas.

I screamed out my location to Al. He responded, saying they were two minutes away. "You don't have to yell," he said.

It was the longest two minutes of my life.

I saw them, five ugly old cars, tearing ass into the lot. I sighed in relief. Drug dealers don't drive cars that shitty.

Smoke and dust billowed around me like I was caught in some massive haboob in the middle of the Sahara. The agents emerged from their cars like they'd just found a ticking bomb underneath their seats, doors swinging open, more dust kicking up as they charged toward the SUV, every one of them had cameras in hand while some were screaming into point-to-point radios; it was complete and utter chaos.

They ignored me, fixated on the trunk. A number of the agents pounced on the SUV, ripping open its rear cab door like it was their only way out of a burning building.

Once that door was opened it was as if they'd all been stunned at the sight of the holiest of Holy Grails. At first no one made a move; I saw a lot of opened mouths, heads shaking, eyes squinting. Some even took a step back as if some wild beast inside might lash out at them, tearing off a limb.

For what seemed like minutes, no one moved. Then, gradually, I heard the sound of cameras clicking. I wondered how many times these poor guys must've been on ops like this that turned out to be total duds.

Suddenly the cheers went up, like the matador had just slain the furious bull.

Pete Davis was one of the first agents to grab hold of me; he squeezed me in a bear hug that felt as though he was trying to send me on the same hospital visit he'd gone through when he, or rather I, helped wreck his car. I actually heard the bones in my back start cracking. He was a very big, strong dude and he was holding nothing back behind his enthusiasm. He let me go and had to scream over the din of the other men who were cheering wildly.

"Dude, I was going to bet you a month's worth of paychecks that this whole thing was just another visit from the kilo fairy. Thank God I didn't!"

More men came to congratulate a man they'd never so much as seen but for a few quick glances the night before. It was as if we'd just won the World Series.

I was the object behind a cacophony of cheers and praise, but for some reason I was bereft of emotion; elation had not filled me as it should have, and I suppose it was because I was as stunned as these guys were, but also because of the way I had just placed Mike's life in danger. I'd done enough damage for two lifetimes already, and to get anyone else hurt just might have sent me over the edge.

For the first time in more than a decade, I could cut the drug world out of my life. I'd taken Tony out and every bridge I had I'd now burned to the ground. And now my case had been worked off.

Yet I wasn't happy leaving it at that. I'd found the job I was meant to do, the only way to attempt to repent for drugs I'd helped flood the streets with. This score was just a grain of sand on an endless beach of cocaine and battered lives. There was so much more I could do.

But I'd given Inez my word that with my case worked off after this bust, I was getting away from the drug world. She was getting her life back, and I wanted to watch her flourish, spread her wings to do all the good she was capable of without me holding her back.

I was handcuffed once we were a few blocks away from the DEA station in Oxnard. Driving there I was numb, and though Pete Davis wanted to drive me there alone so we could talk— and I suppose bury the hatchet—he did most of the talking, most of it about the cases we could do after we wrapped this up in court.

I wasn't listening to him, just watching the passing neighborhoods of Oxnard. Watching the gangbangers set up on corners, taking orders from their shot callers; the hookers that would suck, fuck, or kill for a dime of crack. The little kids with soiled diapers, filthy and undernourished, no more than four years old, running in and out of the street. Where were the parents? Up in some drug den banging, huffing, smoking, snorting their miserable lives into oblivion—*with my product?* I'd been a part of a disease that affects every ghetto in the nation and white America, too.

It was a terrible feeling I had watching the crumbling buildings rolling past me. For a simple seizure of 190 kilos of cocaine and the arrest of a few individuals, all the tiniest of cogs in a much larger machine—I get a pass? That seemed ludicrous.

Pete walked me upstairs in a nondescript building. I was printed and photographed. A wire was placed on me, and it was my turn to stuff batteries into my crotch, as Mike had done. I was briefed to *keep him talking*, the more he talked the more he'd *bury himself.*

Once I was wired up, I asked Pete to give me a hard slap across my face—which he happily agreed to. It stung like hell and left the welt I was hoping it would. I tore some buttons off my shirt, as though I'd resisted the arrest. Once the look was complete, I was, not so gently, thrown into the same cell with Robbie.

When Robbie saw me his eyes widened. For a few moments we both stared at one another with accusatory venom. We were both blaming each other for the takedown. Exactly what I wanted.

He said, "What, you looking at me like I was the one that set this up? You think I'm a rat, you scumbag!"

"Hold it, motherfucker. You came to me, I didn't come to you."

He stood up, moving very close to me. "Guess who was there when the cuffs went on me, you motherfucking *puta.* Your boy Joey Bing or whatever his *real* name is, and that mothafucka wasn't cuffed, how the fuck do you explain that?"

Now I went into what I hoped would be an Academy Award performance, feigning shock and disbelief. I backed away from him, eyes unfocused, stumbling against a bench, falling heavily into it. I stared into the floor, shaking my head. It seemed that Robbie had simply never heard me call Joey "Mike."

"He wasn't arrested with us?" I asked almost to myself. "I watched the guy snort up half of Bolivia. He's killed people before, I'm sure of it." I looked up at him in desperation, "You saw a badge? Are you sure he wasn't collared or turned?"

"I didn't have to see one." Robbie banged the concrete floor with his fist. "I didn't have to see a badge because about fifteen other guys came at me like the pack of dogs they are. And I saw plenty of badges and guns then." He faced away from me, and bent, sitting cross-legged to the floor like he was practicing yoga. I could only hear him mumbling something.

"He was using me, that motherfucker! For years I'd been moving more dope with him than anyone else and we were both selling it. Why wouldn't they just arrest me back then?" I swore. "They must have flipped him. I've been through too much with him on some major scores, but I went on vacation for a week before you and me were put in touch and wasn't dealing with Joey."

"Now that they've got me," Robbie said, "their job is done."

I let him have his moment in the sun. "Well, you are a top distributor for the Fuentes—maybe they'll try and flip us, too?"

He scoffed and spit on the floor very close to my feet. "What of my family in Mexico? I mention one word about my organization, family or not, they'll cut every one of them up, sending me little pieces every other day wherever the fuck I am. And let me tell you something else. Whatever happens to my family or me is going to happen to you and your family. So don't get any ideas."

When he seemed calm and a little more lucid, I asked, "Did you get your phone call?"

He nodded. "I called my people here in California. A lawyer is on the way."

That was good. I knew the phones here had taps on them

and recorded not just everything that was said but also the locations the calls were made to. They now had a telephone number and location to Robbie's number one or number two, and with that number came an address.

But there was one more thing I wanted from Robbie, and it was going to be a dangerous thing to get.

"Robbie," I said. "This is really fucking bad, but we can solve this. The only one who was privy to any of our talks was Bing. None of those cops saw you with the cocaine."

"So what's your point?" Robbie was the type of man who wanted to be in control. He'd see that control in me and by chasing it he'd be placing himself not only in some prison a thousand miles away from California, but rather buried underneath that prison for the rest of his miserable greedy life.

"It's our word against his. And if this goes to trial I'll have my lawyer discredit this soon-to-be-dead rat." In an even lower, more conspiratorial whisper, I said, "You know how easy it'll be for one of my men to get to this piece of shit. If he's alive tomorrow, I'd be shocked. And I already made that call. He knows exactly what he's got to do, and he will because without me this business is over. He knows everything there is to know about Bing—where he lives, girlfriends, safe houses, everything. I'd say there's a team right now watching every exit of this building and his apartments waiting for him to step outside. Once he's spotted, he'll have moments to live. And without him your case goes away, and so will mine."

Robbie held out his hand to stop me, just as I assumed he would. He began to shake his head. "No, we need to do this right. My lawyer is part of our family. When he gets here, I'll have him call my uncle up. We have people down here that will do this right. But they'll need to link up with someone who knows all of this rat's moves. One of your people."

And just like that, Robbie had done it. He had committed a crime that carried as much weight as the 190-key case he was looking at: conspiracy to murder a federal informant, or in this case, a federal agent. It was all on tape.

I could all but see the team inside the office right now jumping up and down.

"Fine by me," I said, clearing my throat, "as long as it gets done soon."

I agreed to allow him to set up the murder—using that exact word so there would be no misunderstanding about his nefarious intent in court. He was going to get his lawyer to link up with one of my guys to act as a conduit to the hit team that would kill Mike Capella, aka Joey Bing.

Soon, I was moved into the agents' bullpen, where Tim and Al retrieved me and brought me into an office where they were chatting with a dapper man, whom they introduced as Special Agent in Charge Hutchinson. Hutchinson proceeded to open a file cabinet, pulling out a thick envelope containing $40,000, a total surprise to me. A happy one, I must say. I'd been told I'd be paid for my services, but what I was being paid was a shock to me.

"Ten thousand should help you relocate for the time being," he said, his voice gruff, but tranquil. "The other $30,000 is a partial payment of the $120,000 we're paying you for the information and help with this case. I personally want to thank you, and if you ever decide to make this a career"—he handed me an elegantly embossed business card from a gold antique box situated on his neat mahogany desk—"don't hesitate to call."

I knew what I should have said—that they'd never see or hear from me again. This dark chapter of my life was finally over. It was time to move on, time to make it right with my family and my God. I thought that's what Inez expected of me, but I just couldn't say it.

I'm sure I appeared a little reticent, even circumspect, though I wanted them to know the door was slightly ajar. So I took my first shot at politicking. "Well, gentlemen, unfortunately that's a longer conversation I'll need to have with my wife. Right now my only agenda is to try and make up all that time I lost with my family. Ten years' worth of time. Though I really want to thank you all for this once-in-a-lifetime opportunity, a second chance at life, but also for your trust and continued belief in me."

I felt Al's hand slowly slip off my shoulder, and I believe at that moment he truly understood what I was struggling with—how close I had come to losing it all.

Did I worry about being chased by these two major cases that occupied my wild introduction into CI work? There was little left to worry about, though as a CI you do always worry.

Tony was sentenced to seventeen years, and, knowing him, he was going to die in prison or start adding up more time by the day while there, so I looked at him as a lifer. He was also completely depleted of all his funds, seized by the government, too broke to even pay a hitter to kill me.

Hector was wanted by the feds, gone and probably never resurfacing until he was caught. If he was smart with his money, which was doubtful, he could stay hidden for the rest of his life living in comfort, and if he wasn't looking to tempt fate twice, stay out of the game for good. But the Beltráns were not going to forget the debt he still owed, and I was sure that would haunt him enough to stay hidden in some spider hole far away.

Raul may have now known who and what I was, but he seemed a minor hazard. I never saw him again, and at times I would wonder if he was alive, clean, or if he'd slipped further into the pit.

Robbie, Miguel, and Joaquin all pled out at twenty years for the drug charges: intent to sell, possession, conspiracy, and a shopping list of other charges. Had they not pled and decided to fight the case, they were all looking at life behind bars without parole. The overwhelming evidence—especially our taped sit-down inside the van—pretty much nailed their coffins closed on the conspiracy charges alone. However, Robbie—the smug overzealous cartel capo—was hit with the bonus charge of conspiring to murder a federal agent, which carried an additional sentence of twenty-five to life.

Sylvia, her son, and that beautiful—I believe innocent—creature, Lourdes, were not charged in the case.

Here's where it gets interesting, and why no matter the precautions you take tying up your cases, you must always watch your back. Once discovery was made available to all the defendants and they found out Robbie was taped in lockup, there no longer was any question or doubt that I was the confidential informant. Sylvia, true to form, placed a $50,000 hit on me. This was not taped or gleaned from any of her phone conversation—if that were the case she'd be sitting side-by-side with her beloved Miguel as a co-defendant for conspiring to kill a federal agent, *me*. No, this was strictly knowledge gained from street talk. When my guys from Alliance Group—now doubled in manpower behind their recent uptick in solved cases and large seizures—paid a visit to the tightly wrapped, pulled, and tucked matriarch, they explained to her, both in Spanish and English, so there could be no mistaking their intent, that if anything should happen to Roman Caribe, anything at all, whether by the hand or the will of God, or as they called it force majeure—anything short of a bolt of lightning shooting out of the sky striking me dead—she would end up not inside the prison, but rather underneath it.

I was told that she received the message loud and clear.

Inez and I had ten days alone to talk over what I would do next. If she was dead set against me continuing to work in this capacity, explaining she couldn't live this life any longer, I was through. We'd move away and start over. I'd apply for our admittance into the witness protection program.

During our ten-day vacation, we headed to Turks and Caicos, and a bungalow and private beachhead on Grand Island with an on-site chef and no one for miles around. It would be the first time we'd been on vacation, totally secluded from the rest of the world, since my daughter was born. After those ten days I was either coming back a civilian or I was coming back a confidential informant working for the United States judicial system.

III
C. S. 96

Game On

For ten perfect days Inez and I did absolutely nothing but lie on the soft white sandy beach of Grand Island, our isolated bungalow just fifty feet from the warm turquoise of the Atlantic Ocean. Every day we slept in, ordered room service, and then walked ten feet onto the beach, where we soaked in the sun until it slipped below the horizon, lighting up the sky in a spectacular explosion of colors.

For the first few days we steered clear of discussing the recent past. Instead, we talked about our children and *their* future. Where would we raise them, the schools we wanted them to attend, while searching out a location with the best medical care for our special needs daughter. We talked about their individual personalities and how we saw their lives playing out, which inevitably brought us to a topic I wasn't looking forward to discussing, though one we could not avoid: how and when would we tell them about my past.

My ten years as a major drug smuggler was without question reprehensible. We both knew that, and Inez felt she deserved some of blame for it, though I realize that I always did it against her wishes, even if my intentions weren't totally selfish. Neither one of us wanted to lie to our children, but we decided they were much too young to understand. You see, from the moment they were able to have simple conversations, I'd preach to them about the devastation of drug addiction, how it ruins not only their lives, but also the lives of everyone around them. It's an endless cycle of misery, wreaking havoc on so many lives until there is nothing left but a hollowed-out shell of a person, every dream and hope abandoned. The irony and hypocrisy of that is so thick that you could choke on it.

Inez and I agreed that revealing any of my past to our children could only render them broken, dispirited, and also ingrain a lasting imprint of distrust upon them for the rest of their lives, something neither of us could live with. We decided to wait until they were much older to bring up this horrible chapter. But, as it turned out, I would need to tell them before too long.

As we moved toward the end of our vacation, Inez became surprisingly curious about what the job of a CI would entail. Most important, she wondered how I could remain safe as well as keep my family safe from the very bad people I'd be locking away.

I explained everything I knew from working the last two cases, but also how it was explained to me. I'd work on cases in locations far away from our new home, but also a great distance from my old stomping grounds, the Inland Empire, San Diego, and parts of LA and San Bernardino County. The good news was that I could work anywhere in the United States I wanted to, places where no one could possibly know me, which helped alleviate some of Inez's anxiety. For any case I decided to take, I explained, not only would the case officers vet the bad guys, but I would do the same long before any case was initiated.

I was lit up like a Christmas tree as I recounted what they'd said to me, and Inez knew it. I'm not going to bullshit here, I *did* want to stay on. For my own sanity, I often felt I needed to continue fighting my past, trying somehow to right some of the wrongs I'd gotten away with. The truth was that beside all the camaraderie, the rush and reward of getting a harmful syndicate off the streets, the real reason I knew I wanted to do CI work is because if I didn't, I'd feel like I'd gotten away with it all and I'd have nothing to tell God about when I faced Him.

But there was also a part of me—a part that I'd rather pretend didn't exist—that was hoping Inez would tell me that life was too dangerous for us, that I needed to give it up and relax for once. A part of me was looking for someone to absolve me for all I'd done without asking me to do my time.

Inez turned up toward me, resting her head on a folded towel. "You need to do this," she said.

Life as C. S. 96

After decimating a large chunk of the Fuentes Cartel, word spread among the government agencies that I had decided to continue working as a confidential informant. I couldn't believe how fast the calls came and how many different agencies and municipalities from all over the country not only knew of me, but wanted me to apply my skills to thwarting and combatting the ever-expanding drug problem in their locales.

There was a lot of work out there and I'd dedicated myself to helping eradicate the problems that I was once a major part of. I wanted to get as close to the flame as I could and then snuff it out.

I quickly signed up with Customs, DEA, and the ATF, as well as many state and local municipalities—large and small—joining forces with their narcotics detectives, though remaining nonexclusive to any one of these entities because I wanted the freedom to pick and choose the cases and subjects I worked. This freedom gave me a unique opportunity to go after those I deemed to be the most heinous and reprehensible, but also allowed me to work in areas where I believed I'd have the greatest impact.

I never wavered in my promise to Inez—throughout my career as a CI, I have made our safety the first priority. But even so, this career is not without huge challenges and personal sac-rifices from CIs and, more importantly, everyone who is close to them. Somehow, we've managed to stick together through all the danger, but there were many times that I'd feared that the life I'd chosen was going to tear us apart. Here are just a few ways we worried it might and how we learned to cope.

Life at Home

After taking out Tony and Robbie, I'd destabilized the operations of two of the major Mexican cartels, and life for my family had to change drastically. For one, this first relocation had a tremen-dous impact on all of us. My children were each at different, but critically important, stages in their lives, from my oldest, who was nine, to my youngest, just barely five months old. They'd moved into a completely different environment, away from their friends and into a new school—all of which occurred basically overnight. This was even tough on Inez, who spent the most time comfort-ing our children and getting them situated in a new school. She'd had to walk away from a life she was very comfortable and happy with—our dream home, her friends, neighbors, family, and her physician's assistant program. Not telling anyone why or where we were moving was not only difficult, but embarrassing as well, and there was no walking this back or creating excuses, because for our own safety no one could know where we were.

We had to live as ghosts.

In fact, even in our next home, we could no longer embrace our neighbors or the community we lived in, all for the sake of operational security. Keeping anyone from my past from finding out where I lived was paramount, and that meant keeping nosy neighbors from learning what I now did for a living.

Inez was an incredibly nurturing mother, friend, and neighbor, and though she remained a loving wife and mother, doting on our children, I could tell this relocation took a piece of her away. We weren't in the witness protection program, but it was damn close to it.

What I didn't realize was how much I'd lose with my kids by deciding to become a CI.

I've always been a firm believer that time heals all, and in a short period of time my children acclimated to their new school and made friends rather quickly, though none of them were ever invited over to the house and they were never allowed to others' houses—it'd be too easy a way to kidnap them and blackmail me. I couldn't lower my guard on these rules, not until I was certain that my cover and new identity were wholly established and intact.

In place of the troop of our children's friends we always used to have at our house, playing everything from wiffle ball to touch football, Inez enrolled our kids in school and community sports programs.

My son quickly became the star of the school basketball team as well as the town's traveling team, earning the nickname "Little Kobe." I tried to make as many of his games as I could, though I'd never go to watch him with Inez, so great were the risks of having him publicly tied to me. Rather, I would travel in a second car and then sneak into the auditorium just prior to the start of each game, find a spot hidden from the other parents and faculty, and watch from afar. It would kill me to watch him make an incredible play or shot and not be able to jump up and down with Inez like the other parents. But beyond that, what hurt even more was watching him after he made that incredible three-pointer then search the auditorium for his dad's smile. I tried to counter that disappointment once he was home by recapping everything he did play by play, but it wasn't the same for him, or any of my other children. At the trophy ceremonies and academic awards, I stayed hidden in the shadows. I can only hope that, in reading this, they understand how I shared in all their glory from afar.

Through it all Inez never complained, but I could tell the pressure behind worrying about me every time I walked out the door was eating at her.

Working Without a Weapon

As a newly minted CI, one of the biggest issues I had to deal with was my safety, as well as my family's well-being. Safety had to be valued above all else—even any sense of personal redemption or paying back the debt I still owed to society—to allow me to keep working the job. One of the stipulations I had to agree to when I signed up, the one that was most frightening for me when I set out to be a CI, was that I was forbidden to carry a firearm—that was the law of the land and there was no way around it. If caught with a firearm, the deal I brokered with the U.S. Attorney's office would be rescinded and I was back to square one.

Yes, I took chances in the very beginning when I was dealing with the Alliance Group during the cases where we'd taken out Tony and the Fuentes clan, always keeping a weapon close by in one of my hides. But I realized how foolish a move that was, because if Tony or anyone from my past wanted—or wants—to kill me, they're going to kill me.

So how could I keep my family and myself safe without a weapon? I needed to learn to rely even more on the power of persuasion. Whenever I'd go to meet a new dealer, I'd wear tight clothes and sit down with my legs crossed so that the person I was meeting could see I didn't have a hidden ankle holster securing a pistol. This immediately brought the level of anxiety down.

In the middle of a conversation I'd stop talking as if I'd just realized something of great importance. Then I'd study the subject, and if they wore clothing that indicated they might have a concealed weapon on them, I'd hold up my hands with the slightest bit of urgency and annoyance and ask, "Excuse me, but did you come to this first meeting carrying a weapon?"

One of two things would happen after that. If the client I was meeting was strapped, he'd apologize profusely, explaining with agonizing prudence that there was no malicious intent, going on and on about how dangerous a business we were in. If that were the case, I'd stand and explain why I never wore a gun, all rehearsed, of course. I'd speak in a tone that conveyed disappointment, like a dad scolding a child he'd caught in a lie. "Not only do weapons breed mistrust, but if someone in this line of work is carrying a strap to a first meeting, the trust I availed to them was not reciprocated and I'm extremely offended." I'd continue the ruse by saying that I was first and foremost a businessman, *not* a gangster, nor would I work with gangsters. That I believed this policy was what kept me in this line of work so long without ever spending one day in jail. Then I'd walk away.

Inevitably, within the next hour, I'd get a call back from the subject, still apologizing for acting with such disrespect, with the added guarantee that at our next meet, *"if I'd still be interested in working with them,"* they'd be unarmed and would agree to be searched if I chose to do so. Once I received that call, I knew I had them, because they now looked at me with very different eyes—as a nonviolent businessman, an educated man, one who detests weapons and all that they breed.

The second scenario was the easiest; they'd smile and start removing their outer garments, proving to me they had come unarmed as well.

Becoming a really good CI meant immersing myself into the character I was portraying, and thinking of every possible scenario that could go wrong and expose me. I had to make these subjects believe every word I said and that they absolutely had to work with me.

Acting the Part

Another major hurdle to Inez's and my social life came not because of the secrecy you maintain as a CI, but the lies you must imply. It wasn't enough for me simply not to talk about what I did for a living; I had to suggest I was a drug pusher. And even then I could never stay totally protected.

I did so with my gold-and-diamond Rolex President, thick gold chains and bracelets, diamond rings, a Gucci silk shirt, a sleek Dolce and Gabbana silk suit, $3,000 saddle leather Prada shoes, capped off with a Louis Vuitton satchel. Well, it wasn't hard to decipher what type of business I was in. The irony of this situation was that, when I was really in the life, I only wore those "flags" at meets with other dealers or out on the town with Tony and other high-end distributors. Once back home, partially in order not to bring attention to myself and partially because it was just my preference, I'd dress down.

The wardrobe made for some awkward situations. For example, as I entered a restaurant with Inez one night, a scene from the movie *Scarface* came into focus. Here I was—Tony Montana in the flesh—and I have to say it bothered me more than I thought it would, being on display like a monkey in a cage. I could only imagine how Inez felt, but she smiled and walked with her head held high.

We were seated, and before the water was even set down, the sommelier dashed to our table, indicating to both Inez and me that this was probably going to be one of the quickest meals we were ever going to order and eat.

We ordered the wine and tried to act like normal people, but my natural instinct kept my eyes moving around the restaurant for anything out of the ordinary, regardless of the fact that I was with Inez living at a remote site for an operation, way off the grid from where I had ever worked before. But you never know. I caught people staring at me, and when I locked eyes with them they'd quickly look away. I also noticed some of the staff near the kitchen huddled together, watching my every move, much the same as when Tony and I were in that Denny's not so many years before. It took about fifteen minutes for the

novelty of the scary drug dealer in the restaurant to wear off—
and that's when it happened.

I noticed a woman, a little older than Inez, hesitantly walking toward our table. Inez's back was to this woman and I
could see she was trying to determine whether she knew Inez
or not. When she was about four feet away from the table, she
nervously held her hands up to me, trying to speak, though
words at the moment seemed hard to come by for her. I smiled
at her, trying to relax her. I was praying she did not know Inez,
but I was wrong.

Inez turned to see what I was smiling at and there was an
instant recognition. This woman was one of Inez's professors
from her physician's assistant program, the one she abruptly
left when we relocated, and I'm certain she had a million questions to ask. I also knew Inez probably was trying to think of
some way to explain to this woman why she just up and left her
studies in the middle of the year. This was not a good situation
because we hadn't talked about a scenario like this occurring
and what to say if and when it did. We would rectify that that
very night, and I'm only glad that it was in time to keep us
from harm, if not to save us from embarrassment.

Once the professor realized it was in fact Inez, I could
immediately sense her disappointment. I knew what she was
thinking: How could Inez, this brilliant mother of four, be
married to or, worse, be having an affair with this obvious
drug dealer? Is he the reason she left school in such a hurry?

The woman's body language was all wrong and Inez noticed;
they had a really wooden exchange, and then Inez tried to introduce me but she was caught up in the awkwardness of the whole

situation and didn't know exactly *how* to introduce me. Should she use my birth name, because that was her married name as this professor knew her, or should she use our alias? I saw Inez turning red with embarrassment, and I was about to introduce myself to her when Inez finally settled with, "This is my husband, Tony." The woman barely extended her hand for me to shake it, which I did. Once this exchange was over, the professor couldn't get away from the table fast enough. Inez stood, hugged her, and then the professor made a beeline toward the exit.

I could see Inez was very upset because she also knew what the woman was thinking. I was embarrassed for the both of us. Though I tried my best to turn the evening around, it wasn't going to happen. Inez barely spoke throughout the dinner and declined dessert—that's when I knew my wife was preparing for a conversation that she would bring up at her own pace.

The moment we were in the car I apologized for placing her in that situation; she said nothing, not a word during the hour-long drive home.

As we approached our home, Inez finally spoke, and in the most plaintive and sad voice, she asked, "Is this the way it's going to be for the rest of our lives?"

It was a really hard question to answer, but I couldn't lie to her. "Yes, Inez, probably."

"You're wearing those clothes for a reason," she said, "because you're thinking that you might run into someone you're trying to arrest, which means that I might meet one of those people, correct?"

I nodded my head. "But the chances of that happening are almost nonexistent because I'm dealing with people who would never be in a place like that, and all my cases are purposely far away. I'm only dressing like this to be totally prepared in case."

She snapped back quickly, "Can't you wear something other than those ridiculous clothes? You know who you look like, don't you?"

Of course I knew. She associated all the bling and silk with Tony, and knowing who I looked like to her stung.

She continued, now with a surge of anger, "And why would you put me in that position. Do you have any idea how embarrassed I am?"

I didn't have the words that could make her feel better. I just told her that when we were out together I would tone down the look so that I wouldn't look so dead on. She just nodded her head without saying anything else and headed into the house.

We didn't go out together alone for a very long time after that—more collateral damage of the work I was now doing.

However, some good did come out of that disastrous dinner. I decided to stick with one alias and would build one legend I'd use for the rest of my career, one that Inez would study and call me whenever we were out.

A Compromised Life

Running into Inez's professor wouldn't be the last time that I, or one of my cases, would be compromised. On two other occasions, after being compromised, I had to relocate my family. The last one occurred fifteen years *after* I had wrapped up a drug gang dealing meth in South Moreno Valley, California, a community in the Inland Empire. And that story points to one of the greatest dangers of CI work that only grows the longer you do it: the chance of having a run-in on the street with someone you've jailed.

When I was out in the street trolling for cases, I learned a number of tricks to get myself noticed. Of course, the cars I drove, my clothing, the bling, my attitude, all of it combined already had heads turning. Dealers know other dealers; they also know heavy players when they see them, and I looked like a heavy player.

One of the tricks to lure these cats in was the cartons of untaxed cigarettes I always kept in the trunk of my car—given to me by my federal friends at the ATF (Bureau of Alcohol, Tobacco and Firearms)—used as chum to reel in the bait that would eventually help me catch the bigger fish I was in the market for.

As I mentioned, I didn't drink, nor did I smoke, but on occasion I had to pick up the nasty habit to draw further attention to myself. For some reason, hood rats, or small-time dealers, loved hanging out in front of corner markets or bodegas. Some of these markets sidelined in felonious businesses such as the tamer numbers racket, and still others would up their unscrupulous game by blatantly selling drugs such as cocaine, crack, meth, weed, or heroin, depending on the *needs* of neighborhood. These were the little markets I'd run surveillance on, sometimes days on end, making certain that they were selling more than just diapers, milk, and beer.

After watching a particular store for a few days I'd determine who was who in the neighborhood pecking order, picking out the lookouts, runners, street dealers, and all the way up to the lieutenants and shot callers.

Once I had all the information on the players, I'd make a

number of runs into the store to buy beer or diapers or baby food, things that gave me reason to be there at some late hour. After a number of these runs at all hours of the day and night the locals would drop their guards and say, "Wussup," or "The little one hungry tonight," indicating the jars or powdered baby food I'd be buying at eleven o'clock at night.

I'd never rush these casual encounters because they were a rare chance to build rapport. I always had to wait for them to think they were approaching me. Seeing all of those flags I wore, and the different super expensive cars I'd roll up in, they knew exactly what my game was—the game I wanted them to think I was in.

Slowly I'd stop to talk, letting them in on my legend: I had a girl in the neighborhood, she just gave birth to our son and I was here to help her for a couple of months until she got on her feet. That gave me reason and purpose to be the new guy in the hood—and not just a dude who showed up out of nowhere, which would be highly suspect. They all bought into it because they wanted to. In the hood, money trumps all, and if you appear to have money, you're either a mark or a guy to earn from.

Eventually, after I was a regular in the store, I'd make my move. I'd wait till the highest-level guys were out in front and I'd roll up.

On this particular day I passed by the players, said my hellos, then went in to buy a forty of beer. Once outside, as opposed to driving away in my luxury ride, I sat on the side of my car, opened the forty, and waited for this one particular dealer to come to me, which I knew he would.

His name was Devon; he was a big man, six-foot-three, easily three hundred pounds, and he was twenty-three years old at the time. He was admiring all of the aftermarket amenities I put into my car, and that's when I opened up the car trunk and tore open one of the dozens of cartons of Marlboro lights that were stacked inside. I made certain to leave it opened until Devon saw the cartons of untaxed cigarettes.

Devon asked why I had so many cartons of smokes, and I smiled, pulled one of the cartons out, and pointed to where the tax stamp should've been. There was none. He immediately understood, laughed, and banged fists with me. He now fully understood I was in the life; what he didn't know was that he was now mine for the taking.

After a while of baiting Devon further—taking him out to lunch or dinners—he let me in on what they were slinging or selling in the area: meth was their drug of choice. He also told me business was slow because it was hard getting the ephedrine to make the meth.

Ephedrine, or "eph" as it's referred to in the street, is the precursor in the drug, and the key component that gives methamphetamine users that "get up and go, go, and keep fucking going!" high. It is found in cold medicines like Sudafed, and since the DEA found out about this precursor, a mandate was sent to stores, pharmacies, and giant retailers, stating that they could only sell one pack of the cold medicine at a time to any one person, hoping to make it extremely difficult for the street cooks to make the drug. Everyone was looking for someone who had a connection for large quantities.

I casually told Devon I had a connect in Mexico, but that it wasn't my game to sell the eph. My game was finding cooks to make the meth, and buyers who wanted to sell the meth.

I knew the San Bernardino Sheriff's Office had recently

made arrests in the desert where much of the methamphetamine was cooked, and large quantities of raw (unprocessed) ephedrine were seized. So I set up a deal with Devon that I'd get him the eph if he found me cooks, and then buyers for the meth, which he did.

This operation lasted for six months, and it turned out to be one of the largest meth busts to date in California. We locked up forty-six dealers and took down a dozen meth labs and the cooks who ran them—and Devon, too, of course.

This was one of those cases where once I started the groundwork and all the potential targets were set up, I slowly worked my way out of the operation by introducing scores of undercovers who acted as my workers. Throughout the six months, I'd show up only occasionally to preserve the appearance that I was still in control of the entire operation. The hierarchy gave me the insulation I needed so that once everyone involved was arrested, the criminals would assume I either left the state or was locked up and charged separately.

I was wrong.

I'd like to think I've honed my skills to a point where I'm undetectable, where you'd sit across from me on the subway reading this and never realize who you'd come face-to-face with. I try to be completely insulated from whomever my targets might be. But as much as I try, something always comes back to kick me back into reality.

About three years ago, a number of years after our second relocation from our home, Inez and I were celebrating my son's win at a state track meet. It was just the three of us at a family-friendly restaurant in Southern California. I was paying the check at the cashier's booth and through a cake display I noticed a very large man staring at the back of my head. I collected my change and pulled Inez and my son in front of me to block them from this man while they walked out of the restaurant.

The bells were going off in my head. I'd been a CI for seventeen years at that point, so I knew the signals loud and clear. In the corner of my eye I noticed the big man slowly walking toward me. "Grab his hand and go to the phone," I whispered in Inez's ear. This was a signal that we had developed for this exact situation many years before. Inez, by this time, had become a pro at escape and evasion, and she knew the moment she was out of sight to call 911.

I took two steps forward then quickly spun on the big man who was now three feet behind me; he was within the kill range—seven to fifteen feet—*if he had a gun.*

And there he was, as big as ever—even bigger.

Devon, from South Moreno Valley, was studying me, unsmiling. I slipped my hand into my coat pocket, indicating to him that I had a weapon, which I of course did not. Nothing had changed, and CIs were still forbidden to carry firearms. I noticed Devon glance down at my hand and he unconsciously took a step backward. He smiled.

"Roman. That you?"

I determined he wasn't carrying a weapon, so I smiled back at him and said, "Holy shit, Devon? How long has it been—twenty years? How've you been?"

He stuck his hand out and we shook. "Yeah, man, damn close to that, I think. I been well. Still with my old lady, the kids are all grown up, doin' they own thing now. You know how it goes."

I nodded my head, pretending to remember everything

about his personal life, but there had been so many "Devons" in between it was impossible.

Devon just nodded his head back. I could now see he was not thinking of rekindling an old friendship, but rectifying a problem he must have been harboring all these years. I felt a drop of sweat run down my back. I needed to move this along because I knew I had been compromised and had to inform my handlers at the DEA. I stuck my hand out and said, "Well, I have to go, long drive home. I'll see you around, man. Was good seeing you!" I couldn't tell if I was maintaining any normal control of my breathing.

His smile was gone. He said, "Yeah, you too, catch ya soon."

Seventeen years of zigzagging through the country, hell-bent on taking out as many drug dealers and their gangs as I could—that had become my life, and I had become the best at it. It stood to reason there were hundreds of men who, just like Devon, would love to know where I was living. As insulated as you are, the more people you put behind bars, the more the law of averages begins to work against you when you leave your house.

The moment I got into the car I called my handler and told him I'd just been made by an old enemy. I waited and watched as Devon got into his car; Inez wrote down the make, model, and plate number, which I relayed back to the agent, along with Devon's name and the dates of his arrest as best as I could remember. The agent told me not to leave, to stay put and wait for the uniforms to come get me. He said, "I'll send out two teams now as well. Where are you?"

I gave him the address of the restaurant, and he said he was getting all of Devon's info as we spoke, including his cell phone information. Technology had become a great friend in seventeen years. Within minutes, with the agent still on the line, three police units surrounded Devon's car, guns drawn. This was all unfolding right in front of us. The agent still on the line told me Devon had made three phone calls already and he ran the names of the people he called: all of them were known predicate felons, two of which had done time for murder. Devon was calling hitters, alerting them where I was, and was probably trying to get them to his location that moment to end an old score.

The cops arrested him on the scene and brought him in for questioning. They did not have a warrant to listen in to his calls so there was no evidence to keep him remanded on a conspiracy-to-murder-a-federal-agent charge. Though my handler told me that he personally went to visit Devon, telling him if anything happened to me they'd make sure that he was going down for it regardless if he did it or not—that didn't change my circumstances. Another home had to be sold, and my younger children had to start all over again.

That night, my daughter and son were picked up and brought to a hotel near the DEA office in north San Diego. The kids were angry about the move, and what broke my heart is that they were taking it out on their mother. It was time to let them know what I did for a living, though not all of it.

I gathered everyone around the bed.

I explained that many years ago I'd made some bad choices and ended up in the wrong business, but eventually—with Inez's support and a stroke of luck—I'd gotten out and started helping the feds catch bad guys like the ones I'd once worked with. I reminded them of our first move and told them that was when I'd began to work for the right side.

I told them a man I'd helped take off the streets had seen us in a restaurant, and he was calling other bad men to let them know I was in the area.

After a thousand questions, they finally nodded off.

Within two weeks we were relocated for the third time, and after my explanation, not one of my children, or Inez, complained. I had a feeling they knew they were a part of something bigger than all of us.

In Search of Redemption

The moment I wrapped my hands around those two suitcases, way back in 1986, each filled with thirty pounds of marijuana, I knew with certainty that my life would never be the same. It was one of those crossroad moments we come upon, and if we're lucky—and smart enough—we choose the right path.

I chose wrong, and my life spun out of control on a downward trajectory that, in its wake, not only helped destroy countless lives—and decimate neighborhoods—but also altered the way my wife and children would live *their* lives.

There is nothing I can say that can change that fact, nothing I can do to force myself to stop wondering how different our lives would've been had I not made those first few mule runs to New York for a measly $6,000. For years after becoming a CI, I clung to the hope that snagging high-profile criminals and working to stem the flow of drugs that I'd once facilitated would quiet that guilt I felt, that feeling that I was falling deeper and deeper into a void. But it turned out that no one could help pull me from this funk, not the agents, who clearly knew something was wrong, nor Inez, who tried everything and whose attempts to brighten my mood would only register as another pang of guilt for what I was continuing to put her through.

Then Inez had an idea. I could take the dirty money that I'd made while in the life and use it to provide an opportunity to friends Inez and I had met through church. Some of these people were barely making it, surviving hand to mouth.

At first I did small things for them, like shopping for groceries for them every week; if they were short on the rent I'd pay it, then I'd buy their children clothes for the year, and when school began I'd buy school supplies. Some looked at me funny, wondering where my money was coming from, but most were grateful for the help. I was grateful to know that I was helping to keep these families from falling into the same trap I fell into. Though I never gave money directly, I made it my business to help these people live better lives, especially their children. One family turned into two, then three, and word spread through the churches in the community. Before I knew it I was helping more than thirty families.

Yet none of this seemed to fulfill this emptiness I still felt in my heart.

I tried harder, visiting the schools in nearby drug-infested neighborhoods. So many of the students wanted nothing to do with these schools, and it was obvious why. The schools looked like they were in war zones, the buildings bombed and cheaply repaired so many times. They were no better than busted-down city jails, infested with roaches and vermin, leaky pipes, cracked walls, broken windows, classrooms without doors, and holes in the ceilings and walls. Beyond all of that, there were no sports or after-school programs to offer incentives to stay off the street.

I knew the children in these neighborhoods would play a major hand in our future, and they could, and would, go one of two ways, my way—the wrong way, where they'd repeat my mistakes and could only hope to escape before it was too late for them—or the right way. And if their surroundings continued to look more like a prison than an institution of learning, I knew it would be that much harder for them to go the right way.

So I began donating, everything from sports equipment to computer workstations, which at the time many of the so-called elite schools in the United States didn't even have. I organized with the school administrations to bring in construction crews and exterminators. Had these been any other schools in the country, I'd have to jump through hoops, and my donations would be kept and dispersed by the school board when they deemed necessary, but to their credit these administrators recognized the needs I described and helped me cut through the red tape.

Taking care of all of these families and schools became a full-time job, and the huge mass of money I'd accumulated in the life began to disappear. With it, my misery began to melt away.

I knew Inez and I would survive just fine. She had graduated and was now a physician's assistant, working at a community clinic in one of those very neighborhoods whose schools we were helping. The money she was making was nowhere near the money she could have earned had she gone into a private practice in an affluent area with a different doctor, but I believe she was, in her own way, quietly working off her own penance. To subsidize her salary, I was getting paid 10 percent on every case

I brought in, or 10 percent of the sum total of the weight of the drugs, and of course the money, confiscated from these arrests.

However, despite all of my efforts to help these folks and the successes that I'd been a part of as a CI, the awards and certificates of achievement that came with it, I remained unable to confront the life I'd led. Lying in bed at the end of the day, I could not escape the suffocating thought that I'd gotten away with it all.

Inez is a very spiritual person, and seeing that I was lacking a deeper meaning in my life, she began insisting that I start going frequently to church again and seek guidance from within.

I went to different churches with her, listened to different pastors, but I always resisted the lessons they were trying to impart. I'd been taken in by a charismatic man before in Tony, someone who claimed he could show me the path to a better life, and some part of me must have worried it could happen again. As the days turned into weeks, weeks to months, my depression began to work its way into my professional life. Every case I started began to somehow fall apart. Soon, with no cases to subsidize Inez's salary, we began to struggle financially.

I was now at the lowest point in my life, yet again on the wrong path and now with nowhere else to turn but inward. When you're at rock bottom you begin to see your mistakes, and I saw how my stubbornness with Inez was hurting me. So I decided to go to church, but this time really listen to the sermons of the pastors.

And then it happened.

I was seated with Inez and our children, listening to a fiery woman pastor preach to a packed church. I sat in the middle of a pew about eight rows back, worrying over what those around us thought of me and my flashy clothes. I hoped they didn't hold my appearance against Inez. The pastor lifted a hand and, without warning, pointed at me and said, "You, I can see you are going to spread the word, and you're going to help so many people."

She proceeded with the rest of her sermon. And though I'd never met this pastor before—and I didn't know why her apparent confidence in me, in all of her congregation, finally got through to me when nothing else could—but somehow I felt that she knew everything I was going through. It hit me like a thunderbolt: I needed to open up my heart to God.

And I did.

The next day, I visited the pastor of the church where I was a regular at the time, and I opened myself up to this man. He explained to me that no one can earn salvation. It is a gift bestowed upon us at birth, and once you've given yourself to God, you will understand that a man cannot atone for his sins—one man, Christ, has already done that for us. And once you begin to imitate God on Earth by helping others, that is when you will find eternal bliss.

The pastor asked me what I wanted to do, and I didn't know. "Think on it," he said, "and you will find where your path leads."

That night, putting my kids to bed, I realized that I wanted to help children—to get to know them one to one and do whatever I could to help them achieve their dreams, and I decided that working to become a pastor was the best way for me to reach at-risk children in my community. I went back to the pastor and told him everything.

It turned out I had a lot to learn. You can't just *decide* one day that you're going to become a pastor or a deacon of a church. Countless questions need to be asked and answered, and not only of me, but of my family and the limited friends that I have, questions about my morality, my character.

I poured myself into answering these questions, studying the Bible, and preparing myself for the life ahead. Many months later, I was officially ordained as a minister.

I started out slowly, because at first I didn't know how to find the children who most needed help, but I did have four little disciples to help me—my kids. They all had friends in school, many that were troubled, and they told these kids about me, that maybe by talking to their dad they might come to understand what's troubling them.

My ministry started with one boy and has grown into dozens of kids and their parents coming to my home on two, sometimes three nights a week to talk through their problems. We brainstorm potential solutions together and reach back into the stories of the Bible for inspiration. After we have these discussions in an open forum, we cook a large meal together. Everyone has to help, whether it's chopping up vegetables, helping prepare the food, or setting the table.

Someday, when I've finally retired from CI work, I'll tell my little ministry about the wild course my life took, how I led myself and my family down the path of despair and lost myself, how I cozied up to murderers and drug lords, and how, when my situation got so bad that I would wake in the night fearing for my life, I met a sheriff's deputy who showed me the way out. How I've spent more than two decades trying to undo the damage I did in only one.

When that happens—when I'm done with my work and able to tell the world who I really am—I'll need to go deeper into hiding. Until then, I'll be walking the same streets you walk, trying to see into you without ever being seen, doing my best to pick up the shattered pieces that my drug life left behind.

APPENDIX

To Whom It May Concern,

I began working with ███████████ in March or April of 1996 when I was a Special Agent with the U.S. Customs Service. ███████ worked as a confidential source of information, initially regarding a drug smuggling organization that was involved in moving narcotics across the international border in the San Diego, California area, the narcotics initially moved into the Los Angeles area, then dispersed to points across the United States, primarily though into Detroit, Michigan and New York, New York.

███████ also worked on many other investigations, sometimes posing as a transportation specialist for narcotics, and sometimes posing as a buyer or seller of narcotics.

During the 13 years I worked with ███████, he was involved in numerous cases, and was instrumental in scores of felony arrests and the removal of large amounts of narcotics off the streets. He often times put himself at risk in these investigations.

███████ was always controllable, unlike most other sources I worked with, and never created any signification problems to those who worked with him. He not only worked well with the agencies he assisted, but offered sometimes helpful insights into the various targets we were investigating.

He worked not only with my agency, but I was involved with him on investigations co-worked with The Drug Enforcement Administration, with several local police departments, and I know he also worked with the Bureau of Alcohol, Tobacco and Firearms.

I am also aware that ███████ continued to work with other law enforcement agencies following my retirement in October 2009, as I maintained semi-regular contact with him.

███████████

Supervisory Special Agent

Homeland Security Investigations

Immigration and Customs Enforcement (retired)

October 7, 2015

To Whom It May Concern,

My name is Detective Richard Fagan, recently retired from the New York City Police Department's Organized Crime Investigations Division. I spent the last 20 years in this unit of the 32 years I spent with NYPD. My duties and responsibilities there were to investigate, infiltrate and prosecute crimes associated with Organized Crime on a high level. In August of 2000, I had the opportunity to meet CS96. I refer to him as CS96 because NYPD regulations restrict me from ever putting his real name on any piece of paper or identify him as such in any manner. I have many years of experience dealing with Confidential Informants as they pertain to narcotics, extortion and murder. After debriefing CS96, I knew I was dealing with someone on a scale way bigger then I was used to and immediately went through the laborious paperwork and background checks to sign him up as a NYPD registered Confidential Informant. He was assigned a CI number and a code name for meetings and any other subsequent paperwork. From that day forward we used him for numerous high level narcotics cases. Placing him in many undercover roles from street guy to high echelon narcotics transporter, buyer and seller. He was able to penetrate numerous groups and organizations that we were unsuccessful in infiltrating in the past. These cases all were highly successful and resulted in millions of dollars in currency seizures and enormous amount of drug seizures. He would work alone or we would send him in with undercover officers. His cases also resulted in subsequent cases and off-shoot drug seizures and wiretap cases that were all very successful. I spent most of my career doing covert operations in several units and have not to this date and probably will never meet a more competent, resourceful and successful Informant again. Since these cases I have recommended him to several other agencies on a local and federal level and they too have has enormous results with him.

Detective First Grade Richie Fagan (ret) NYPD

ACKNOWLEDGMENTS

Roman Caribe

First and foremost I want to thank my LORD. My path was hazardous until my LORD changed my life. Today, I am a new man. As the LORD says in Psalm 23:2–3, "He leads me beside still water. He has restored my soul. He has led me in a path of righteousness for his name's sake."

I'm grateful to DEA, ICE, ATF, FBI, and all the local police and state agencies across the United States that I have been blessed with the opportunity to work with. Thank you for giving me the opportunity to prove myself.

A special thanks to special agent MD of DEA and Richie Fagan, a first-grade gold shield detective of the NYPD, and his partner, BG.

I also want to thank Richard Abate of 3 Arts Entertainment—you are the best literary agent in the world.

What can I say about Robert Cea? Robert, you, have been given a special gift to write. Thank you, brother, for bringing my book to life. And to your very funny and extremely smart business partner, David Goldberg, thank you.

I also want to send my gratitude to Mauro DiPreta, publisher of Hachette Books, and his assistant, David Lamb, for allowing me to tell my story. Thank you for believing in me.

To my wife and children, I thank you for your unconditional love and support through thick and thin. Your faith has inspired me to become the man I am today. Without you, this book would never have been possible.

Robert Cea

First and foremost I'd like to thank "Roman Caribe" for having the faith and trust in my abilities, thus allowing me to record and write your truly amazing story. It was an incredible adventure reliving *"the life"* with you and I thank you and your family for the opportunity. You're truly a brave man, and beyond question have not only redeemed your past, but have become a man I'm truly proud to call my friend.

This book would not have come to fruition had it not been for NYPD detective first-grade, Richie Fagan, ret. His introduction to CS96 and his continued help and support throughout the entire process was insurmountable, and I thank you for all you've helped me accomplish. I also send my thanks to Richard Abate and Rachel Kim at 3 Arts Entertainment for their incredible foresight from the very beginning—my appreciation is endless. A big thanks is in order to Lisa, Nicky, and Liv for allowing me the time away to write this book. I love each of you deeply and owe you so much. You've made me the man I am today—a proud dad. A huge thank you as well to David Lamb at Hachette Books, whose thoughtful insight and incredible editing skills helped turn this book into something that, I believe, is very special. You are truly a gifted man—again, thank you for all of your help and wisdom throughout, and I so look forward to working with you again. I can't thank Mauro DiPreta of Hachette Books enough for the opportunity to work together once again. His inspiration and stalwart leadership made the entire process seamless and—above all—fun. I'm grateful for all of his support over the years and continued faith in me.

To Jeff and Dawn Cea, thank you for all your support throughout our long and loving history together. You've always been there for me, and the comfort you both so generously give time and time again is, well…words can't describe my gratitude to and love for you both. To Dawn Dolce, you, too, have always been there for me, and though we don't see each other enough, you're always on my mind—I love you dearly. I also want to send my thanks to Michael, Vincent, and Dana, who are always with me and always will be—I love you all very much. To Danny Gray, you'll always be in my heart and will forever remain my buoy in a life that contains so many dark storms. Our friendship remains as strong as it did when we met so many years ago—I love you. To my business partner and dearest friend, David Goldberg, what is there to say? Without you I'm just another guy with an idea, and I thank you for helping turn those ideas into hundreds of hours worth of quality television and film as well as for the books you've helped with and so generously allowed me to write while you steer the ship. You've always been there for me with a simple word of inspiration or a pep talk to help get me back on track, and my gratitude for your friendship and our lasting partnership is incalculable. Thank you for being on point, day in and day out, and for running the business for the year I was away, and most importantly, thank you for being the most sincere, honest, and truest friend a man could ever have. I'm proud to call you my partner, prouder to call you my friend.